Discourse Representation of Temporal Relations
in the So-Called Head-Internal Relatives

Hituzi Linguistics in English

No. 1	Lexical Borrowing and its Impact on English	Makimi Kimura-Kano
No. 2	From a Subordinate Clause to an Independent Clause	Yuko Higashiizumi
No. 3	ModalP and Subjunctive Present	Tadao Nomura
No. 4	A Historical Study of Referent Honorifics in Japanese	Takashi Nagata
No. 5	Communicating Skills of Intention	Tsutomu Sakamoto
No. 6	A Pragmatic Approach to the Generation and Gender Gap in Japanese Politeness Strategies	Toshihiko Suzuki
No. 7	Japanese Women's Listening Behavior in Face-to-face Conversation	Sachie Miyazaki
No. 8	An Enterprise in the Cognitive Science of Language	Tetsuya Sano et al.
No. 9	Syntactic Structure and Silence	Hisao Tokisaki
No.10	The Development of the Nominal Plural Forms in Early Middle English	Ryuichi Hotta
No.11	Chunking and Instruction	Takayuki Nakamori
No.12	Detecting and Sharing Perspectives Using Causals in Japanese	Ryoko Uno
No.13	Discourse Representation of Temporal Relations in the So-Called Head-Internal Relatives	Kuniyoshi Ishikawa
No.14	Features and Roles of Filled Pauses in Speech Communication	Michiko Watanabe
No.15	Japanese Loanword Phonology	Masahiko Mutsukawa

Hituzi Linguistics in English No. 13

Discourse Representation of Temporal Relations in the So-Called Head-Internal Relatives

Kuniyoshi Ishikawa

Hituzi Syobo Publishing

Copyright © Kuniyoshi Ishikawa 2009

First published 2009

Author: Kuniyoshi Ishikawa

All rights reserved. Except for the quotation of short passages for the purposes of criticism and review, no part of this publication may be reproduced, stored in a retrieval system, or transmitted in any form or by any means, electronic, mechanical, photocopying, recording or otherwise, without the written prior permission of the publisher.
In case of photocopying and electronic copying and retrieval from network personally, permission will be given on receipts of payment and making inquiries. For details please contact us through e-mail. Our e-mail address is given below.

Book Design © Hirokazu Mukai (glyph)

Hituzi Syobo Publishing
Yamato bldg. 2F, 2-1-2 Sengoku Bunkyo-ku Tokyo, Japan
112-0011

phone +81-3-5319-4916 fax +81-3-5319-4917
e-mail: toiawase@hituzi.co.jp
http://www.hituzi.co.jp/
postal transfer 00120-8-142852

ISBN978-4-89476-406-4
Printed in Japan

To my dear mother Kimiko Ishikawa and my late father Naonosuke
and to my beloved family: Emiko and Tomonori

PREFACE

The present book is a slightly revised version of my doctoral dissertation that I submitted to Yale University. I have kept the overall structure of the presentation intact, although minor revision and expansion were made in some chapters. The goal of this book is to present a model of the representation of interpretation for an untensed nominal complement construction in Japanese, the so-called Head-Internal Relative (HIR) construction. In spite of its name, I claim that the alleged HIR clause is in fact a nominal complement clause on the grounds that it is gapless, that certain corresponding relative clause formations are impossible, and that the apparent head nominal -*no* does not convey meaningful content. Furthermore, the clausal complement is claimed to be untensed.

Based on the observations through which the untensed HIR clause proves to be somehow associated with its main clause of the construction, I demonstrate that the aspectual compatibility between the two predicates affects the interpretation processes. An event-based approach to the interpretation of the temporally underspecific constructions will be proposed. The temporal interpretation of this construction necessarily involves access to the discourse representation of event units, due to the underspecified temporal indication with HIR predicates. I examine the construction in the light of discourse event representation. The most serious problem about the complex clause construction in question has been the apparent fact that a referential head of the assumed relative clause is missing. As a result, despite the construction's being intuitively interpretable, the 'how' of this interpretation is not clear. Through the discussion developed in the book, the referent of the head turns out to be identified within the HIR clause as a participant of two contiguous event units represented in discourse.

With observations of the core meanings of the aspectual predicates that inevitably appear in the HIR, I present a specific reasoning process of what I call *default matching* and argue that such a matching process is vital to the interpretation of the temporal ordering relation between the two events in the HIR, since tense is unspecified in the clause. Furthermore, by incorporating a representational theory of discourse interpretation, I attempt to present an integrative model of discourse representation for untensed clausal constructions such as the HIR.

I further investigate the core property of the subject marker -*ga*, which is the only possible case marking in the subject position of the HIR clause. I demonstrate that the existential nature of -*ga* contributes to the thetic introduction of the first event that is connected to the second event in the information-updating processes of discourse: an existentially presented event in the preceding discourse and a newly introduced event in the discourse update. I conclude that the HIR sets up an existential condition sufficient for the consequent event, which is contiguous with the first event, to occur.

The theoretical implications are that certain interpretation processes of underspecified complex constructions inevitably require the involvement of such discourse inferential systems as default reasoning for sequences of events evoked by complex constructions.

ACKNOWLEDGMENTS

I am indebted to Sergey Avrutin, Larry Horn, Dianne Jonas, Seiichi Makino, Eric Potsdam, and Young-Suk Lee for their valuable written comments on different versions of the earlier chapters of this dissertation. During the initial period of the writing of the earlier chapters, Dianne Jonas and Sergey Avrutin gave me invaluable comments and advice without which the dissertation could not have been finished. I am much obliged to Seiichi Makino for reading all the drafts patiently and providing me with his insights during the long stretch of time, in spite of his busy academic schedules. I am also obliged to Maria Babyonyshev. She supported me with detailed comments for the elaboration of my dissertation. Louis Goldstein supported me not solely as a director of graduate studies but also as one attentive, earnest scholar and educator since I had started my research at Yale. I am also thankful to my departmental chairperson Steve Anderson and to the following scholars: Bob and Willa Abelson, Andrew Dillon, Caroline Heycock, James Huang, Alec Marantz, Samuel Martin, Mamoru Saito, Junko Shimoyama, Chioko Takahashi, Satoshi Tomioka, John Whitman, and Caroline Wiltshire for their helpful comments. I am grateful to Lizanne Kaiser, Matthew Richardson, William Vance, Paula Resch, Rosemary Jones, Catherine Manning, and Sean Orourke for checking my English and giving me valuable comments. I have benefited also from the following people who kindly sent or gave me papers: Masaaki Fuji, Koji Hoshi, Yuki Matsuda, Keiko Miyagawa, Kunio Nishiyama, Kyoko Ohara, and Asako Uchibori. Not to mention, for their friendship and encouragement I am grateful to all the fellows with whom I shared my life in the linguistics department, and especially to Casandra Murphy for her invariable support. For their support in Japan, I would also like to express my gratitude to Tadashi Yoshizawa, Masatomo Ukaji, Akira Ikeya, Minoru Nakau, Masaru Nakamura, Tiaki Kumakura, and Arimichi Makino. For their long-lasting friendship and support, I thank: Yoshiaki Koshikawa, Michiaki Murata, Larissa Chen, Minjung Son, Hosung Nam, Sean Orourke, and Irene Iezzi. My special gratitude should be expressed to Lisa Thomas for her insights and patience with which she discussed the dissertation topic extensively at various stages of my research. For proofreading of my manuscript, Tammy Harshbarger and the Hadler family, i.e. Eliza, Alice and Jim, were a "great" help to me.

My foremost and deepest gratitude goes to 'Larry,' that is, my adviser Laurence Horn, who taught me things about a variety of academic disciplines, commented on most of my writings throughout my study at Yale, and guided me through my overall coursework and further steps to the Ph.D.

Finally, I express my thankfullness to Isao Matsumoto of Hituzi Syobo for giving me an opportunity to publish this book, and to Koitiro Yoshimine for planning and Takashi Moriwaki for editing and scheduling with patience. This research was partly supported by a Yale University Dissertation Fellowship. The publication of this book was partly supported through Japan Society for the Promotion of Science, by KAKENHI, a Grant-in-Aid for publication of Scientific Research Results (205040, 2008) of The Ministry of Education, Culture, Sports, Science, and Technology.

Kuniyoshi Ishikawa

CONTENTS

PREFACE i
ACKNOWLEDGMENTS iii
GLOSSARY OF TERMS ix

Chapter 1 Introduction to the so-called Head-Internal Relatives (HIR) in Japanese   1

1.1 Introduction   1
1.2 A structural sketch of the HIR   3

Chapter 2 An analysis of the so-called HIR as a prenominal complement construction and its interpretation   11

2.1 Properties of the Japanese HIR: an argument against LF-movement   11
2.2 Gapless HIRs as prenominal complements   14
2.3 Problems with the interpretation of the Japanese HIR   18
     2.3.1 The functions and category of *no*   18
     2.3.2 Problems with *pro* approaches to the interpretation of the HIR   22

Chapter 3 Modeling the event representation of temporal interpretation   35

3.1 The HIR as an untensed clause   35
3.2 Discourse representation for the interpretation of untensed constructions   40
     3.2.1 Unindexed T and its consequence in untensed constructions   40
     3.2.2 Summary of the Event File Card approach   42
     3.2.3 Interpretation of untensed RIs   43
3.3 The Japanese HIR in discourse representation   46
     3.3.1 Temporal relations between two events in the HIR   46

    3.3.2 Aspect representation in the HIR   48
    3.3.3 E-cards introduced by presupposed events   50
    3.3.4 Interpretation of the HIR by means of E-cards   53
3.4 Summary of the chapter   55

Chapter 4   Interpreting complex predicate *-te iru*: the interaction of event relations with eventualities and tense   59

4.1 Introduction: ambiguities of the Verb-*te iru*   59
4.2 The existential reading of state, as opposed to continuative aspect, with the *-te iru*   61
    4.2.1 A persistent reading of the 'existence of a state' with the Verb-*te iru*   62
    4.2.2 An invariable reading of the Verb-*te iru* and problems with Nitta's tripartite classification   64
4.3 Further arguments for the *-te iru* form as existential: comparison with the English present perfect   72
4.4 A system of reasoning processes for the temporal interpretation of the Verb-*te iru*   78
    4.4.1 Matching of events for the temporal contiguity in discourse: a system of interpretation for the Verb-*te iru* predicate   79
    4.4.2 The matching process for temporal interpretation of the Verb-*te iru* in the HIR construction   85

Chapter 5   Resolving the underspecified meanings: default reasoning in discourse interpretation   91

5.1 Introduction   91
5.2 Two distinct defaults: lexical and discourse   92
    5.2.1 Lexical defaults versus discourse defaults   93
    5.2.2 Defaults in discourse representation   99
        5.2.2.1 SDRT: a theory of discourse structure that constrains conflicting defaults   99
        5.2.2.2 Discourse event relations: linking defaults to discourse interpretation   104

5.3 Interpreting the underspecification without a presupposition trigger: a case for default matching ... 108
   5.3.1 Identifying the missing antecedent of a discourse referent: *Bridging* as a subsumed process in SDRT ... 108
   5.3.2 Default matching for interpretation without a presupposition trigger ... 110
5.4 Default matching to interpret the HIR in discourse ... 114
   5.4.1 Discourse relations between the two events in the HIR ... 116
   5.4.2 Apparent exceptional examples as more grounds for the involvement of default matching ... 118
5.5 Summary of the chapter ... 122

Chapter 6   *Ga* and information structure of the HIR   125

6.1 Introduction ... 125
6.2 Analyses of the subject marker *-ga* ... 127
6.3 Existential individuation of *-ga* ... 137
6.4 Exhaustive Listing (EL) as a reflection of prosodic highlighting ... 140
6.5 Implicature of preferred readings of EL examples ... 147
6.6 The HIR to represent sequenced events ... 150
6.7 Summary of the chapter ... 152

Chapter 7   Final remarks   157

BIBLIOGRAPHY ... 159
INDEX OF TOPICS ... 169
INDEX OF AUTHORS ... 171

GLOSSARY OF TERMS

HIR	head-internal relative (clause)
NOM	nominative
ACC	accusative
DAT	dative
PR(E)S	present (tense)
PST	past (tense)
FUT	future
Prft	perfect
Imprf(t)	imperfect
Prog	progressive
Evd	evidential marker
N	nominal
NP	noun phrase
VP	verb phrase
AP	adjective phrase
PP	prepositional/postpositional phrase
CP	complementizer phrase
IP	Infl phrase
TP	tense phrase
DP	determiner phrase
AspP	aspect phrase
COMP or C	complementizer
D	determiner
Infl	inflection (head)
P	preposition/postposition
T	tense
LF	logical form
SUB	subject
OBJ	object
TOP	topic
CPL	copula

Ptcl	particle
NEG	negation
Op	(null) operator
Hon	honorific
Pol	politeness
Q	question marker
e	event variable.

Chapter 1

Introduction to the so-called Head-Internal Relatives (HIR) in Japanese

The objective of this dissertation is to examine the structure of a so-called Japanese head-internal relative clause (hereafter HIR) and to propose a model of the representation for the interpretation of the HIR. I will claim that, although it is called 'relative clause', the alleged HIR clause is in fact a nominal complement. Further investigations also reveal that the HIR in Japanese is untensed and aspectually organized. Consequently, I will argue that the construction must inevitably have access to discourse for the temporal interpretation. I will examine the construction in the light of discourse representation in which the interpretation is achieved through the representation of event units indicated by the clauses. I will present a certain reasoning process for the ordering relation between the two events and I will propose an integrative model of discourse representation for untensed clause constructions such as the HIR. Hereafter throughout the discussion, I will continue to use the term the HIR to refer to the prenominal complement clause with a head *no* in Japanese, since that is the only and commonly used terminology.

1.1 Introduction

The structure of the HIR Construction has been associated with that of a relative clause. The Japanese HIR is also treated as equivalent to a canonical relative clause at some level of representation in Ito (1986), Ishii (1988), and Watanabe (1991). With its unique properties being investigated, however, I will argue that the alleged HIR in Japanese is not a relative clause, as has been claimed. I will instead claim that it is a prenominal complement clause with a contentless nominal -*no* as a head. Before discussing in detail the construction in Japanese, I will quickly give an outline of what is generally termed as an HIR in some other language. First of all, in Japanese and other languages such as Quechua languages and Lakhota, both HIRs and relatives lack an overt Wh-relative marker, in contrast to relatives in a language such as English. Second and more importantly, HIRs do not indicate any explicit relativized noun outside the clause, which contrasts with canonical relatives in the same language. The following examples illustrate these points.

(1)a.   Canonical Relative Clause in Ancash Quechua
       [$_{NP}$ [$_{S'}$ nuna t_i ranti-shqa-n] bestya$_i$]   alli   bestya-m   ka-rqo-n
           man   buy -Prft-3   horse(NOM) good horse-Evd be-Pst-3
       'The horse the man bought was a good horse.'
   b. Head-Internal Relative (HIR) clause in Ancash Quechua
       [$_{NP}$ nuna bestya-ta   ranti-shqa-n] alli   bestya-m   ka-rqo-n
           man horse(ACC) buy-Prft-3   good horse-Evd be-Pst-3
       'The horse the man bought was a good horse.'
                           [from Cole 1987: 279, 5 and 1 respectively]

The examples in (1) taken from Ancash Quechua (Cole1987) show that there is no obvious syntactic clue to identify a missing argument, i.e. a subject or an object, of the matrix verb in the HIR sentence (1b), since there is no relativized noun appearing to the right of the embedded NP *nuna bestya-ta ranti-shqa-n*. In contrast, in the canonical relative clause (1a), the apparent relativized noun *bestya* 'horse' occurs outside the modifying relative clause.

Past analyses of the HIRs involve LF movement of an internal noun out of the subordinate clause domain. Thus, Williamson (1987), Cole (1987), and Basilico (1996) basically regard the structure of the HIRs as identical to that of canonical relatives in that they both involve movement of an internal noun. In (1b), Cole (1987) argues that *bestya* 'horse' in the HIR clause moves covertly at LF to the right, i.e. outside the subordinate domain *nuna bestya-ta ranti-shqa-n*. Consequently, according to his account, the structures of the HIRs and relatives would be equivalent at LF. They would both have the structure in (1a) at LF.

However, I argue that Japanese HIR counterparts are not relative clauses but untensed prenominal complements. I propose the association of the

Japanese counterpart with the HIR to be immaterial to the discussion of the construction in question. I instead claim that access to discourse is required for their interpretation due to the lack of tense indication with the alleged HIR in Japanese. I will present a model of discourse representation by means of events and show that Japanese HIRs can adequately be interpreted through the event representations.

In the next section, I give a brief sketch of the structures of Japanese HIRs. I continue to use the term the HIR to refer to the alleged HIR in Japanese unless specified otherwise. However, I will later claim that it is a misnomer.

1.2 A structural sketch of the HIR

In this section I look first at the basic structure of the HIR in comparison with relatives. Then, I point out how the alleged HIR in Japanese is similar to and different from the HIRs in other languages.

In Japanese, both subordinate and main clauses are verb-final. Therefore, the embedded verb marks the clause boundary between main and embedded clauses on the surface. Now let us see how NP positions differ between the HIRs and relatives in Japanese. The following examples illustrate this point.[1]

(2)a. Japanese HIR
John-ga   [NP [IP/CP Mary-ga   ringo-o   katta]   -no]-o
   -NOM [[Mary-NOM apple-ACC buy-Prfct]-no]-ACC
tabeta.
ate
'lit., Mary bought an apple/apples, which John ate.'
Approximate translation is: 'John ate an apple/apples that Mary just bought (and she did not intend to give it/them to him).'
 b. Japanese relative clause construction
John-ga   [[Mary-ga   katta]   ringo]-o   tabeta.
   -NOM [[Mary-NOM bought] apple]-ACC ate
'John ate an apple/apples Mary bought.'

c. (= 2b)

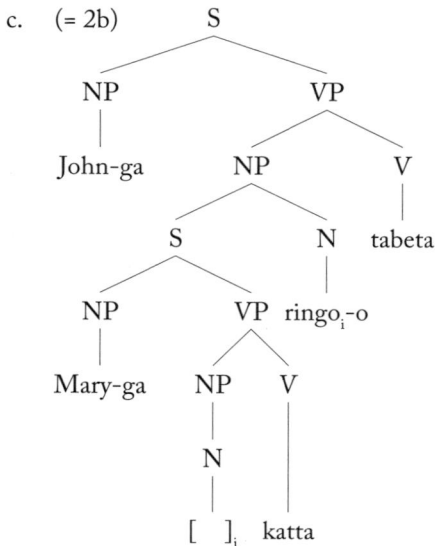

[The structure is adopted from Tsujimura 1996, 170: 18; the specific examples are mine]

The translation of (2a) is not precise at its best, and it can be described as 'John ate something of [Mary's having bought a cake]' in ungrammatical English. The meaning indicated in the English translation of the HIR is obtained only after the compatibility of the two events indicated by the two clauses is reasoned. I will discuss, in chapters 2 and 3, the properties of the HIR that cause such difficulties with translation.

Note that the case assigned to an NP internal to the HIR is determined by the subordinate HIR predicate. In the HIR (2a), the accusative case assigned to the underlined NP *ringo* 'apple' is the same case that should assign to an object NP by the HIR predicate *katta* 'bought'. In addition, in (2a), the position corresponding to that for the relativized noun *ringo* 'apple' in the relative clause (2b) appears to be filled instead by *no*.[2] This apparently relativized element of the HIR is a morpheme that lacks semantic content, so it cannot indicate the semantic content of the argument, i.e. the internal argument in (2a), of the matrix verb. In contrast, in (2b), the relativized noun *ringo* is outside the relative clause and functions as the head of the object NP of the main predicate. Canonical relative clauses in Japanese have been represented with "a gap" internal to them, and the gap corresponds to the head (= relativized) noun (Tsujimura 1996, 266), as is illustrated in (2c). In (2c), *ringo* 'apple' is interpreted as the direct object of the subordinate verb *katta* 'bought' (Tsujimura 1996, 172 & 266). On the other hand, in the HIR example of (2a) one of the nouns, i.e. *ringo* 'apple', inside the HIR should be inferentially selected as a referent of the argument of the matrix verb *tabeta* 'ate,' instead of *no*. The noun selected as the referent of the argument of the matrix verb depends on semantic restrictions imposed by the verb. Therefore, the logical choice in this case would be *ringo* 'apple.'

On the surface, *no* in an HIR appears to serve two functions: 1) as a head of the argument NP of the main predicate; and 2) as the relativized noun if the subordinate HIR is indeed a relative clause. Semantically, a selected NP in the HIR also has two functions: 1) it is interpreted as a referent of the argument of the main predicate; and 2) it serves as an argument of the subordinate predicate. For example, in (2a), the NP *ringo* 'apple', functions as an object, with an accusative case marker -*o* assigned by the subordinate verb 'bought.' It is also interpreted as a referent of the object of the main predicate 'ate' as well, with the accusative -*o* after *no* being associated with the NP *ringo*. This interpretation process involves ambiguities. In (3), *no*'s position syntactically appears to correspond to that of a relativized noun in the relative clause construction.

(3) An approximate structure of HIR Construction in Japanese:
(....)[$_{NP}$ [$_{IP/CP}$ ...SUB...(OBJ)...Predicate] [$_N$ *no*]]-{NOM/ACC}... Main Predicate

It is possible that the syntactic requirements regarding case and a theta role are met with the NP, i.e., the HIR plus *no*. However, *no* lacks explicit content.[3] In other words, the entity of the argument of the main verb is not identified. It must be inferentially interpreted. Therefore, ambiguity occurs with the interpretation of the HIRs when an HIR clause includes more than one NP within its clause, as in (2a). One must decide which NP corresponds to the content of the argument that the main predicate requires. Note that the ambiguity is not derived from the reference of the semantic content that an ordinary relativized head nominal is lexically encoded with. On the contrary, because -*no* is not equipped with semantic content, the corresponding head candidate must be identified somewhere else. In this regard, the alleged HIR is unique and no other relatives in Japanese seem to show this property. When

I use the term *referent* with *-no* in the HIR examples, it refers to an entity that exists in discourse and is reasoned through discourse interpretation processes. In later chapters, I will claim that the referents of the NPs in the HIR can be interpreted through the event representations in discourse. Otherwise, I will not discuss the referentiality or anaphoricity of a nominal in general, especially in cases where it appears as a relativized head in a canonical relative construction. That is beyond the scope of this study. In chapter 2, I discuss the analysis of *no* and the identification of the referent of an argument of the main predicate.

In order to analyze the HIR structures, I need to define the term *head* here. A head usually refers to an X^0 category in the X' convention. However, in the literature, the terms *semantic head* (Ohara 1992, 1994) and *internal head* (Williamson 1987) are also used to refer to an NP inside the HIRs. In this case, the NP is interpreted as a referent of an argument for the main predicate. Terms such as *head-internal* or *headless* are used to describe the apparent structure, referring to the superficial lack of the relativized head element that should be overt in the relative construction. In this book, I will use the term *semantic head* to refer only to the NP that is internal to the HIR and inferentially selected as the referent of an argument of the main predicate. I will use the term *relativized head*, on the other hand, to refer to a nominal outside the relative clause. Therefore, a noun such as 'apple' in the relative construction (2b) is termed a relativized head, a noun that is modified by a relative clause and situated outside of it. *No* is termed a head to its HIR.

At the surface level, it seems that the function of a semantic head is not identical to the function of a relativized head in Japanese or in the languages discussed in Cole (1987): Ancash Quechua, Imbabura Quechua, and Lakhota. The question should then be whether the semantic head and the relativized head have anything in common in Japanese at some level of representation such as LF. I will discuss this issue in chapter 2.

Now I turn to the discussion of one interesting property of Japanese HIRs. Japanese HIRs do not allow certain adverbs to appear in their clause domains. As discussed in Kuroda (1992, 148: 9, 12) and Murasugi (1994, 432: 18), temporal adverbs such as *kinoo* 'yesterday' cannot occur with the assumed past-tense predicate, as (4a) shows.

(4) a. The HIR in Japanese
John-ga   [[Mary-ga   {*kinoo/*senjitu}   ringo-o
John-NOM [[Mary-NOM {*yesterday/*the other day} apple-ACC
katta]-no]-o   tabeta.
bought]]-ACC ate
Intended: 'Mary bought an apple yesterday/the other day, which John ate.'

b. Relative Clause in Japanese
John-ga   [[Mary-ga   {kinoo/senjitu}   katta] ringo]
John-NOM [[Mary-NOM {yesterday/the other day} bought] apple]
-o   tabeta.
-ACC ate
'John ate an apple which Mary bought yesterday/the other day.'

c. The HIR in Japanese with the same temporal adverbs in the main clause
John-ga   [[Mary-ga   ringo-o   katta]-no]-o
John-NOM [[Mary-NOM apple-ACC bought]]-ACC
{*kinoo/*senjitu} tabeta.
{*yesterday/*the other day} ate
Intended: 'Mary bought an apple, which John ate yesterday/the other day.' or 'Yesterday/the other day, John ate an apple, and Mary bought an apple for that.'

d. Relative Clause in Japanese
John-ga   [[Mary-ga   katta] ringo]-o   {kinoo/senjitu}
John-NOM [[Mary-NOM bought] apple]-ACC {yesterday/the other day} ate
tabeta.
'Yesterday/the other day John ate an apple which Mary bought.'

In contrast, there is no such restriction in the relative clause counterpart, as (4b) shows. In addition, an ambiguity occurs in (4c), but not in (4d). When the day of Mary's purchase of an apple is interpreted as that of John's eating it, the sentence is felicitous. That is, both events happened yesterday. However, the sentence is infelicitous when the two events are interpreted as occurring non-contiguously on different days. Such an ambiguity does not occur in the relative clause in (4d). Note that the HIR example in (4c) cannot have a solid translation in English. The given one in (4c) is an approximate translation, i.e., the closest one that I can do to the original Japanese sentence. At least three factors are involved in the difficulty of the translation of the HIR construction, as seen in (4a) and (4c): first, the indefinite head *no* does not have a meaningful content; second, an argument of the main predicate is missing; and, third, the HIR clause does not seem to indicate an explicit tense, as observed in (4). All these missing elements in the HIR do exist in the English translations in (4a) and (4c). Therefore, the English translations for the HIR examples are usually the ones I get only after I determine and select one of the plausible meanings with the HIR, depending on the mutual compatibility of the meanings between the two clauses.

This kind of ambiguity with the HIR, as in (4c), is understood to be due to a particular property discussed in the literature. According to Kuroda (1992) and Murasugi (1994), the temporal restriction in the HIR is due to a kind of temporal contiguity or, to put it in Kuroda's (1992, 148–9) terms, *simultaneity* of the two events indicated by the main and subordinate clauses. For example, in (4a), Kuroda and Murasugi both claim that Mary's buying of an apple/apples and John's eating of the apple/apples have to be temporally associated with each other. They argue that, if 'yesterday' is added in the HIR, the two events become disjointed in time, and the sentence becomes uninterpretable. Therefore, the tense in the HIR must be dependent on that of the main predicate. In chapter 3, I will discuss the interpretation of the contiguity of two events and the temporal restriction in Japanese HIR.

Overall, I ask, the following questions: first, whether or not we can account for the structures of Japanese HIRs in the same manner as we do for relatives; second, how we can interpret their other properties.

Endnotes

1. The categorical status of the HIR clauses and the accompanying *no* is controversial. The HIR is analyzed as CP in Tsubomoto (1981) and Uchibori (1992), and IP in Ishii (1988), Horie (1993), Matsuda (1993), Murasugi (1994), and Hoshi (1995), depending on how the function and structure are analyzed. *No* in the HIR is also analyzed as: 1) C(=COMP) in Kuroda (1992); 2) a pronoun in Tsubomoto, Uchibori and Matsuda; and 3) a noun in Murasugi and Hoshi. I will discuss *no*'s status in section 2.3 of chapter 2.
2. In section 2.3 of chapter 2, I argue that *no* is a noun. I also argue that case must be assigned to the HIR-*no*, since I reject a claim that a null pronoun is located between the

HIR-*no* and the case marker.

3   Japanese has this class of incomplete nominals, often referred to as formal nouns or pseudo nouns. Some of them are bound morphemes, and others are not. *Kata* 'way/direction' in *yari-kata* 'how to do ...', and *you* 'manner/way' in *sigoto no yari-you* 'the way to do the job' are bound morphemes, whereas *koto* 'event/fact' in *hakari-goto* 'conspiracy' can be an independent unit as a free morpheme.

Chapter 2

An analysis of the so-called HIR as a prenominal complement construction and its interpretation

In this chapter, I present data that show the fundamental difference between the HIR and relatives in Japanese. I argue that Japanese HIRs are not involved in NP movement. Then, I demonstrate a diagnostic test for complement clause status and claim that, in Japanese, the noncanonical HIRs in question are in fact prenominal complement clauses that do not have motivation for NP-movement, unlike canonical relative clauses.

In section 2.1, I summarize one approach to HIRs in general. I then discuss problems this approach poses, as applied to Japanese HIRs. Further in section 2.2, I argue that Japanese HIRs are prenominal complements, and that past approaches describing the structure in terms of relativization do not adequately account for Japanese HIR's complement structure. In section 2.3, I discuss problems with the interpretation of the HIRs. I examine the nature of *-no* in the HIRs. I will then show that recent analyses such as a *pro* approach discussed by Murasugi (1994) and Hoshi (1995) are not adequate for the identification of missing argument NPs in the main predicates. I claim that access to a discourse representation is required to interpret the NPs.

2.1 Properties of the Japanese HIR: an argument against LF-movement

In this section, I discuss the LF-movement approach to HIRs proposed by Cole (1987) (and also by Ito (1986), Williamson (1987), Ishii (1988), Culy (1990), Watanabe (1991, 1992), and Basilico (1996)). I argue that the interpretation of Japanese HIRs and their relative counterparts differ markedly in Japanese under certain circumstances.

The LF NP-movement approach, as exemplified in Cole (1987) and Basilico (1996), relies on the assumption that HIRs are identical to relatives at some level of representation, namely LF.[1] This approach is illustrated in (1).

(1)a. S-structure of HIRs b. LF-structure of HIRs

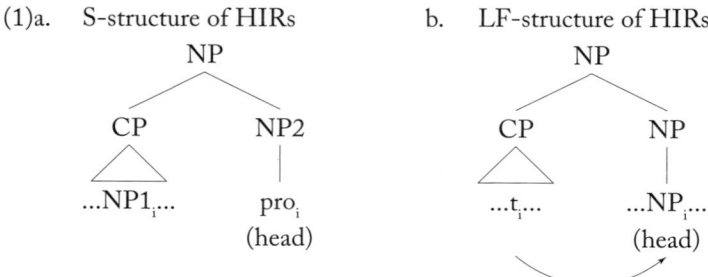

c. [= (1b)]
[$_{NP}$ [$_{CP}$ nuna [$_{NP1i}$ bestya-ta] ranti-shqa-n] pro$_i$] alli   bestya-m
man horse(ACC) buy-Prft-3   good horse-Evd
ka-rqo-n.
be-Pst-3
'The horse the man bought was a good horse.'
        [Cole (1987, 278: 3 & 4). Author changed *e* to *pro* and S' to CP]

In (1a), NP1 in CP is coindexed with a null pronoun at S-structure (and at D-structure as well in Cole (1987, 278)) before NP movement. Cole argues that at LF the NP1 in CP covertly moves to fill the NP2 position shown in (1b).[2] (1c) is the reiterated example (1b) of the Ancash Quechua HIR in chapter 1. The NP1 'horse' in the HIR clause will move to the coindexed pro position at LF. The main point of this approach is that NP1 covertly moves out of the original position internal to CP. As seen from these diagrams, Cole reasons that HIRs in Ancash Quechua have the same structure at LF as relatives. Therefore, according to Cole's analysis, at LF the HIRs have relativized lexical heads, just as relatives do.[3]

Since both structures are presumed identical to each other at LF, it follows that the interpretations of comparable relatives and the HIRs should be identical propositionally in Ancash Quechua. However, their meanings are significantly different in certain cases in Japanese. In fact, the canonical relative counterparts of the HIRs are infelicitous in examples (2).

(2)a. the HIR Clause in Japanese
　　　Mary-wa [John-ga　　Kanada-san　no　komugiko-o
　　　　　　-TOP　　-NOM Canada-made GEN flour　　-ACC
　　　yaita] -*no-o*　tabeta.
　　　baked]-*no*-ACC ate
　　　'*lit.,* Mary ate what became of John baking/heating Canada-made flour.'
　b. Relative Clause
　　　#Mary-wa [John-ga　　yaita] Kanada-san　no　komugiko-o tabeta.
　　　　　　-TOP　　-NOM baked Canada-made GEN flour-ACC　ate
　　　Intended: 'Mary ate the Canada-made flour John baked.'

In (2a), the object that 'Mary ate' is not directly interpreted as the 'Canadian flour' itself; the NP 'Canadian flour' is in the subordinate HIR clause. It is interpreted as the object, *i.e.* internal argument, of the verb 'baked', not as the object of the main predicate 'ate'. In contrast, in (2b), the 'Canadian flour' is outside the subordinate clause, and is therefore interpreted as a constituent of the object argument NP of the matrix verb, with a theta role assigned to the object by the matrix verb 'ate'. Thus, in the relative clause (2b), the relativized 'Canadian flour' must be interpreted as cooked food for eating because of the verb 'ate.' However, 'Canadian flour' can only indicate a raw material. This leads to the oddity of the meaning: 'Mary ate Canadian flour' in the given context in (2b). Raw materials such as Canadian flour may exist in two different states: i.e. the states before and after the cooking of the flour. When 'Canadian flour' is directly forced to stand for its state after cooking, as in the case of the relative (2b), the sentence becomes odd. On the other hand, in (2a) 'Canadian flour' is not directly connected to the main verb 'ate' but to its subordinate verb 'baked'. Therefore, the sentence is felicitous, as opposed to (2b).

The contrast in (2) contradicts the presumed structural equivalence of the HIR and relatives, as proposed in the LF-movement approach. The felicity of (2a) can be explained only if we assume no movement of the semantic head in the HIR, i.e. only if the semantic head in question remains internal to the HIR at LF.[4]

In conclusion, the contrast in (2) suggests that the structure of the HIR must be different from that of the corresponding relatives in Japanese, at least in examples which contain certain nouns, e.g. flour, oranges and soy beans, in the semantic head positions. In the next section, I will discuss the real nature of this construction, examining Matsuda's argument.

2.2 Gapless HIRs as prenominal complements

In the last section I have argued that the LF NP-movement approach cannot explain certain HIR examples, and have claimed that Japanese HIRs are not involved in NP movement. I further develop this claim in this section and discuss the structure of Japanese HIRs. I argue that Japanese HIRs are not relative clauses but prenominal complements.

Hereafter, I will continue to use the common term *the HIR* unless specified otherwise to refer to the Japanese prenominal complement clauses in question that have been analyzed as relative clauses in the literature. Matsuda (1993) claims that the name *Head-Internal Relative Construction* is a misnomer, and she analyzes the construction as consisting of a complement followed by *no*. I adopt part of Matsuda's complement analysis in this subsection but argue against her analysis of *no* as a pronoun later. In support of my analysis of the HIR in Japanese as a complement, I discuss data on LF-extraction of *naze* 'why'.

In discussing the differences between complement clauses and relative clauses, Fukui (1988) argues that LF-extraction of phrases in each case displays an interesting grammaticality contrast. Fukui argues that a noun complement clause shows a weaker Empty Category Principle (ECP) violation when a phrase is extracted at LF than a relative clause does. Fukui explains this in terms of L-marking.[5] L-marking is defined as follows:

(3) α L-marks β iff α is a lexical category that θ-governs β.

[Chomsky (1986, 15: 28)]

Fukui (1988) illustrates his point with (4) and (5) and attributes the grammaticality contrast between the two sentences to L-marking.

(4) Complement Clause as Subordinate Clause
?*Kimi-wa [NP [S' Taroo-ga girlfriend-to   naze wakareta] koto]-ni
you-TOP   (*m.* name)-NOM -with why broke-up thing/fact-at
sonnani odoroite-iru-no?
such   be surprised Q
'Why are you so surprised at the fact that Taro broke up with his girlfriend *t* ?'

(5) Relative Clause as Subordinate Clause
*Kimi-wa [$_{NP}$ [$_{S'}$ Taroo-ga   naze wakareta] onnanoko]-ni kinoo
you-TOP   (*m.* name)-NOM why broke-up girl   -to yesterday
party-de atta-no?
    -at met Q
'Why did you meet the girl at the party yesterday whom Taro broke up with *t* ?'

[Lasnik & Saito (1984, 244)]

In both examples, a narrow-scope reading is not available to the adjunct why-phrase *naze*. Only in (4), does the adjunct *naze* 'why' have an interpretation in terms of its wide-scope reading.[6] The adjunct *naze* is interpreted as a constituent of the main clause in (4). In contrast, the same adjunct *naze* in (5) cannot have an interpretation in either a narrow- or wide-scope reading.

Fukui argues that the extraction of *naze* from the same category S'(= CP) results in a different grammaticality, depending on whether S' is L-marked or not. He argues that, in (4), the rightmost head noun *koto* L-marks its clausal complement to its left. The head is a lexical category, i.e. N(= noun) and is in a sister relation with the complement. Further, the head noun assigns the theta role of Theme to the complement.[7] Thus, in Fukui's account, the head noun theta-governs the complement and therefore L-marks it.[8] When L-marked, the clausal complement is not a barrier that blocks movement of an internal element out of it, nor is it a barrier that blocks the association of two coindexed elements. Therefore, when the adjunct *naze* is extracted at LF for a wide-scope reading, sentence (4), which contains an L-marked complement, is more acceptable than sentence (5). The covert extraction of *naze* is not blocked by the complement clause from which it originates. In contrast, (5) is not interpretable because the covert extraction of *naze* is blocked by the relative clause. Thus, Fukui argues that the relative clause in (5) is a barrier because it is not L-marked.

Now in order for the moved adjunct *naze* to be interpreted with a wide-scope reading, the following conditions must be met. When *naze* is extracted in (4), it moves out of the S' clause to its matrix clause, leaving a trace in its original position. The Empty Category Principle (ECP) states that traces must be properly governed (Chomsky 1986, 250: 11; Haegeman 1994, 442: 12). Proper government is defined as follows:

(6)   α properly governs β iff α θ-governs or antecedent-governs β.

[Chomsky (1986, 17: 31)]

In (4) and (5), *naze* and its trace must be coindexed without an intervening barrier under the antecedent-government; otherwise, the trace is not properly governed. In (4), the adjunct *naze* antecedent-governs its trace. There is no intervening barrier in (4). In contrast, the relative clause is a barrier in (5). The relativized head *onnanoko* 'girl' does not L-mark the relative clause in (5) because it does not assign a theta role to the relative clause which is an adjunct to the head *onnanoko*. Therefore, Fukui argues that LF-extraction of *naze* is blocked by the intervening barrier, i.e. the relative clause, between *naze* and its trace in (5). The adjunct *naze* cannot antecedent-govern its trace. Neither a wide-scope nor a narrow-scope reading is allowed for *naze* in (5). This covert extraction of *naze* that Fukui proposes explains the fact that a wide-scope reading is possible with *naze* only in (4).

I will now turn to the HIR and follow Fukui's (1988) proposal regarding the *naze* extraction. I use his conclusion to test whether or not Japanese HIRs are complement clauses. If the HIRs are complements, they should display a weaker violation of ECP than relatives in the examples similar to (4) and (5). The following examples (7) and (8) show the anticipated contrast.

(7)   HIR as Subordinate Clause
      ?Mary-wa [$_{NP}$ [John-ga   syoonen-o <u>naze</u> nagutteiru]-<u>no</u>]-o osaeta no?
            -TOP   -NOM boy-ACC why hitting-ACC   caught Q
      'Why did Mary catch John hitting a boy?'
(8)   Relative Clause as Subordinate Clause
      *Mary-wa [$_{NP}$ [John-ga   <u>naze</u> nagutteiru] syoonen]-o osaeta no?
            -TOP   -NOM why hitting   boy-ACC caught Q
      'Why did Mary catch the boy who John was hitting?'

The contrast between (7) and (8) is somewhat clearer than that between (4) and (5). The adjunct *naze* in (7) has a wide-scope reading, whereas *naze* in (8) is not interpretable with either a wide- or narrow-scope reading. I account for this contrast in the following manner. A relative clause such as the one in (8) is not L-marked and is therefore a barrier, as discussed regarding (4) and (5). When *naze* is extracted, the relative clause blocks the coindexation of *naze* with its trace. The trace cannot be properly governed. Thus, the ECP is violated. A wide-scope reading is not available to *naze* in (8). A narrow-scope reading is not availabe to either (7) or (8). Consequently, the sentence is not interpretable in (8). On the other hand, the HIR clause in (7) is L-marked. The head *no* assigns a theta role to its complement, i.e. the HIR. The extraction of *naze* out of the clause is thus possible. The sentence allows the extracted reading, i.e. a wide-scope reading and therefore shows a weaker infelicity in (7).

Overall, (7) with an HIR and (8) with a relative clause show the same grammaticality contrast as that between (4) with a noun complement and (5) with a relative clause. The contrast between the examples is explained only if we analyze an HIR as a complement clause to the head *no*.[9] Therefore, following Matsuda (1993: 16–26), I claim that the HIRs are clausal complements to *no*.[10] On the other hand, I consider a canonical relative clause as an adjunct, which cannot be L-marked by its head.

Mihara & Hiraiwa (2006) argue, following Murasugi (1994), Mihara (1994), and Hoshi (1995), that the HIRs function as an adverbial, but the points I have so far made here in this section demonstrate that the HIRs are distributed quite differently from an adjunct. Adverbial complements correspond to adjuncts. Thus, the above-mentioned literature that favor the HIR as adverbial will face problems with two sets of contrasts: the contrast between (4) and (5) and the contrast between (7) and (8). In the next section, I will discuss Murasugi's adverbial analysis, but in the following chapter, I will claim that, due to the untensed nature of the HIR, the interpretation of the HIR construction must have access to discourse.

Before I conclude, I will clarify two points. First, my argument here is based on the empirical data showing contrasts between the HIRs and relatives in Japanese: these contrasts must be accounted for by any approach. I have given an account consistent with the contrasts observed in the data. Secondly, even if L-marking itself is proven to be problematic, the distinction between a complement and an adjunct in general seems to be a well-defined one, given the fundamental principle of theta-role assignment.[11] Complements but not adjuncts are assigned theta-roles. Since both the gapless status concerning argument positions at LF and the extraction restrictions are present in both the HIRs and *koto*-complements, it seems plausible that the HIRs are associated with complements irrespective of the discussion of L-marking. As a consequence, I conclude that Japanese HIRs are prenominal complements, not relatives.

Overall, I have discussed the structure of the HIR clause, and have argued that Japanese HIRs are not relatives but complements to the head *no*. Therefore, LF NP movement approaches based on the structures of relatives are not applicable to the HIRs. There is no gap internal to the HIR. In the next section, I will further discuss the possibility of postulating a null element position out of the HIR-*no* domain.

2.3 Problems with the interpretation of the Japanese HIR

I now turn to the question of how the HIRs are interpreted. In section 2.3.1, I discuss the head *no*. In 2.3.2, I discuss a *pro* approach which is another possible alternative to the interpretation of the HIR. I claim that, as a whole, a coindexation-based approach postulating a *pro* cannot account for the interpretation. These arguments lead to the introduction of a discourse representation to the interpretation of the HIR, which I will propose in chapter 3.

2.3.1 The functions and category of *no*

So far I have argued that Japanese HIRs are prenominal complement clauses, and I have claimed the following. First, the HIRs in Japanese are markedly different from relatives that come with overt relativized head nouns. As discussed before, in Japanese the canonical relative clause has been represented with a gap internal to it in an argument position (Tsujimura 1996, 266). This gap is associated with the original position of movement of a nominal. Japanese HIRs do not display such an internal gap position. Later, I will also discuss the possibility of a gap position for the null element of a nominal outside the HIR. Second, the head *no* assigns a theta-role to the HIR (complement), as the test in the previous section demonstrates. Therefore, the HIR complements have no motivation to move an argument out of their domains, unlike relative clauses. For these reasons, the structure of the HIRs cannot be equated to that of canonical relative clauses in Japanese.

I now turn to the question of how the HIR as a complement plus a noun can be properly interpreted. I first discuss the question of what the head *no* is. I mentioned earlier that one of the arguments of the main predicate appears to lack a referent because the head *no* in the whole NP, i.e. the HIR-*no*, cannot represent an explicit meaning. In this section, I discuss the nature of *no* by examining past analyses. I also discuss an analysis of *no* and the interpretation of Japanese HIRs in the light of this analysis.

In the earlier sections, I have assumed that *no* is a nominal, based on my analysis of the HIR as a prenominal complement and on the case-marking attached to the whole NP, i.e. the HIR-*no*. However, there are controversies in the literature about whether *no* in the HIR is either a noun, a pronoun, or a COMP. I examine the analyses in the literature and claim that *no* in the HIR is indeed a noun, following Murasugi's (1994) and Hoshi's (1995) claims.

Murasugi (1994) gives examples of pronominal *no* quoted from Ito (1986) and Kuroda (1992) and claims that *no* in the HIRs is a noun.[12] Kuroda (1992) points out that, when *no* functions as a pronoun, it shows a derogatory connotation indicating a lack of respect for its human referent. Note that *no* appears in a variety of syntactic environments. Pronominal *no* primarily refers to an object, not a human. Therefore, when *no* is used as a pronoun to refer to a person in an honorific context, the result is unacceptable, as shown in (9b). Kuroda compares (9b) with the acceptable sentence (9a) in a non-honorific context.

(9)a. Asoko-ni tatte iru kodomo$_i$-o soko-ni suwarasete,
     (over) there stand-be child-ACC there sit-make (and)
     mukoo-ni tatte iru-*no*$_i$-o koko-ni suwarasete kudasai.
     over-there stand-be here sit-make please
     'Please have the children standing over there sit there near you and have those standing far over there sit here.'
  b. *Asoko-ni tatte irassyaru go-roozin$_i$-o soko-ni oyobi-site,
     (over) there stand be-Hon Hon-aged-ACC there have-come (and)
     mukoo-ni tatte irassyaru *no*$_i$-o koko-ni oyobi-site kudasai.
     over-there stand be-Hon-ACC here have-come please
     'Please have those honorable aged persons standing over there come there near you and those standing far over there come here.'
                              [Kuroda (1992: 159, 10 & 11)]

On the other hand, the nominal *no* does not display any derogatory connotation, as shown in (10). The nominal does not indicate any derogatory connotation that conflicts with the honorific context.

(10) otosi-no sensee-ga otabeni-narisugiru no-wa yokunai
    old-GEN teacher-NOM eating-too-much(Hon)-TOP is-not-good
    'It is not good for the old teachers to eat too much.'
    [Murasugi (1994: 428, 9a, b)]

Note that 'the old teacher' and *no* cannot be coindexed in (10). The difference between (9) and (10) indicates that the two *no*'s are distinctive: nominal *no* vs. pronominal *no*. The important difference between the pronoun *no* in (9) and the nominal *no* in (10) is that the nominal cannot be connected directly to any individual entity, thereby being immaterial to the derogatory or non-derogatory distinctions, and instead connected to an event described in the preceding clause. Therefore, *no* in (10) should be distinctive and analyzed as a noun, not a pronoun. Similarly, *no* in the HIR also does not show any derogatory connotation, as seen in (11).

(11) HIR: Sensee-ga kenkyusitu-kara dete irassyatta no]-ni guuzen
    teacher-NOM office -from out-came (Hon)-DAT accidentally
    oaisuru-koto-ga dekita
    meet (Hon) able (PST)
    'I happened to be able to meet the teacher who was coming out of his office.' [Ito 1986]

The morpheme *no* in the HIR (11) shows the same non-derogatory connotation as the nominal *no* in (10). In other words, it shows a connotation different from that of the pronominal *no* in (9b). Therefore, with these examples such as (9), (10) and (11), it is demonstrated that *no* in the HIR is not a pronoun but a noun, following Murasugi's claim, since *no* in the HIR is not relevant to any derogatory connotation, as the pronominal *no* is in (9).

Now I will briefly mention the possibility that *no* is a complementizer (COMP). In Japanese, certain nominals are analyzed as COMPs. Murasugi (1991 & also 1994: 426) argues extensively that so-called *rentai syuusyoku* clauses (prenominal clauses) such as the HIRs in Japanese are IPs, not CPs, and therefore claims that *no* is not a COMP but a noun. Murasugi includes both a clausal complement to a noun and a noun-modifying clause in discussing prenominal clauses. Similarly, Hoshi (1995: 9–10) analyzes the HIRs as IPs. Thus, *no* cannot function as a COMP if the structure of a prenominal clause such as the HIR is an IP. Therefore, without further argument, I follow Murasugi (1994) and Hoshi (1995) in this respect.[13]

As I pointed out, *no* in the HIRs has been analyzed as either a COMP, a pronoun, or a noun. In addition, Matsuda (1993) analyzes *no* as a proform of two particular nominals: *tokoro* and *mono*. However, Horie (1993: 451–4) explicitly shows exceptions to the correspondence relation between *no* and the two nominals, *tokoro* or *mono*. This crucial example is taken from Horie (1993: 454, 24).

(12) Taroo-wa [Hanako-ga   siken-ni gookakusita {no/koto/*tokoro/*mono}
     -TOP   -NOM exam-in passed   ?/ fact/ place/ thing
     ]-o   sitta.
     -ACC learned
     'Taro learned that Hanako had passed the exam.'

In (12), *no* is paraphrasable only by *koto*, not by *tokoro* or *mono*. *No* demonstrates the clear distributional distinctiveness from *tokoro* or *mono*, which is claimed to be a proform of *no* at issue. Thus, I reject Matsuda's (1993) analysis of *no* as a proform of either *tokoro* or *mono* and exclude it from my discussion here. I have already shown that *no* in the HIR is neither a pronoun nor a complementizer.[14] Therefore, *no* must be a noun. This is the only possibility after all other claims are eliminated.

If *no* is a noun, then it should occupy the head position of the complex NP that contains the HIR as a complement, shown schematically in the following manner.

(13) [[_{NP} [_{IP} .....HIR.....] [_N *no*]]-Case (NOM, ACC, etc.) ...Main Predicate]

I hereafter treat *no* as a noun and it is structurally the head of the preceding HIR complement. The subordinate clause as a whole is an argument NP of the main predicate.

I now turn to the interpretation of *no* and the semantic head. The subordinate HIR-*no* is assigned a theta-role, since it is analyzed as an argument NP. However, the head *no* of the argument NP does not represent an explicit meaning. An English equivalent of *no* might be 'one' or 'being.' As a result, a referent of the argument NP of the main predicate must be inferentially interpreted. In addition, syntactically *no* is a head noun of N^0 category and therefore cannot be coindexed with any other NP, which is derivable from the fact that it cannot have a demonstrative "this", "that" or any adjectival element before it, whereas a typical relative head NP can. The evidence that a referent of the argument NP must be inferentially interpreted may be drawn from the ambiguity observed in (14).

(14) [[Hasi   no ue de, **keikan**-ga **doroboo**-to momiatte ita]-<u>no</u>]-ga
 bridge on-the   cop-NOM thief-with wrestling-Prft   -NOM
 ayamatte   kawani   otita.
 mistakenly river down-to fell
 'On the bridge, a policeman was wrestling with a thief, who mistakenly fell down into the river.'

Ambiguities in the HIR become conspicuous when more than one referent in the HIR can be interpreted as the referent of an argument NP of the main verb. In (14), the agentive referent of the main verb *otita* 'fell' can be either the policeman, the thief, or even both. This ambiguity depends on the availability of a specific context that contains a referent of the argument of the verb *otita*, 'fell.' If three contexts are available that correspond to the three referents, i.e. the policeman, the thief, or both, the degree of ambiguities increases. This ambiguity in the example suggests that the interpretation of a referent of the main predicate argument involves inferential processes. In the next chapter, I will argue that in order for the head *no* to receive its interpretation concerning a reference, it needs to access discourse. Before discussing the interpretation in discourse, however, I examine how the recent possible approach for interpretation, i.e. what I call a *pro*(-based) approach, would explain the HIR construction.

2.3.2 Problems with *pro* approaches to the interpretation of the HIR

I have pointed out in section 2.1 that the postulation of *pro* in the HIR poses problems. However, because a *pro*-based approach is a possible alternative to the interpretation of Japanese HIRs, I examine the approach more in detail in this section. Murasugi (1994) and Hoshi (1995) adopt Harada's (1973) Double-*O* Constraint, and argue for the occurrence of *pro* in the argument position of the main predicate in the Japanese HIR Construction.[15] Harada

(1973) proposes the following constraint on the occurrence of case *o*.

(15) The Double-*O* Constraint (DOC)
A derivation is marked as ill-formed if it terminates in a surface structure which contains two occurrences of NPs marked with *o*, both of which are immediately dominated by the same VP.   [Harada (1973: 138, 55)]

In short, the DOC means that more than one occurrence of *o* leads to an ill-formed clause. The morpheme *o* is regarded, for the most part, as the realization of accusative case. In the following discussion, however, note that Harada's classic DOC is an observational fact on the surface. As a general principle, I maintain that accusative case assignment can be multiple with a single predicate concerning double objects, since there is no verification that the marker -*o* (typically as accusative) and -*ni* (typically as dative) in Japanese equally correspond structurally with accusative and dative respectively. There are idiosyncratic instances in which -*o* functions as quirky case: for example, such an idiosyncrasy is observed with *aruku* 'walk', as seen in the example of the following paragraph. This verb marks accusative with a locative phrase, *miti* 'road'. The effect of the DOC is understood to be an observational fact on the surface only. Therefore, I assume the general principle that accusative case can be multiply assigned for double objects, in spite of the apparent constraint of the DOC in Japanese. The DOC could in fact constitute a subpart of the principle, along the line of Larson (1988). The weak effect of the DOC in the following discussion may deserve more attention to such an attempt as DOC at the generalization of case system in Japanese.

Extending Harada's (1973) proposal of the DOC, Murasugi (1994: 433) argues that the DOC has a weak effect when one of the two *o*-marked NPs is an adverbial, whereas it has a much stronger effect when the two NPs with *o* are both arguments.

(16)a. Causative Construction with 'read' [double *o*]
    *Mary-ga   sono hon-o John-o   yomaseta.
      -NOM   the book-ACC -ACC made-read
    'Mary made John read the book.'

b. Causative Construction with 'walk' [double *o*]
?Mary-ga   sono miti-o John-o   arukaseta.
    -NOM the road-ACC -ACC made-walk
'Mary made John walk on the road.'
[Murasugi (1994: 25b, and 24b respectively) with author's modification of the ordering of the two NPs with *o*]

Murasugi states that (16a) is completely ungrammatical according to the DOC since the two NPs are arguments, with each marked with *o*. In contrast, (16b) is less ungrammatical, or marginal, since *miti* 'the road' is not an argument but an adverbial. The DOC has a weak effect on (16b).[16]

Furthermore, with the postulation of *pro* in *tokoro* 'place'-phrases, Murasugi explains the marginal grammaticality of the phrase with the double *o* in (17b) in the same manner as in (16b).

(17) a. *Tokoro*-phrase with *pro*
Keikan-wa   [[doroboo$_i$-ga ginkoo-kara detekita] tokoro]-o
policeman-TOP robber-NOM bank-from   came out scene/place-ACC
pro$_i$ tukamaeta.
    arrested
'The policeman arrested the robber coming out of the bank.'
b. *Tokoro*-phrase with an added overt object [double *o*]
??Keikan-wa   [[doroboo$_i$ -ga ginkoo-kara detekita] tokoro]-o
policeman-TOP robber-NOM bank-from   came out scene/place-ACC
soitu$_i$-o   tukamaeta.
the fella/guy-ACC arrested
'The policeman arrested the robber coming out of the bank.'
                                    [Murasugi (1994: 20, 22 respectively)]

Murasugi argues that a *tokoro*-phrase has a *pro* in the argument position of the main predicate, as in (17a). Murasugi claims that the *tokoro*-phrase is an adverbial, not an argument, despite it being marked with *o*. Because the *tokoro*-phrase is not an argument, (17b) is claimed not to be completely ungrammatical when a lexical pronoun *soitu* 'the fella/guy' appears in place of *pro*, thereby introducing a second *o*. Murasugi claims that the DOC applies only weakly when one of the two *o*'s is a non-argument.

Furthermore, Murasugi (1994) applies the above argument to the HIR. She argues that the meanings of the HIRs and *tokoro*-phrases are identical when the sentences consist of the same lexical items. Therefore, she treats both constructions uniformly, postulating *pro* in the HIR as well.

(18) HIR with *pro* in the argument position:
Keikan-wa   [[doroboo$_i$-ga ginkoo-kara detekita] no]-o
policeman-TOP robber-NOM bank-from came out-ACC
pro$_i$ tukamaeta.
    arrested
'The policeman arrested the robber coming out of the bank.'
[Murasugi (1994: 21)]

Murasugi observes that the *tokoro*-phrase in (17a) and the HIR-*no* phrase in (18) are quite similar. Then, based on this observation, she claims that the HIRs plus *no* are also adverbial, and the DOC has a weak effect on the HIRs. The following sentence illustrates her account.

(19) HIR with *sore* 'it' as an argument [double *o*]
??Mary-wa [[syasin$_i$-ga   teeburu-ni oitearu] no]-o *sore*$_i$-o mita.
 -TOP picture-NOM table-on is-put-ACC   it -ACC saw
'Mary saw a picture that is put on the table.'   [Murasugi (1994: 28)]

Murasugi's point rests on the subtle grammaticality differences when the pronoun *soitu* 'the fella' in (17b) and *sore* 'it' in (19) replace *pro*'s in the assumed argument position. Her claim is that *tokoro*-phrases and the HIRs are both adverbial and should show the same partial grammaticality in double *o* examples. However, contrary to her argument, there is an example in which the HIR shows a strong violation effect concerning the double *o*, as in the following.

With two sets of data, I argue against Murasugi's analysis of the HIRs as adverbial and her *pro*-based approach to the HIR.[17] I first present an example in which the DOC displays a strong effect on the HIR. According to Murasugi's approach, the DOC should show a weak effect on the HIRs when they occur with the double *o*. However, in (18), when I replace the alleged *pro* with its antecedent NP *doroboo* 'robber' in the subordinate clause and further replace the original antecedent *doroboo* with a *pro* (under its identity with its now replaced NP) in the main clause, the resultant HIR with the double *o* is totally ungrammatical, as in (20).

(20) HIR-*no* phrase [double *o*]
    *Keikan-wa   [[pro$_i$ ginkoo-kara detekita]-no]-o
    policeman-TOP [[(SUB) bank from   came out]   ]-ACC
    doroboo$_i$-o   tukamaeta.
    robber-ACC arrested
    'The policeman arrested the robber coming out of the bank.'

The three examples, (17a), (18), and (20), should display the same kind of grammaticality, i.e. a mild violation, if Murasugi is right. Contrary to her argument, the resultant HIR sentence (20) is totally ungrammatical with the double *o* and strongly violates the DOC. The result suggests that the HIR is not an adverbial, and her approach does not apply to the HIR in the same manner as it is applied to the *tokoro*-phrases. The point is that the total ungrammaticality of (20) is contradictory to her analysis of the HIR as adverbial.

    Alternatively, I argue that the result can be explained if we analyze the HIR-*no* phrase as an argument, not an adverbial. The DOC's weak effect that is claimed to apply to adverbials does not apply to the HIRs. Note also that the subtle grammaticality is a little problematic in the cases of (17b) and (19), and I do not discuss whether Murasugi's argument does or does not apply to the *tokoro*-phrases. The important fact is that the HIR (20) is completely ill-formed with the occurrence of double *o*, which is contrary to Murasugi's argument. One may argue that any instance of the above operations, as in (20), that result in double *o* may be ill-formed. As a result, the weak/strong effect of the DOC that Murasugi proposes may be irrelevant to the observed ungrammaticality variations. However, the example in (21b) is grammatical after the same operation by the postulation of *pro* as in (20). Observe (21a).

(21)a. Yamada-wa [[huusen-ga   sonomamade umaku   hukuramu]
        Yamada-TOP   balloon-NOM as-it-is   successfully swell
        mono]-o tsubushita.
        thing-ACC burst
        'Yamada burst the balloon which could successfully swell.'

b.(?)Yamada-wa [[*pro*ᵢ sonomamade umaku hukuramu] *mono*]-o
Yamada-TOP (SUB) as-it-is successfully swell thing-ACC
huusenᵢ-o tsubushita.
balloon-ACC burst
'Yamada burst the balloon which could successfully swell.' [double *o*]

We can attribute this grammaticality to the adverbial nature of the *mono* subordinate clause in (21b). Therefore, it seems that we need Murasugi's claim of weak/strong effects as an observational fact in Japanese at this stage. The weak effect of the DOC may turn out to be the surface realization of the multiple accusative assignment regarding the double objects. However, I do not discuss this general issue. In addition, it is true that in certain cases double *o* does not result in the total ungrammaticality in the same schematic anaphora as in (20).

The same fact that I have discussed earlier can also be seen when the antecedent noun *doroboo* 'robber' precedes its coindexed *pro* in the subordinate clause.

(22)a. *Tokoro*-phrase [double *o*]
?Keikan-wa dorobooᵢ-o [[*pro*ᵢ ginkoo-kara
policeman-TOP robber-ACC [[(SUB) bank from
detekita] -*tokoro*]-o tukamaeta.
came out] place]-ACC arrested
'The policeman arrested the robber coming out of the bank.'
b. HIR-*no* phrase [double *o*]
*Keikan-wa dorobooᵢ-o [[*pro*ᵢ ginkoo-kara detekita]-no]
policeman-TOP robber-ACC [[(SUB) bank from came out]]
-o tukamaeta.
-ACC arrested
'The policeman arrested the robber coming out of the bank.'

The HIR example (22b) still remains ill-formed, whereas (22a) is not unacceptable. Contrary to Murasugi's claim that the HIRs are adverbial, the occurrence of the double *o* in the HIRs results once again in the strong violation of the DOC. The result here also suggests that the HIR-*no* phrase is an argument, not an adverbial. If we maintain the discussion of the DOC's strong/weak effect, the ungrammaticality of (22b) should be attributed to the occurrence of the two *o*-marked arguments in the HIR sentence. The two arguments with the double *o* in the HIRs strongly violate the DOC, irrespective of *pro* in the main predicates. Based on my observations concerning both (20) and (22), I conclude that the HIRs are arguments and reject the analysis of the HIRs as adverbials.

Another point to mention is the grammaticality contrast between (22a) and (22b). This contrast suggests that the HIRs and *tokoro*-phrases differ from each other. Although *tokoro*-phrases can be analyzed as adverbials and thus have *pro* in the argument positions, the HIR-*no* phrases cannot be treated in the same way. The postulation of *pro* in the HIRs results in the wrong prediction as to the grammaticality of the double *o* occurrence. The existence of *pro* in the HIRs must be questioned. In the following paragraphs, I discuss this issue.

The second problem with the *pro*-based approach to the HIRs is the heavily restricted distribution of *pro* in the HIRs with respect to the argument position in which it appears. Murasugi (1994) and Hoshi (1995) consider the HIRs as adjuncts. Therefore, if we follow Murasugi's *pro* approach, *pro* should occupy an empty argument position, either an object or subject position. Observe the grammaticality of such examples in (23) and (24).

(23) a. HIR-*no* with nominative case *ga* and *pro* in the object position
 *John-wa [[sensee_i-ga aisatu-sita]-<u>no</u>]-ga *pro*_i musi-sita.
 -TOP   teacher-NOM bowed   -NOM (OBJ)   ignored
 Intended meaning: 'John ignored the teacher's bowing,' or 'The teacher bowed, which John ignored.'
 b. HIR-*no* with accusative case *o* and *pro* in the subject position
 *[[John_i-ga kawa-no   watasi-o   hasitte-ita]-<u>no</u>]-o   *pro*_i
       -NOM river-GEN bridge-ACC run-be-PST   -ACC (SUB)
 otita.
 fell
 Intended meaning: 'John was running along the bridge over the river, and he fell.'

(24) a. HIR-*no* with accusative case *o* and *pro* in the object position
 John-wa [[sensee_i-ga   aisatu-sita]-<u>no</u>]-o   *pro*_i   musi-sita.
      -TOP teacher-NOM bowed   -ACC (OBJ)   ignored
 'John ignored the teacher's bowing,' or 'The teacher bowed, which John

ignored.'
b. HIR-*no* with nominative case *ga* and *pro* in the subject position
[[John$_i$-ga   kawa-no   watasi-o   hasitte-ita]-<u>no</u>]-ga   *pro*$_i$
　　　　-NOM   river-GEN bridge-ACC run-be-PST   -NOM (SUB)
otita.
fell
'John was running along the bridge over the river, and he fell.'

I have marked the grammatical functions for *pro* with parentheses in each gloss. It turns out that, as shown in (23), in the light of grammatical functions, asymmetric combinations cannot occur between the HIR-*no* phrase and *pro*. The only possible combination would be the one when both serve as the same grammatical function such as subject or object, as in (24). If the HIR-*no* is marked with accusative *o* which should be marked onto an object, *pro* must be an object, as in (24a). If the HIR-*no* is marked with nominative case which should be marked onto a subject, *pro* must be a subject, as we see in (24b). The *pro* approach cannot explain this parallelism in (24). In other words, the *pro* approach cannot account for why the other combinations cannot occur, as seen in the ungrammaticality of (23).[18] However, if we discard *pro* and simply assume that the HIR-*no* is a syntactic argument of the main predicate, as I claim, we do not have a problem with accounting for the above examples. Those examples are ungrammatical simply because the HIR-*no* is assigned a wrong case-marking which contradicts the argument structure that the main verb requires. In (23a), the verb *mushi-shita* 'ignored' requires an internal Theme argument, i.e. an object, as well as *John* as an external argument. However, the logical object, i.e. the HIR-*no*, is marked with nominative case and cannot be an object. Therefore, the sentence is ungrammatical. Likewise, in (23b) the verb *otita* 'fall' should have an external Agent argument, i.e. a subject, but the logical subject HIR-*no* is marked with accusative case and therefore cannot be a subject. No other external argument is available. Consequently, the sentence is ungrammatical. Importantly, if the HIR-*no* phrases in (23) are marked with the case appropriate to their functions in the sentences, the sentences are grammatical, irrespective of the existence of *pro*. Those appropriate examples in fact correspond to the examples in (24). For example, if nominative case *ga* attached to the HIR-*no* is replaced with accusative case *o* in (23a), the sentence becomes grammatical, as in (24a). Likewise, if accusative *o* is replaced with nominative *ga* in (23b), the sentence becomes acceptable, as in (24b). Therefore, I conclude that *pro* cannot exist in the argument positions of the main predicates in the HIR construction.

In this section, I have shown that Japanese HIR-*no* phrases are arguments, not adverbials. I have argued that the *pro*-based approach cannot account for the problems of two separate issues: first, the problem of the strong violation of the DOC when the HIRs occur with the double *o*, and, secondly, the problem of the biased distribution of *pro* that would occur if the empty element were postulated in the argument positions in the HIR examples. Thus, I have shown that the *pro*-based approach is not adequate for the interpretation of Japanese HIR construction. In the next chapter, I seek an alternative solution to the problems regarding the interpretation of the construction at issue.

Endnotes
1   This assumption is made under the studies of Ancash Quechua, Imbabura Quechua, Diegueno, and Lakhota in Williamson (1987), Cole (1987), Culy (1990), and Basilico (1996).
2   Note that in principle an NP cannot move to an NP position already occupied by another NP. Therefore, the target position of NP movement in this case should not be that of the null pronoun, but I do not discuss this here, as it is not relevant to the argument in the section.
3   Cole and Hermon (1994) cite Culy's (1990) alternative claim that HIRs lack a syntactic head at either S-structure or LF. They also state that Culy proposes LF movement of an internal NP to an A' position external to the HIR clause.
4   Similarly, Matsuda (1993, 7–10) argues that the interpretations of comparable relatives and the HIR cannot be identical in the following pair of examples.

   (a) HIR Clause: John-wa [[Mary-ga   mikan-o   shibotta] no]-o nonda.
                    -TOP   -NOM orange-ACC squeezed-ACC drank
       'John drank the product of Mary squeezing oranges.'
   (b) Relative Clause: #John-wa [Mary-ga   shibotta] mikan-o   nonda.
                         -TOP   -NOM squeezed oranges-ACC drank
       'John drank the oranges that Mary squeezed.'   [Matsuda (1993, 7–8: 11a, b)]

   In both examples, what John actually 'drank' after Mary's squeezing is not the whole portion of an orange but the juice. The 'orange' is involved in the relevant event in two ways, just as the 'flour' in (2) is. However, because the semantic head is internal to the HIR even at LF, the 'orange' is interpreted only as the object of the subordinate verb 'squeeze', and not of the main verb 'drank.' The object of 'drank' must be indicated,

instead, by the HIR-*no*. Example (a) is thus felicitous, in contrast to (b). I argue that a referent of the object must be inferentially interpreted in discourse.
5   Fukui (1988) adopts this line of arguments from Chomsky (1981, 1986).
6   Relatively low grammaticalities in both sentences are partly due to the preference for the in-situ , i.e. narrow-scope, readings with Wh-phrases in Japanese. In (4) and (5), a narrow-scope reading is not possible. Therefore, both sentences sound awkward.
7   As discussed in Iida (1987) and others, certain classes of nominals in Japanese apparently assign theta roles to the preceding NPs or complements.

Sensei-ga   suugaku-(w)o   koogichu-ni   John-wa sando-mo
Teacher-NOM mathematics-ACC lecture-middle-at/in John-TOP 3-times-Intnsfr
inemurishita.
doze-Pst
'John dozed off three times during the teacher's lecture of mathematics.'

In this example, (*koogi*)-*chuu* assigns accusative case -(*w*)*o* to a nominal *suugaku* and nominative -*ga* to *sensei*. This class of nominals is discussed in Iida. Grimshaw (1990) also discusses the processes of theta assignment with deverbal nouns.
8   Chomsky (1986: 35) states that the extraction of an element from a noun-complement results in a weaker subjacency violation than that of relative clauses. He argues that the noun-complement is L-marked by its head noun and, therefore, not a barrier to the extraction (Chomsky 1986: 35–6). Fukui adopts this analysis and argues that the head noun *koto* in Japanese assigns a theta role to its complement, as in (4). I do not argue whether nouns can generally assign theta roles to their complements in Japanese, but, given the example of the theta assignment with a class of nominals in the preceding footnote, I follow Fukui (1988) and Matsuda (1993) in assuming that *koto*, *no* and this class of formal nouns can assign theta roles to their complements. The given examples of the theta assignment of Nominative and Accusative cases with a head noun support an argument for the possibility of theta assignment to an IP structure in Japanese, as I discuss later in section 2.3.1.
9   One would argue that the complements in question here are adjuncts to the head noun, as in Stowell (1981). However, the head nouns presented in this section belong to formal nouns or pseudo nouns, as I mentioned earlier in the footnote. These nouns usually need a complement to which they attach, as in the examples below. No intervening element is allowed as well: adjacency is observed, as Matsuda (1993) argues. Korean also has a similar class of nouns called "incomplete nouns."

a. *(John-wa)   koto-o   sitta.
          -TOP thing-ACC knew/recognized
    'John recognized a thing.'
a.' John-wa [Mary-ga   hon-o   kaita]-koto-o   sitta.
       -TOP   -NOM   book-ACC   wrote thing-ACC knew
    'John recognized that Mary wrote a book.'
b. *(John-wa)   no-o   tukutta.

-TOP one?-ACC made
'John made one(?).'
b.' John-wa [sensee-ga kougeihin-o osieta]-<u>no</u>-o jibunde tukutta.
teacherNOM handcraft-ACC taught one?-ACC by himself made
'John made a handcraft, which a teacher taught.'

I do not discuss this, but suggest that these nouns may have specific lexical information on subcategorization regarding the sentential complements they require. *Koto* may not be a complementizer, but that does not affect our argument. It suffices here that *koto* is a nominal.

10 Though Matsuda (1993: 16–23) also argues for the view that the HIRs are complements, not relatives, she divides the HIRs into two types of subclasses and proposes that *no* is either a proform of a noun *tokoro* 'place' or a proform of *mono* 'thing.' However, as Horie (1993: 451–4) discusses, there are other examples in which these paraphrases do not work. Moreover, *no* seems to be paraphrased also as *koto* 'thing/event' in some cases. It is not clear how Matsuda's argument can be supported. Another problem with Matsuda (1993: 26–8) is that she analyzes the rightmost head *no* as a pronoun. I discuss the issue in section 3.1, but it is not clear, in general, how a pronoun can be a head to a complement clause, as Matsuda claims. I nevertheless adopt her core claim that the HIRs are complement clauses to nouns.

11 It should be emphasized that adjuncts cannot be assigned a theta role. As an adjunct, canonical relatives in Japanese cannot be assigned the theta role. In contrast, I analyze the HIR as a complement, and therefore it can be assigned a theta role, as discussed earlier. Furthermore, the direct relevance condition, or contiguity restriction in my terminology, between the two events would not be accounted for if the HIR is analyzed as a relative clause.

12 The morpheme *no* can be either a genitive case marker, or a pronoun, or a nominal. However, Murasugi (1994: 426–7) shows crucial evidence against the analysis of *no* in the HIR as a genitive case marker. In a Japanese dialect called Toyama dialect, the nominal *no* is phonetically realized as *ga*, while the genitive case marker is realized as *no*. Since the head *no* in the HIR is realized as *ga* in the dialect, she concludes that *no* in the HIR is not a genitive case marker. I adopt her analysis and only discuss whether it is a noun or a pronoun here.

13 In the literature, it is argued that only CP, but not IP, can be referential in general. In this respect, the HIR apparently poses a problem with its structure analyzed as IP. Without further discussion of this issue, however, I just point out that certain classes of nominals in Japanese can assign theta roles for both subject and object NPs without any other predicate, as already shown earlier in the footnote. It seems possible therefore that IPs without tense features can reach a referent in certain constructions in Japanese, although the general question of the referentiality with the IPs' structures has yet to be solved. I will only discuss the referent available in discourse as a participant of indicated events.

14 Concerning the complementizers in Japanese, Horie (1993) extensively examines the different distributions of those alleged complementizer candidates in Japanese. That suggests that, except typical complementizers such as -*toiukoto*, some more studies need

15 Hoshi (1995, 9–10) actually proposes an empty argument NP [e] outside the entire HIR-*no* phrase, and he argues that [e] is base-generated as an argument of the matrix predicate. He then states that the empty NP [e] is a kind of anaphoric element along the lines of Cole (1987). It is not clear how a null NP in a head-governed argument position can be both base-generated and anaphoric. A null element that is base-generated and anaphoric would be PRO, but PRO must not be governed and cannot meet this condition. Rather, the empty NP [e] in this environment seems to be a *pro* with a feature [-anaphor]. A null argument NP, if base-generated and head-governed, would only be analyzed as a *pro*. Therefore, I assume that Hoshi's [e] is a *pro* here.

16 As Maria Babyonyshev (personal communication) points out, the DOC does not have any effect on the multiplicity of accusative assignment for double objects in the examples: Murasugi's example sentences are both acceptable, if *John-o* is replaced with dative *John-ni*. In the replaced examples, two objects are held as acceptable. Note, however, that in certain cases clear distributional differences are observed between -*o* and -*ni*.

    a. John-wa/ga   miyage-o   Mary-ni   ageta.
       John-TOP/NOM souvenir-ACC Mary-DAT gave
       'John gave Mary a souvenir.'
    b. John-mo/*wamo/*gamo; miyage-mo/*omo; Mary-{*mo/nimo}

When an intensifier like -*mo* 'also' is added to them, as in (b), they are overridden by the intensifier only with the subject/topic markers -*ga/wa* or the object marker -*o*. The dative -*ni* cannot be overridden; instead, only the addition of the intensifier is possible just like the cases with the other postpositional case markers like -*kara*, -*de*, etc. This suggests that there are features or elements that distinguish markers -*ga/wa* and -*o* from -*ni* in Japanese, as in (b). Some more studies have yet to be done on this phenomenon.

17 Mihara (1994) and Hoshi(1995) also analyze the HIR-*no* construction as an adverbial and posit *pro* in the argument position of the main predicate. I do not examine them, but in the following paragraphs I point out that their adverbial analysis cannot be maintained.

18 Along the same line of the *pro*-based approach, Murasugi would have to stipulate a constraint such as "Double *ga* (NOM)-Case Constraint (DGC)" in order to account for the marginal example with the pronoun *sore* 'it' below.

    ex. [[Hon$_i$-ga   teeburu-ni oite atta]-no]-ga (Ø/??*sore*$_i$-ga)   nakunatta.
        book-NOM   table-on   put existed-NOM it/that-NOM disappeared
        'A book/books that had been put on the table (by someone) disappeared.'

In this HIR example, *sore* replaces *pro* in the alleged argument position, with the second *ga* (NOM)-case assigned. The marginal grammaticality of the sentence would be accounted for by resorting to the DGC, i.e. the constraint on the occurrence of double *ga*-case. Then, grounded in the DGC, the *pro*-approach would state that the marginality is due to the weak effect of the constraint when one of the two *ga*'s is marked onto an adjunct. The DGC applies weakly to the HIR example because the HIR-*no* phrase is an adjunct. However, this contradicts the well-formedness that the above example shows when it lacks a subject. In fact, the whole HIR-*no* phrase properly functions as a subject, i.e. an argument. Moreover, the *pro*-approach is contradictory to the fact that multiple *ga*'s do occur, as in the following example. The well-formed example below has two *ga*'s, which contradicts the DGC.

ex. Shiatoru-ga   koohii-ga   umai.
    Seattle-NOM coffee-NOM good
    'Coffee is good in Seattle.'

Therefore, the *pro*-based approach that postulates *pro* in the argument position in the HIR is untenable.

Chapter 3

Modeling the event representation of temporal interpretation

In chapter 2, I have argued that Japanese HIRs are not involved in NP movement. I have claimed that the noun *no* cannot be coindexed with any other NP in a sentence. Instead, I have analyzed *no* as a head noun of an argument NP of the main predicate, although *no* does not indicate an explicit referent in its semantic content. Furthermore, I have rejected the postulation of the null element *pro* in the argument position. Now, having established that previous approaches are inadequate, I will discuss how the HIRs can properly be interpreted. In section 3.1, I show that the HIRs display an interesting tense/aspect representation. I claim that, because of the temporal restriction of the subordinate HIR as an untensed clause, access to discourse is necessary for their interpretation. In section 3.2, I discuss a discourse representation approach based on Russian examples and argue that the discourse-based approach can represent the interpretation of Russian untensed constructions. In section 3.3, I show how NPs in Japanese HIRs can also be interpreted by means of the proposed approach to the event representation in discourse. I show how the temporal restrictions will be accommodated in the approach. Overall, in chapter 3, I will present a skeleton of the model of the discourse representation for the interpretation of untensed clauses such as the HIR.

3.1 The HIR as an untensed clause

Earlier in chapter 1, I mentioned that Japanese HIRs show a restriction on the occurrence of temporal adverbs. I repeat the example here.

(1)a. The HIR in Japanese
John-ga   [[Mary-ga   {Ø/*kinoo/*senjitu}   ringo-o
John-NOM [[Mary-NOM {Ø/*yesterday/*the other day} apple-ACC
kat*ta*]-no]-o   tabe*ta*.
bought]]-ACC ate
'Mary bought an apple yesterday, which John ate.'
b. Relative Clause in Japanese
John-ga   [[Mary-ga   {-Ø/kinoo/senjitu}   kat*ta*]
   -NOM [[-NOM {-Ø/yesterday/the other day} bought]
ringo]-o   tabe*ta*.
apple]-ACC ate
'John ate an apple which Mary bought yesterday.'

In the HIR clause in (1a), the temporal adverbs which indicate past time cannot occur. In contrast, there is no such restriction in the relative counterpart, as in (1b). It is generally understood that the *-u* form indicates the present or future tense, while the *-ta* form indicates the past tense.[1] However, this dichotomy cannot explain the ungrammaticality of (1a). The HIR in (1a) exemplifies the conflict between the past tense form *-ta* and the adverb *kinoo* 'yesterday'. In fact, past researchers have demonstrated that there are irregularities in the Japanese tense system. Soga (1983) summarizes the problem in this way:

(2) The *-ta* form or so-called 'past tense form' normally refers to events in the past, and the *-ru* form or so-called 'non-past tense form,' to those in the present or the future. Aspectually, *-ta* most normally indicates the completive aspect, and *-ru*, the incompletive aspect. In some cases, however, their reference does not conform to the normal pattern, when these forms may be more significant from the aspectual viewpoint, regardless of the time relations. Thus, *-ta* may be used to indicate the completive aspect although the event referred to may happen in the future, and *-ru* may be used to indicate the incompletive aspect of a past event.
[Soga (1983, 36)]

As Soga states in (2), the two tense markers, *-ta* and *-(r)u* can also indicate aspect oppositions such as the completive/perfective and the incompletive/ imperfective respectively. Examples of such uses of the tense markers are shown below.

(3) a. Karakat-*ta* nara, sumanai.
Tease-TA Conditonal tolerate-Neg
'(I) won't tolerate it if (you) tease (me).'

b. Ashita-no eiga-wa san-ji kara-dat-*ta*.
Tomorrow-GEN movie-TOP 3 o'clock from Cplr-TA
'Tommorow's movie turns out to start at 3 o'clock.'

c. Ani-wa honbako o moo nijukko mo kanzen-ni
elder brother-TOP bookcase-ACC already 20-Clssfr also completely
tukut-*te*-ir-*u*.
make-TE-Asp-NONPAST
'My elder brother (by now) has made as many as 20 bookcases completely.'
[(3c) is quoted from Iwasaki 2002: 114, 23, with my addition of 'completely']

In (3a), the speaker indicates the completion of an addressee's teasing in the conditional clause. He declares that he will not tolerate if the addressee teases him later. Therefore, the sentence does not indicate past, but the aspectual information of prefect(ive) is marked with *-ta* in the conditional clause. In (3b), with *-ta*, the main clause represents information about the time for tomorrow's movie that the speaker is concerned about. Therefore, the marker *-ta* is involved in the future event of the movie taking place at 3 o'clock tomorrow. In (3c), there is some more complexity with the complex predicate, *-te ir-u*. The complex predicate as a whole indicates a resultative state, and the sentence indicates that the brother's making of as many as 20 bookcases has been completed prior to the reference time (which coincides with the speech time). The point is that a variant form of *-ta* represents the completion, not pastness, since the time that the whole sentence indicates is 'now' with a non-past marker *-u*. This *-u*, together with *-ir-*, represents imperfective, i.e., a state (of change), in (3c). Note that the adverb *kanzen-ni* 'completely' represents the completion of an act, and the occurrence of the adverb endorses the perfective meaning of *-ta* with the act of having made 20 bookcases by now. Such a complex combination of aspectual information is derived from the opposition between imperfective and perfective with *-u* and *-ta*. I will discuss the complex predicate, -*te ir-u* in detail in chapter 4. I suggest here that, in the HIR clause, i.e. the embedded clause, -*ta* may indicate the completive/perfective aspect instead of the past tense.

As we have already seen, in the relative construction (1b), the sentence is grammatical even when both the past verb form *teni-ire-ta* 'got' and the temporal adverb indicating the past event occur. In this case, we must consider the role tense plays in the relative clause. It is then arguable that -*ta* serves as the past tense marker in both the subordinate relative clause and the main clause in (1b). However, the same adverbs cannot appear in the case of the subordinate HIR in (1a). We can now see the cause of the ungrammaticality arising from the inclusion of the temporal adverbs *kinoo* 'yesterday' and *senjitsu* 'the other day.' If -*ta* in fact indicated the past tense, in this case these adverbs would be acceptable. However, the adverbs cannot occur with the perfective aspect marker -*ta* in the subordinate HIRs. The perfective/imperfective aspect in subordinate clauses cannot be associated with specific time reference for the event. Comrie (1976) claims that "aspect is the internal temporal constituency of a situation" (Comrie 1976: 3), "where ... it [= time reference of aspect] is relative time reference" (Comrie 1976: 2) or "relative tense" (Chung and Timberlake 1985). Time reference of aspect is not grammaticalized. Instead, the external temporal indication, i.e. the specification of a time-point, is carried out by the tense of the main predicate. Based on these observations, I claim that aspect is indicated by -*ta* and -*u* in the subordinate HIRs, but tense is indicated by the same forms in subordinate relative clauses.

The same line of discussion of the -*ta* form in (1a) also applies to the -*u* form in (4).

(4)   The HIR in Japanese
  a. Mary-wa [[John-ga   kusatta ringo-o   {Ø/*ashita/   *yokujitsu
         -TOP   -NOM   rotten apple-ACC {Ø/*tomorrow/*next day
     /*kyoo/*kinoo}   kuti-ni   irer-*u*]-no]-o   tome-*ta*.
     /*today/*yesterday} mouth-in put (Pres?)-ACC stopped
     'Mary stopped John from putting the rotten apple in his mouth.'
  b. Mary-wa *kinoo*   [[John-ga   kusatta ringo-o   kuti-ni irer-*u*]
         -TOP yesterday [[-NOM   rotten apple-ACC moth-in put]]
     -no]-o tometa.
     -ACC stopped

'Yesterday Mary stopped John from putting the rotten apple in his mouth.'

In (4a), we observe the alleged present/future marker -*u* in the HIR. The sentence is grammatical when the temporal adverbials of either the present/future or past do not appear. However, the sentence is ungrammatical if these adverbials are associated with the subordinate event, i.e. John's putting the rotten apple in his mouth. We cannot explain this fact if we assume that -*u* indicates the present/future tense.

As mentioned above, -*u* may indicate the imperfective aspect. In the grammatical counterpart of (4a), i.e. the one without an adverbial, the subordinate event must be interpreted as incomplete. This interpretation applies whether the main event takes place in the present, future, or past. The issue here is that John's act of putting something in his mouth is indeed in the middle of being carried out. Thus, the temporal representation with -*u* indicates that the event in the subordinate clause is in progress in relation to the main event. The -*u* form in (4) leads us to the interpretation that John's putting the apple in his mouth was not over when Mary's action to stop it began. Subordinate clauses with -*u* are tenseless, but indicate the imperfective aspect. In contrast, in (4b), with the addition of the past time adverb 'yesterday' in the main clause, the sentence is well-formed. Therefore, the main clause of the HIR construction allows the tense indication. In general, subordinate clauses in the HIR construction lack tense indication. Instead, they only indicate the internal temporal organization of the subordinate event in relation to the event represented by the main clause.

Concerning my characterization of -*u* and -*ta* in the HIRs in terms of aspect, there is a supportive fact found in classical Japanese. The form -*ta* was used exclusively for the perfective until the sixteenth century. Soga (1983) states as follows:

(5) In classical Japanese, the form *tari* and *nu* as well as *tu* were used to express the meaning of completive aspect. Past tense was expressed by different forms such as *ki* or *keri*. However, by around the middle of the sixteenth century, *tari* had changed to *ta* and has survived to this day, taking on the function of the past tense marker as well as the completive aspect marker.

[Soga (1983, 39–40)]

It is therefore arguable that the assumed tense markers *-ta* and *-u* serve as aspect markers in certain constructions in modern Japanese.

In this section, I have argued for the aspectual organization of Japanese HIRs. As support for my argument, I have discussed the tense asymmetry between the HIRs and relative clauses, and have mentioned also the historical change of the use of *-ta* form. Based on these discussions, I conclude that the Japanese HIR clauses lack tense. I have also observed that the imperfective and perfective aspects are indicated by the *-u* and *-ta* forms respectively. Note that the English translations of the HIR examples are at best approximate ones obtained through some reasoning. As I have already discussed, the following factors are at least involved in the observation: first, the head nominal *no* does not have a meaningful content; second, an argument of the main predicate is apparently missing in the main clause; and, third, the HIR clause itself is untensed, i.e., no temporal relation is explicitly determined through the tense indication. Given these, the English translation is obtained only after the meaning of the sentence is reasoned in discourse as to which NP can be the argument of the main predicate, on the one hand, and what temporal ordering can be legitimate between the two events indicated by the two clauses, on the other hand. Later in section 3.3, I will discuss how other properties of the HIR can be accounted for uniformly in light of their untensed status, but in the next section 3.2, I will first discuss how the untensed HIR can be interpreted.

3.2 Discourse representation for the interpretation of untensed constructions

I base my arguments in the following section on research conducted on Russian data. Once the discourse representation model is explained, I will return to the Japanese language and explain how this model can be used for the interpretation of Japanese HIRs.

3.2.1 Unindexed T and its consequence in untensed constructions

I now turn to the question of how an untensed clause can properly be interpreted. Hyams (1996) argues that an infinitive clause, i.e. an untensed clause, cannot have an index on Tense head (hereafter T). On the other hand, T must bear an index in a finite clause. Gueron and Hoekstra (1995) and Hyams (1996) argue that T can either be coindexed or contraindexed with

Tense Operator (hereafter TO) which forms a Tense chain with T through C. When T is coindexed with TO, the present tense will be indicated. When T is contraindexed with TO, the past tense will be indicated. In the case of an unindexed clause, T does not have an index, according to Hyams. As a result, T without an index cannot form a Tense chain with TO. Therefore, sentences with underspecified T should have no temporal interpretation as either the present or past tense.

Now let us assume, following Chomsky (1995), that T must also have Spec-head agreement in TP with its subject NP because the NP bears D feature. The consequence of Hyams's argument is that an untensed clause cannot have the feature of the NP checked off by T. Consequently, the untensed sentence should be uninterpretable. However, there are certain cases in which untensed clauses can indeed have an interpretation, with both T and a subject NP unindexed.[2] If untensed sentences are allowed as grammatical ones, the above theories alone cannot explain how the subject NPs and T without indices are interpreted. Avrutin (1997a, b) argue that untensed sentences can be interpreted through access to discourse representation where they are interpreted as event units. In the following discussion, I give examples of untensed sentences and present how they can be interpreted by means of a model of discourse representation which Avrutin proposes.

Avrutin (1997b) argues that certain root-infinitives (hereafter RI) in Russian can indeed have interpretation by non-syntactic means. Infinitival forms of verbs do not indicate tense and are generally ungrammatical in Russain, as in (6).

(6)a.   Ivan begal/begaet/*begat'.
      Ivan {ran   /runs   /*to run}   [Avrutin(1997a, 2: 1)]

Likewise, the RI sentence in (7) could also be identified as ungrammatical. Under some specific discourse related circumstances, however, Russian does allow RIs such as (7).

(7)   Carevna (tut) xoxotat'.
     Princess (here/at this point) to langh
     'The princess started to laugh (right after something funny happened)'
                                                [Avrutin(1997a, 2: 2)]

As we see in the gloss in parentheses in (7), the verb indicates the beginning of an action that immediately follows some event assumed to be known. In other words, a preceding event exists in the discourse when the infinitival sentence (7) occurs. In response to such discourse-rooted phenomena, Avrutin (1997a, b) proposes Event File Cards (hereafter E-cards) for discourse representation of linguistic utterances. Before I discuss how the RI example (7) can be interpreted, I summarize the E-card approach.

3.2.2 Summary of the Event File Card approach

Following Heim's (1982) individual file card (hereafter I-card) approach, Avrutin claims that, in discourse, E-cards represent the events indicated by utterances. Diagrammatically, the representation of the sentence *John ate an apple* will be:

(8)　An Event File Card representation of *John ate an apple*

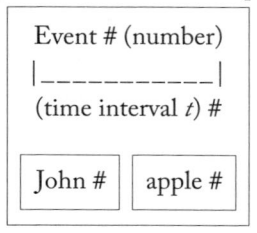

```
┌─────────────────────────┐
│  Event # (number)       │
│  |_____|          │
│  (time interval t) #    │
│                         │
│  ┌────────┐ ┌─────────┐ │
│  │ John # │ │ apple # │ │
│  └────────┘ └─────────┘ │
└─────────────────────────┘
```

[Avrutin (1997b, 11: 13)]

In (8), the E-card contains a time interval during which the event holds, i.e. lasts, and also contains two I-cards representing participants in the event. Avrutin argues that the number of each I-card is the instantiating constant of the variable index on the subject or object NP. The number of the E-card is also the instantiating constant of the variable index on the event argument introduced by the predicate. Following Davidson (1967), Higginbotham (1983, 1985), Kratzer (1989), and Parsons (1990), Avrutin claims that clauses involve reference to events, and he incorporates the notion of an event argument/variable into his theory. He adopts the theory of Tense chains developed by Gueron and Hoekstra (1995). They argue that T and the event argument e are elements of the same Tense chain. Following this hypothesis, Avrutin claims that T and e must necessarily be coindexed at LF in order to allow for the interpretation that a certain event holds during a particular time interval.

Furthermore, Avrutin (1997b) claims that, in discourse, the argument NPs, i.e., *John* and *an apple*, in (8) are interpreted and have referents due to the corresponding numbers on their I-cards. In other words, the presence of an index on an NP means that this NP can introduce a discourse referent by way of an I-card. Consequently, the NPs must bear indices. In addition, their referential features must be checked off by the relevant heads. For example, D feature of the subject NP *John* in (8) must be checked off by T. Such indexation processes are illustrated in the sentence *John ate an apple* in (9a). Avrutin assumes that the semantic representation of the event will be like (9b).

(9)a. John$_k$ T$_j$ ate (e$_j$) an apple$_m$

   b. $\exists e \exists x (eat(e) \wedge Agent(e, John) \wedge Theme(e, x) \wedge apple(x)) \wedge e < S$
      [S = speech time]   [Avrutin(1997b: 12, 14)]

In (9a), T and *John* are both indexed, which allows the subject to be interpreted. T is also coindexed with the event variable e, which is discussed and incorporated in Ishikawa (2000). Therefore, the sentence has a temporal interpretation as well.

3.2.3 Interpretation of untensed RIs

I now return to the question of how the untensed RI sentence can be interpreted. Given the above E-card approach, the untensed sentence in (7) should be uninterpretable, since T does not have an index. If only the variable e had an index, the chain of the unindexed T and the indexed e would count as contraindexation that would violate the coindexation requirement for the same Tense chain. Therefore, the event variable must also be unindexed. Consequently, the event cannot be anchored in time. In addition, an NP cannot be interpreted without the index of T, as discussed. However, Avrutin (1997b) presents the interpretation process in the case of such RIs in the following manner. He claims that spec-head agreement is not relevant when both T and a subject NP have no index, and thus there is no violation of the indexation. He proposes that in such a context an RI can be interpreted as a result of some other event that is assumed to be known to the speaker and hearer in the conversation.

Avrutin claims that in an RI sentence such as (7) a preceding event has culminated or ended and introduces a resultant state. Parsons (1990) presents two aspectual stages of events in semantic representation: Ongoing events and *Culminated* events. Ongoing, or progressive, events introduce *In-progress* states, whereas Culminated, or perfective, events introduce *Resultant states*. Avrutin hypothesizes that a Culminated event projects an additional E-card. For example, if the preceding context is expressed by an utterance such as *King (has) told a joke*, as in (10), this Culminated event projects two E-cards: the projecting E-card for its own 'King has told a joke' and the other projected E-card for a new Resultant event that later fulfills it like 'The princess (starts) to laugh.'

(10) Korol' rasskazal anekdot.　　　Carevna xoxotat'.
　　　King (has) told a joke. [That causes] Princess to laugh.
　　　　　　　　　　　　　　　　　　　　　　[Avrutin(1997b, 16: 22a)]

The evidence that only Culminated events project additional E-cards can be observed in the contrast between (a) and (b) in the following.

(11)a. (=(10) Korol' rasskazal anekdot. Carevna xoxotat'.
　　　　　　King (has) told a joke.　　Princess to laugh.
　　b. Korol' rasskazyval anekdot. *Carevna xoxotat'.
　　　　King was telling　a joke.　　Princess to laugh.
(12)a. Fokusnik　　　pokazal　　fokus. Zriteli applodirovat'.
　　　　Magician (has) performed a trick. Spectators to applaud.
　　b. Fokusnik pokazyval　　fokus. *Zriteli applodirovat'.
　　　　Magician was performing a trick. Spectators to applaud.
　　　　　　　　　　　　　　　　　　　[Avrutin (1997b, 16: 22 and 23)]

Only the (a) discourses are grammatical because the preceding events have culminated. In the (b) discourses, the ungrammaticality is not due to their inherent structure; it stems from the linkage of the two events. The progressive sentences are grammatical in themselves in both (11b) and (12b).[3]

Regarding the NPs in the RIs, Avrutin claims that they can be interpreted indirectly as participants in the events represented by the projected (new) E-cards: the princess in (10) can be interpreted as a participant of the resultant event that occurs right after the projecting event 'King (has) told a joke,' as in the gloss in parentheses in (7). Since the NP does not have an index, it cannot be represented by a numbered I-card. Therefore, the indirect participation in the projected E-card is the only way for the NP to be interpreted in discourse.

Concerning the NP's case marking, nominative case cannot be marked in an untensed clause. Therefore, the fact that the untensed RI sentence (7) is grammatical without nominative Case must be accounted for. Avrutin shows that Russian displays default nominative case marking. As seen in (13), the default lexical case in Russian is nominative, not accusative.[4]

(13)a. It's her/*she. [English]
    b. Eto ona/*ee. [Russian]
       it (is) she/*her
    c. Eto   Marija/*Mariju/*Marii.   [Russian]
       it (is) Marija [NOM]/*[ACC]/*[DAT]   [Avrutin(1997b:25, 35)]

This suggests that a subject NP can bear nominative case without an index in an RI sentence.

Let us turn to the interpretation of the temporal relation between two events in RIs. As discussed, both T and e are unindexed in RIs. Therefore, the events of RIs cannot be anchored in time and, consequently, they do not have temporal interpretation in themselves. However, in the proposed E-card approach, the temporal reading between two events in RIs can be interpreted in terms of the left/right boundaries of event time intervals. The notions of the left/right boundaries are discussed in detail by Giorgi and Pianesi (1997). Avrutin proposes that Culminated events, i.e. the projecting events in the case of RIs, specify both ends of the event time intervals. Assuming that the two events must be connected, he argues that the projecting event shows the left boundary of the projected (second) event in terms of its own specified right boundary. Therefore, the adjacent or contiguous relation between the two events is represented. In fact, the RIs interpreted as the projected events indicate inception: the left boundaries of the events are specified. This means that the second event is expected to take place at a particular time t which is identical to the time for the culmination of the first event. Thus, the interpretation of (10) in which the princess starts to laugh just when the king has told a joke is accounted for by the E-card approach in discourse representation.

3.3 The Japanese HIR in discourse representation

I now turn to Japanese HIRs to see how the E-card approach as a model of discourse representation can be applied to their interpretation.

3.3.1 Temporal relations between two events in the HIR

As Avrutin argues with examples such as (7), Russian RIs always imply another event contiguous to the RI sentence. In response to such discourse-rooted phenomena, Avrutin has claimed that the RI is interpreted as a result of some other 'completed' (Culminated) event assumed to be known in the preceding discourse. In fact, a similar temporal ordering condition is observed in Japanese HIRs as well. Regarding the temporal ordering relations observed in the HIRs, Kuroda (1992: 147) proposes a condition (14).

(14) The Relevancy Condition:
For a p.-i. relative clause [= HIR] to be acceptable, it is necessary that it be interpreted pragmatically in such a way as to be directly relevant to the pragmatic content of its matrix clause.   [Kuroda (1992: 147, 6)]

Kuroda's observation is that a sentence containing an HIR will be infelicitous unless the content of the HIR clause has a kind of direct relationship in discourse to the meaning of the matrix clause, as defined in the condition (14). Although Kuroda has not further defined or formalized the condition, he also uses the term "simultaneous interpretation" (Kuroda 1992: 148–9) to describe the situation in which two events must be interpreted as occurring simultaneously. (15) illustrates the relevancy condition.[5]

(15) a. #John-ga   [[Mary-ga   nanni-demo   kasikoi]-no]-o   hometa.
     John-NOM [[Mary-NOM anything-about clever]   ]-ACC praised
     'Mary is clever about everything, and John praised her.'
   b. [[Suri-ga   Mary-no   saihu-kara   kane-o
     Pickpocket-NOM Mary-GEN wallet-from money-ACC
     nukitoru]-no]-o   John-ga   tukamaeta.
     pull-out]   ]-ACC John-NOM caught
     'A pickpocket pulled Mary's money out of her wallet, and John caught him.'

c. #[[Suri-ga jyuuniji-ni Mary-no saihu-kara kane-o
   Pickpocket-NOM 12 o'clock-at Mary-GEN wallet-from money-ACC
   nukitoru]-no]-o   John-ga   niji-ni   tukamaeta.
   pull-out]   ]-ACC John-NOM 2 o'clock-at caught
   Intended: 'A pickpocket pulled Mary's money out of her wallet <u>at 12 o'clock</u>, and John caught him later <u>at 2 o'clock</u>.'
d. Relative Clause:
   John-ga   [[nanni-demo   kashikoi] Mary]-o   hometa.
   John-NOM [[anything-about clever]   Mary]-ACC praised
   'John praised Mary, who is clever about everything.'

As seen in the ill-formed (15a), Mary does not actually seem to perform a particular act that is "directly relevant" or tied to the action of 'praising.' Being clever is an individual-level predicate and is inherent to Mary. Therefore, there is no clear indication of a temporal ordering relation between the two events. In contrast, in (15b), by pulling Mary's money out, a pickpocket's crime is directly tied to the action of John's catching him; John's act is triggered by the pickpocket's act. The HIR clause sets up a condition sufficient for the consequent event to happen in (15b). In (15c), however, the sentence is not acceptable, with the time gap between the two events indicated by the adverbials, 'at 12 o'clock' and 'at 2 o'clock'. This contrast between (15b) and (15c) demonstrates some kind of direct relevancy between the two events in the HIR. The example (15d), which is the canonical relative counterpart of (15a), is acceptable, with a predicate of inherent property. This fact demonstrates that a relative clause like (15d) does not require such temporal restrictions. In fact, in the HIRs, only stage-level predicates appear in both the main and subordinate clauses.[6] Then, the question is how the temporal relations between the two events in the HIRs will be represented in discourse.

As I have discussed before, untensed constructions such as the HIRs can be interpreted only in certain contexts, and through discourse access. A Russian RI example such as (7) inherently requires a Culminated causal event, and this Culminated event projects an additional E-card for a new Resultant event. The event represented by an RI can be interpreted by means of this additional E-card. However, in the case of Japanese HIRs, the two events may be connected in a temporal relation different from those in the Russian RIs. In fact, there are two different temporal relations that are expressed in Japanese

HIRs. (16) illustrates such cases.

(16)a. John-wa [[Mary-ga hako-o tukutte-ir*u*]-no]-o kowasi*ta*.
    -TOP   -NOM box-ACC make-remain   -ACC broke
    'Mary was making a box, and John broke it.'
  b. Taro-wa   [[Yumi-ga   keeki-o   yai*ta*]-no]-o   tabete-
    (*m*. name)-TOP (*f*. name)-NOM cake-ACC baked   -ACC eat
    simat*ta*.
    finished
    'Yumi baked a cake, which Taro ate.'

The HIR in (16a) indicates that the first event is still ongoing at the beginning of the second event. The *-u* form with the subordinate predicate demonstrates the imperfective, or the In-progress state in Parsons' terms, and the making of the box is ongoing when the second event 'John broke it' started. The two events clearly overlap each other. Thus, the first event indicates an In-progress state with the imperfective aspect. Conversely, in (16b), the subordinate event is completed at the initiation of the main event. There is no overlap between them, because the *-ta* form of the subordinate predicate *yai-ta* 'baked' indicates the perfective, i.e. a Resultant state. The two events are interpreted as adjacent, but without any overlap.

So far, I have assumed that *-u* and *-ta* correspond to the imperfective and perfective aspect respectively. However, more complex cases are observed in the HIR predicates, in which case the dichotomic account for the functions of *-u* and *-ta* poses a problem.

3.3.2 Aspect representation in the HIR

In Japanese, there are no grammaticalized progressive or perfective forms. As a result, the progressive and perfective aspects cannot be represented by one corresponding form in a predicate. In the following examples, one auxiliary form can express either a progressive or perfective meaning.

(17)a. (Watasi-wa) kaisya-ni ir*u*.
    -TOP office at stay/exist
    'I am at the office.'

b. John-wa   tabemono-no essee-o   kai<u>te-ir</u>u.
    -TOP food-GEN   essay-ACC write-remain
    'John is writing an essay on food.' [progressive/durative] or 'John wrote an essay on food (before).' [perfective/resultative]
c. John-wa   ·ie   -ni kaet<u>te-ir</u>u.
    -TOP home at   return-remain
    'John (has) already returned home (and is home now).' [perfective/resultative only]
d. HIR: Shuppansha-wa [[John-ga   tabemono-no essee-o
        publlisher-TOP [[-NOM food-GEN   essay-ACC
    kai<u>te-ir</u>u] no]-o   shuppan-shita.
    write-remain]   ]-ACC published
    'John (once) wrote an essay on food, which the publisher published.' [perfective/resultative only]

Complex verb forms are often used in Japanese to represent a variety of modal and aspectual meanings. *Te iru* is one such form and is often used to indicate a sort of progressive meaning in the present tense. (17a) shows that *iru* is an existential verb in itself and indicates the existence of a subject. (17b) shows the ambiguity of a complex predicate with the *-te iru* form. Although the *-te iru* form is often used to indicate the progressive meaning, the predicate in (17b) can indicate either a perfective/resultative state or a progressive state. In general, most predicates with the *-te iru* form bear the same kind of ambiguities. In fact, when this ambiguity occurs, the default reading is the perfective/resultative, though the reading can be influenced by the individual verb's aspectual meaning. (17c) is the instance of an inherent perfective reading.

The same complexity applies to HIR predicates with *-te iru*. In (17d), the HIR predicate *kai-te iru* is interpretable only with the perfective reading 'wrote an essay before.' The HIR clause in (17d) is identical to (17b), in which either the progressive or perfective reading is possible. Therefore, *-te iru* cannot be associated with one aspectual category such as progressive. Moreover, my earlier statement that the *-u* ending in an HIR predicate represents progressive aspect must also be reformulated: *-u* appears in the complex form *-te iru* of the HIR predicate in (17d) where the predicate has only the perfective reading.

However, with two semantic concepts, In-progress states and Resultant states, the above complex examples can be uniformly described. Aspect is represented by means of either In-progress or Resultant states in the HIRs, independent of variable forms, i.e. *-u, -ta, -te iru,* or *-te ita.* For example, aspect in (17b) can be described by means of the two state distinctions. In addition to the default Resultant state, the In-progress state can also be indicated with its context given in (17b). In contrast, in the HIR (17d), epistemically, the event with an In-progress state cannot be connected to the act of publishing the essay. Therefore, by default the Resultant state is indicated. In order to account uniformly for such variable interpretations at issue in the HIRs, it seems necessary to utilize the concepts of In-progress and Resultant states. Later, I will use these concepts to explain temporal relations between two events.

3.3.3 E-cards introduced by presupposed events

As discussed earlier, only a Culminated event can be claimed to introduce two E-cards. The unculminated event in the HIR, as in (15b), should introduce only one E-card. Therefore, the overlapped temporal relations in the HIRs cannot be accommodated in the same way as the adjacent relations in RIs. How can they be interpreted?

Avrutin (1997b: 33) argues that another kind of untensed construction introduces a new E-card by means of presupposition. The so-called Mad Magazine register gives rise to the expressions in (18).

(18)a. John dance. Never in a million years!
    b. Herman eat bean sprouts. Why?   [Avrutin 1997, 31–2: 51a, c]

Avrutin points out that certain attitudes are expressed toward presupposed events in these expressions. Therefore, a presupposed event introduces a new E-card in the discourse that will represent the event of this kind of Mad Magazine register clause. In fact, Japanese HIRs also show robust presuppositions. The evidence may be drawn from the exclusively existential readings with the HIR clauses.[7]

(19)a. A presupposed proposition for the HIR in (16a):
    There is at least one box which Mary was making at the time of the main event.
    b. A presupposed proposition for the HIR in (16b):
    There is at least one cake which Yumi already baked at the time of the

main event.

Moreover, Japanese HIRs do not allow any universal quantification, as we see in (20).

(20) HIR with 'every'
    a.?*Keikan-ga [[<u>subeteno</u> **doroboo**-ga dete -kuru]-no]-o tukamaeta.
        policeman [[every thief-NOM get-out-come]]-ACC arrested
        '*lit.*, Every thief came out, who(m) a policeman arrested.'
    b.?/*John-ga [[Mary-ga <u>subeteno</u> **ringo**-o katta]-no]-o
        John-NOM [[Mary-NOM every apple-ACC bought]]-ACC
        tabeta.
        ate
        'Mary bought every apple, which John ate.'

In fact, existential quantification is the only quantification allowed in the Japanese HIR. It is well known that presupposition is not canceled by the negation of the whole proposition. This fact should be evident in the HIRs if the evoked meanings in (19) are presuppositions.

(21) Negated sentences of (16a) and (16b):
    a. John-wa [[Mary-ga hako-o tukutte-ir*u*]-no]-o kowasa
        -TOP -NOM box-ACC make -remain -ACC break
        -nakat*ta*.
        -<u>NEG</u>-PST
        'John did not break the box Mary was making.' [Therefore, Mari's box may still be there.]
    b. Taro-wa [[Yumi-ga keeki-o yai*ta*]-no]-o tabe
        (*m.* name)-TOP (*f.* name)-NOM cake-ACC baked -ACC eat
        -nakat*ta*.
        -<u>NEG</u>-PST
        'Taro did not eat the cake Yumi baked.' [Therefore, Yumi's cake may still be there.]

As expected, the presuppositions depicted in (19a, b) are maintained, even if the main predicates are negated, as indicated by the remaining contents within square brackets. Therefore, the existential HIRs inherently evoke presupposition. Concerning the existential nature of the HIR, which bans universal quantification, non-generic reading that the subject marker *-ga* indicates will turn out to be relevant. In fact, later with some more investigations of the components in the HIR, the existentiality results from the combination of different but closely related properties those components represent. I will examine those properties of the HIR in the following chapters: the existentiality with aspectual complex predicates in chapter 4; and non-generic individuation that the subject marker *-ga* is equipped with in chapter 6 in relation to indefiniteness/definiteness. Based on the above observation, however, I claim that the presupposition of the existential HIR as a whole introduces the second event representation in discourse, as discussed earlier with regard to Mad Magazine register. A presupposed event introduces both an E-card on its own and a new E-card that can represent the (second) event asserted in the main clause.

I have earlier discussed existential readings in the HIRs. In light of the HIR's untensed status, we can account for the impossibility of universal quantification in the HIRs. In general, a universal operaror such as *subeteno* 'every' cannot bind a variable which does not have an index. This would be the case with the HIR since an NP which the variable should belong in is unindexed in the HIR. Consequently, the variable without an index would be uninterpretable without access to discourse, which is what Avrutin proposes, as discussed in the earlier sections.

Along the line of Avrutin (1997b), as introduced in 3.2.3, let me assume that Object Agreement (AgrO) head moves to T and checks its features in the case of tensed clauses. However, AgrO cannot have its features checked by the unindexed T in the case of the HIR. Therefore, AgrO cannot have an index. An object NP in the HIR is unindexed just as is a subject NP. This coincides with the fact that no NP can be universally quantified in the HIR.[8]

Likewise, a time adverb in general is restricted in the HIR because Tense operator is unindexed and therefore cannot bind a temporal variable introduced by the time adverb. When the operator does not bind any variable, the adverb is uninterpretable. The event represented by the HIR is not anchored in time. In other words, as discussed before, two events must not be disjointed in time. Now I will illustrate how such untensed HIRs can be interpreted by means of E-cards introduced by presupposition.

3.3.4 Interpretation of the HIR by means of E-cards

I have argued that the second events in the HIRs should either overlap or be adjacent to the presupposed (first) events. However, how is it that the two events must be interpreted as temporally connected to each other? The temporal connections between two events in the HIRs are different from those in the Russain RIs. We cannot simply use the RI analysis which depends on Culminated events. Drawing on Josephs (1976, 344), I claim that *no* plays a role in sharing the same time intervals between the two E-cards introduced by presupposition. When the referent of *no* is selected in the first E-card, creating identical referents in the two E-cards, the time intervals for the two E-cards should share the same number. Consequently, the two events are invariably contiguous with each other. To be more precise, one of the relevant argument NPs that is presupposed is likely to be selected as a referent when *no* becomes a ***participant*** of the relevant E-card. The referent must meet the semantic features and theta role of the argument NP of the main predicate. For example, in the case of (16a), based on the presupposition (19a), the identification of a referent for the main clause object can be satisfied by selecting 'a box,' since a box is breakable. Likewise, the identification for the object which Taro eats in (16b) can be achieved on the grounds of the presupposition (19b): 'a cake' is selected as a referent. As a result, the time interval of the first event shares the number of the time interval of the second event where the referent replacing *no* has become a *participant*. The two events are thus connected because of *no*'s referent identification process. Then, depending on the indication of either an In-Progress state or a Resultant state in the first event, the two events will be interpreted as either overlapped or adjacent.[9] For example, in (16a), John starts to break the unfinished box while the making of the box is still in progress. The *-u* form indicates an In-progress state, and its right boundary is open. Therefore, the two events are interpreted as overlapping, as in the diagram (22) for (16a).

(22) [←(16a)] 'Mary is [Asp] making a box'   'John broke *no* (something).'
        (presupposition)

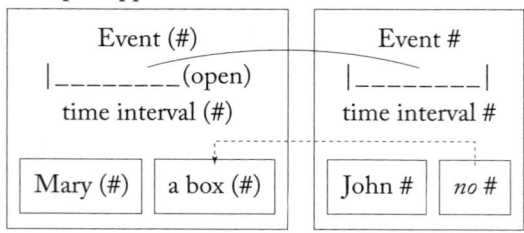

Event (#)	Event #
|_____(open)	|_____|
time interval (#)	time interval #
Mary (#) | a box (#)	John # | *no* #

On the other hand, an adjacent interpretation occurs when a Resultant state indicates the closed right boundary of the first event, as in Russian RI cases. The first event is complete when the second event in the main clause occurs. The right boundary corresponds to the left boundary of the second event, as illustrated in (23) for (16b).

(23) [←(16b)] 'Yumi (has) [Asp] baked a cake'   'Taro ate *no* (something)'
        (presupposition)

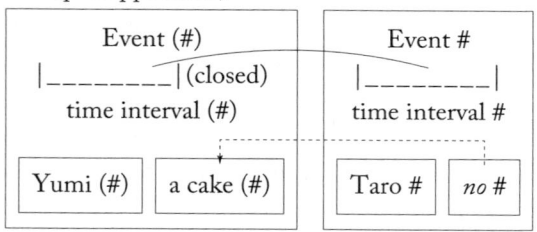

Event (#)	Event #
|_____|(closed)	|_____|
time interval (#)	time interval #
Yumi (#) | a cake (#)	Taro # | *no* #

In summary, two events indicated in the HIR construction can be adjacent or overlapping, depending on the following time-interval scheme (24).

(24) In the time-interval representation of the first Event Card:
   (i) when the right boundary of the time-interval is open, 2 events are overlapping;
   (ii) when the right boundary of the time-interval is closed, 2 events are adjacent to each other.

We have seen how *no* connects two events and is involved in the selection of a referent for the argument NP of the main predicate. This referent is chosen from among the available NPs in the HIR. What then happens to the remaining unindexed NPs in the HIR?

As I have discussed in 3.2.3 concerning RIs, the NP *Mary* in (16a) can be interpreted indirectly as a **participant** of the **presupposed** event that should be connected to the **asserted** event "John broke *no* (something) (at the time of t)." The same process applies to the unindexed NPs in the HIR in (16b). In other examples of the HIRs, the identification of a referent may involve more complex processes and ambiguities because of other contextual factors. I will discuss those more complex cases in later chapters.

Overall, in this chapter, I have applied the E-card approach to the interpretation of Japanese HIRs, especially to the identification of both the temporal relation and non-referential participants between two events, and I have developed and partially modified Avrutin's (1997b) E-card approach for boundary specifications in the E-cards. The modification is necessary for Japanese HIRs, due to the fact that their temporal relations are affected by two different states that the first event may indicate. I have indicated that the core properties of the untensed constructions can uniformly be accounted for by the modified version of Event File Cards as a model of discourse representation. In later chapters, I will further elaborate my approach to discourse representation and propose the skeleton of an integrative model of event representation for the HIR.

3.4 Summary of the chapter

In this chapter, I have argued that certain constructions must have access to discourse for interpretation. I have presented a representational model of the interpretation of the untensed HIR construction. I have shown that sentences are interpreted as event units in discourse representation, and I have indicated that Japanese HIRs, the interpretation of which was not analyzed properly in past approaches, can be represented with a slight modification of the file card approach. The event-related phenomena such as the temporal contiguities between the HIRs and their main clauses typically require the involvement of the interface domain between syntax and discourse. Given the existential nature of the HIR discussed with the examples in (20), presupposition is evoked for its temporal relation to the new event indicated by the main clause. Access to event representation in discourse plays an essential role in the elucidation of underspecified structures.

In the next chapter, I will further discuss some complex phenomena observed in one of the components of the HIR predicate structure, and develop my approach to the event representation for the interpretation of the untensed HIR.

Endnotes
1. I note that *-ta* and *-u* forms are the only morphological markers for tense in Japanese. Also, there is no grammaticalized form for the progressive/imperfective or the perfect/perfective per se. Furthermore, there is no agreement in tense (*i.e.* sequence of tenses) between main and subordinate clauses in Japanese, as shown in (25a) in chapter 2 and in (3a) in this chapter.
2. Hyams (1996) also points out that in certain cases T will be given a tense interpretation without an index. She calls such an interpretation *temporal coreference*. Hyams (1996, 17) states, "I am suggesting that a present tense T can be either anaphoric ... or it can enter into coreference, in which case there is no binding relation between the operator and T. We thus have temporal anaphora and temporal coreference, analogous to nominal anaphora and nominal coreference, as described in Reinhart (1983)."
3. Both in (11) and (12), (b) examples seem to improve their acceptability, with *tut* 'here' added to the beginning, just like the one in the princess sentence (7). However, the example (7) is acceptable without the deictic expression, whereas (b) examples seem not to be acceptable without it.
4. Object NPs in the RIs must have their referential features checked by AgrO, but I will focus on the relation between unindexed T and subject NPs. The object NPs are claimed to bear indices in RIs in Russian.
5. Concerning the nominalizer *no*, Josephs (1976, 344) points out that *no* is characterized as representing a "directly perceived, simultaneously occurring event."
6. Although this stage-level predicate restriction is important to the HIR, we will later, in chapters 4 and 5, see some complex examples of the HIR, where the identification of an argument NP and/or the temporal ordering relation must be reasoned through discourse event representation, not in terms of predicate properties. See also section 2.3.1 for a complex example.
7. The same view that Japanese HIRs only allow existential readings is seen in Uchibori (1992: 3–4). She (1992 4–5) also states that the HIRs require stage-level predicates.
8. As discussed earlier, default case marking is possible with a subject NP in English and other languages. However, as Maria Babyonyshev (personal communication) points out, it may be problematic whether the same line of argument applies to the object NP that is not indexed. In English, an untensed clause seems to allow universal quantification to an object NP, although the HIR does not.

"What? Him push *every* girl?" "Never."

I do not have any solution to the problem at this stage. However, in general, case assignment in Japanese seems to be much more complex than in English, due to the fact, at least, that some intensifying particles like *-mo* or *-wa* override the subject and object markers, but not other case markers, and due also to the fact that case marking is often ellipted. The issues about case assignment have yet to be solved in future research.

9   One may argue that *no* functions as a connective or conjunction, and that its lexicon specifies the temporal relations between the two events indicated by the main and subordinate clauses in HIRs. *Ato* 'after, behind, back, etc.', *mae* 'front', or *aida* 'in-between, middle, etc.' appear to be examples of the same class of conjunctives. In this case, those temporal connections could be a matter of lexicon. However, under such an analysis, it is not clear how *no* could be both a noun and a conjunction at the same time. I do not pursue that view here.

Chapter 4

Interpreting complex predicate *-te iru*: the interaction of event relations with eventualities and tense

4.1 Introduction: ambiguities of the Verb-*te iru*

In the preceding chapter, I have proposed two distinct states, *In-progress* and *Resultant* states in identifying the temporal meaning of the HIR predicate. I have claimed that, with the two semantic concepts In-progress and Resultant states, more complex examples will be uniformly described. I have then pointed out that complex temporal forms such as *-te iru/ita* could take over the positions of the aforementioned temporal markers, *-u* and *-ta*, as seen in (1a, b), repeated here from (17b, d) in the previous chapter, and (2a, b).

(1)a. John-wa   tabemono-no essei-o   kaite iru.
       -TOP food-GEN   essay-ACC write-remain/be
      'John is writing an essay on food.' [progressive/durative] or 'John {has written/wrote} an essay on food (before).' [perfective/resultative]

   b. [HIR] Shuppansha-wa [[John-ga   tabemono-no essee-o
      publisher-TOP [[-NOM food-GEN   essay-ACC
      kaite iru] no]-o   shuppanshi-ta.
      write-remain/be] N]-ACC publish-PST
      'John (once) wrote an essay on food, which the publisher published.' [perfective/resultative only]

(2)a. John-wa   tabemono-no essei-o   kaita.
       -TOP food-of   essay-ACC write-PST
      'John wrote an essay on food.'

b. [HIR] Shuppansha-wa [[John-ga   tabemono-no essee-o
       publisher-TOP [[-NOM food-GEN   essay-ACC
   kaita] no]-o   shuppan-shita
   write-Prf]N]-ACC   published
   'John wrote an essay on food, which the publisher published.'

This predicate *kaite iru* is, in fact, ambiguous in general without further context, as shown in (1a). It can indicate either progressive/continuative or perfective/resultative meaning, depending on the whole utterance. The literature analyzing the uses of the temporal marker *-te iru* vary in the classifications. In contrast, however, the ambiguity observed in the same clause does **not occur** when *-te iru* occurs in the HIR construction, as seen in (1b). Intuitively, it makes sense to have the interpretation of contiguous events due to the clear cause-effect relation reasoned between the two events, as in the gloss of (1b), rather than the reading of apparently unrelated events. Even so, it is not clear how the observed ambiguity disappears, once the same clause is accommodated as a subordinate clause in the HIR construction. One thing to point out here is that there is no sequence of tenses, *i.e.* no agreement in tenses, between main and subordinate clauses in Japanese (endnote 1 in chapter 3). The two clauses in a complex clause construction do not necessarily have to be constrained so that the two events may be contiguous temporally with each other. Note also that, when the aspectual markers are replaced with the simple past counterparts, as in (2a, b), no such contrast occurs. It seems plausible to think that the source of the occurrence and disappearance of the ambiguity can be sought somewhere in the structures of the predicate Verb-*te iru* and of the HIR complex clause construction. With the observed ambiguities in (1a) and the contrastive readings between (1a) and (1b), questions arise as to why and how such complex cases can be described in terms of the generalized dichotomy, In-progress and Resultant states, as I have proposed in the previous chapter. Aside from the simple temporal predicate forms, Verb-*u* and Verb-*ta*, the only temporal predicate forms occurring in the HIR clause are the complex predicate forms, Verb-*te iru/ita*. Therefore, in this chapter I will exclusively examine them and answer the above questions.[1]

Most importantly, concerning the difference of how the two events are temporally connected between the RIs (root infinitives) and the HIRs discussed in chapter 3, I will demonstrate that the existential presupposition derived from the In-progress state can be rooted to one core nature of the complex predicate, -*te iru*. I examine closely the complex predicate form that appears in the HIR. I will discuss varied analyses of the complex predicate observed in the literature. First, in 4.2, by examining the classification of the uses of Verb-*te iru* in the literature, I will discuss the uses of Verb-*te iru* predicate in simplex clause examples. I will analyze the ambiguities of the internal complex eventualities with the -*te iru* form, on the one hand, and the interactions of their meanings with external temporal operators such as tense and time adverbs, on the other hand. One core meaning of the use of -*te iru* will be proposed. In 4.3, properties of the English present perfect will be examined comparatively with those observed in the literature concerning the uses of -*te iru*. I will then show, in 4.4, how the system of time-interval boundaries in an event representation introduced in chapter 3 will indicate the temporal meanings by the form Verb-*te iru* predicate. Finally, I will apply the above discussion to the examples of the HIR construction in which the Verb-*te iru* predicate occurs.

Overall, in chapter 4, I will explicate where the existential meaning discussed in chapter 3 comes from in the HIR, and will then demonstrate that both Resultant states/In-progress states distinction and the existential property are central to an integrative interpretation process with the HIR that I will propose. I will present a particular process of interpretation in discourse in the context of the apparently varied temporal meanings of complex predicate Verb-*te iru*. The discussion of the interpretation process will be passed on to chapter 5, where I will propose an extended integrative approach to the event representation for underspecific constructions such as the HIR. Those temporal meanings result from the interactions among eventualities, temporal elements, and the preceding discourse contexts.

4.2 The existential reading of state, as opposed to continuative aspect, with the -*te iru*

In section 4.2, I will examine the analyses of the use of form -*te iru* combined with a verb. Different classifications have been proposed based on the distinct analyses in the literature, most of which are based on some kind of eventualities of verbs with which -*te iru* is combined. I will discuss the problems with those analyses and their classifications of the uses of -*te iru* in the first group of the treatments in the literature. I will then introduce the second group of the analyses of -*te iru* that share a view that I argue for concerning the core meaning. Supportive arguments will then be given.

4.2.1 A persistent reading of the 'existence of a state' with the Verb-*te iru*

The auxiliary aspectual marker -*te iru* consists of two morphological units: -*te* and *iru*. The second morphological unit is a verb, full or auxiliary, *iru* 'be (as a full verb), exist'. The first part, -*te*, is analyzed under different categories in the literature but is most generally understood as connective, apart from the controversy of its taxonomy.[2]

The literature analyzing the markers -*te iru* mostly attributes the distinct uses to the kind of aspectual classes that the combined verbs belong in. There is a consensus that -*te iru* as a whole unit indicates some kind of state. However, I have observed disagreement with the views of what constitutes the fundamental use of the -*te iru* form.

The first group of the treatments in the literature [Suzuki 1979: 7 & ff.; Okuda 1984: 89; Moriyama 1988: 141; Takahashi 1990: 48–9], mostly following the traditional arguments for aspectual oppositions between Perfective Aspect and Continuative Aspect in Japanese, analyzes the fundamental use of -*te iru* as *Continuative*. Some others classify it further into subcategories: Continuative and Resultant State, as in Hashimoto 1969; Masuoka & Takubo 1989; and, with further classifications, Nitta 1997, which I will discuss later. The first group bases the claim on the oppositions between simplex markers -*u* (present/future) / -*ta* (past/perfective) [as Perfective Aspect], on the one hand, and complex markers -*te iru* (present continuative) / -*te ita* (past continuative) [as Continuative Aspect], on the other hand. [For example, Suzuki 1979, Okuda 1984, and Takahashi 1990]

(3)a. [the result of a change continues — with a verb of change]
       To-ga   shimatte-iru.
       door-NOM close-TE IRU
       'The door {is/has been} closed.'
   b. [an action continues — with a verb of activity]
       Inu-ga   hashitte-iru.
       dog-NOM run-TE IRU
       'A dog is running.'   [Takahashi 1990: 49]

(4)a. Taro-wa hon-o yonde-iru.
 Taro-TOP book-ACC read-TE IRU
 'Taro is reading a book.'
  [the continuation of a monotonous activity]

 b. Akachan-wa suya-suya-to nemutte-iru.
  baby-TOP calmly sleep-TE IRU
  'The baby {has fallen asleep/is asleep} calmly.'
   [a continued state after a change]

 c. Shujin-wa ie-ni kaette-iru.
  Husband-TOP home-to return-TE IRU
  'My husband has already returned home.'
   [a continued state after a change of location]
   [Suzuki 1979: 13–4]

They label all these subcategorized examples as "Continuative" aspect. However, it turns out that the analysis does not always hold. In (3b), an ambiguity occurs: the sentence can also indicate the state or fact after some activity in the past, whether it was complete or not. That reading will be clearer with (3b) when context is added, as in (5).

(5) Sannenmae-no inu-no reisu-de ano inu-ga hashitte iru.
 Three-years-ago-GEN dog-GEN race-at that dog-NOM run-TE IRU
 '(I now report to you.) That dog ran in a dog race three years ago.'
   [the existence of a state/fact]

In contrast, the reading of "the state after an act (*i.e.*, falling asleep)" does not seem to vary in (4b).

In the same manner, the other example above with the reading of "continuation" of an action/activity, *i.e.* Continuative, can indicate a *state after the initiation* of an action, whether the act is complete or not.

(6) [← from (4a)]
 Sannen-mae-mo shiken-ni ochita-toki Taro-wa hon-o
 Three years-ago-also exam-LOC failed when Taro-TOP book-ACC
 yonde-iru.
 read-TE IRU

'When he failed in another exam three years ago, Taro read {a book/books} (as he did this time).'

The sentence may refer to the repeated failure Taro experienced, even though he read books for exams. Therefore, with additional contexts, the meanings in each subcategory in the literature can change in their examples. In particular, the two examples above, with additional contexts, turn out not to fall under the proposed category, "Continuative". Note that, in all the above examples of (3) and (4) that I have shown for the classifications in the literature, the reading of "(an existence of) a state" seems to persist and even more so when contexts are added, as observed in (5) and (6). Along this line, Shirota (1998: 208) states that in the case of continuative predicates, which include Activity verbs and Accomplishment verbs, meanings vary in the Verb-*te iru* construction, depending on what part of a state is focused on concerning the entities of the subject NP in the duration of their acts in contexts. Considering the apparent variable meanings within the defined "continuative" class and also considering the persistent reading of "the existence of a state after an act or process" that I have observed, I tentatively analyze a fundamental meaning of Verb-*te iru* as *existentiality of a state after the initiation of an act* for my first approximation.[3] In the next section, I will examine some more detailed classifications of the aspectual marker -*te iru* in Nitta (1997), and see if my tentative analysis will be able to account for the phenomena concerning the apparent distinct meanings displayed in the Verb-*te iru*.

4.2.2 An invariable reading of the Verb-*te iru* and problems with Nitta's tripartite classification

Nitta (1997) argues that the fundamental meanings of the form Verb-*te iru* are classified as: (A) the middle of an action, (B) holding of a resultative state, and (C) experience/completion.

(7) a. Minna soto-de ason-de iru. [(A)]
everyone outside-at play-TE IRU
'Everyone is playing outside.'
b. Shiroi inu-ga buru-buru-to hurue-te iru. [(A)]
white dog-NOM tremblingly shiver-TE IRU
'A white dog is shivering in a trembling manner.'

(8)a. Tsuma-mo hutari-no   kodomo-mo nemutte ita. [(B)]
       wife-also two-person-GEN children-also sleep-TE IRU-PST
       'My/His wife and two children also {have fallen asleep/are asleep}.'
   b. Karera-wa kesakara   hutari-de   Tokyo-e
       they-TOP this-morning-since two persons-with Tokyo-to
       itte   iru. [(B)]
       go-TE IRU
       '*lit.*, They have gone/been to Tokyo together since this morning.'
(9) Kare-wa gan-no   shinyaku-o   hakken-shite   iru. [(C)]
    he-TOP cancer-GEN new-drug-ACC discovery-do-TE IRU
    '(It is true that/I tell you) He has discovered a new drug against cancer.'
                                                    [Nitta 1997: 236–7]

Examples (7), (8), and (9) correspond to (A), (B), and (C) of the above subcategories in their order. Nitta states that his classification above is based on distinct classes of eventualities that the verbs are associated with. Therefore, the aforementioned three subcategories of the meaning patterns that Verb-*te iru* displays appear to be akin to the kinds of eventualities: activity, accomplishment, and achievement. That is, (A) seems to belong to activity/process class, (B) to accomplishment, and (C) to achievement. However, in the examples in (10) of the verbs he lists, *atatameru* 'warm', *shimeru* 'shut', *amu* 'knit' and some others in (10a) do not seem to match Nitta's classification of [non-change] and [process], although other verbs such as *aruku* 'walk', *ugoku* 'move', *utau* 'sing', *odoru* 'dance' typically indicate those features he describes.

(10)a. Group (A) Middle of action: *aruku* 'walk', *ugoku* 'move', *utau* 'sing', *odoru* 'dance', *oyogu* 'swim', *arau* 'wash', *hashiru* 'run', *taberu* 'eat', *nomu* 'drink', *kowasu* 'destroy', *maku* 'roll', *atatameru* 'warm', *shimeru* 'shut', *amu* 'knit'
                                                    — [-change] and [+process]
    b. Group (B) Holding of a resultative state: *nemuru* 'fall asleep', *iku* 'go', *kumoru* 'cloud', *aku* 'open [vi.]', *ukabu* 'float', *umareru* 'be born', *okiru* 'wake up', *ochiru* 'fall down', *owaru* 'end', *kawaru* 'change [vi.]'   — [+change]
    c. Group (C) Experience/completion: *hakken-suru* 'discover', *nakusu* 'lose', *hatasu* 'achieve', *au* 'encounter', *okosu* 'cause/trigger', *sumasu* 'finish', *shikujiru* 'miss'   — [-change] and [-process]
                                                    [Nitta 1997: 236–7]

In a classic test with telicity-oriented temporal adverbs such as "in ... hours", the problem is highlighted.

(11) a. #John-wa   nijikan-de   odotta.
         John-TOP in-two-hours danced
         ?'John danced in two hours.'
     b. #Hutori-gimi-no otoko-wa   nijikan-de   aruita.
          stoutish-GEN   man-TOP in-two-hours walked
          ?'A stoutish man walked in two hours.'
(12) a. Kyouryokuna eakon-wa   nijikan-de   hiroi kyougijyou-o
         powerful air-conditioner-TOP in-two-hours wide stadium-ACC
         atatame-ta.
         warmed
         'Powerful air-conditioners warmed the wide space of the stadium in two hours.'
     b. Jyoshi-koukousei-wa sono-otokonoko-no   tameni nijikan-de
         girl-highschool-TOP that-boy   -GEN for   in-two-hours
         sukaahu-o an-da.
         scarf-ACC knitted
         'A high-school girl knitted a scarf for that boy in two hours.'

As the contrast shows, with *nijikan-de* 'in two hours,' sentences with *odoru* 'dance' and *aruku* 'walk' are not well-formed, as in (11), whereas sentences with *atatameru* 'warm' and *amu* 'knit' are, as in (12). They are all classified under Group (A). The same kind of problem is observed also in Group (B) in (10b), where *okiru* 'wake up', *ochiru* 'fall down', *owaru* 'end' and *iku* 'go' do not seem to indicate the same kind of eventualities as other members such as *kumoru* 'cloud', *aku* 'open [vi.]', *ukabu* 'float' do. These verbs may instead belong to Group (C) with *hakken-suru* 'discover', *hatasu* 'achieve', *au* 'encounter (an accident)', *okosu* 'cause/trigger', since the denoted acts are **momentary** and indicate the ending of acts. Even after those problematic members of Group (B) and (C) are replaced or removed, a question still remains as to how the feature [-change] can be held when the result of the acts of verbs, *hatasu* 'achieve', *au* 'encounter (an accident)', *okosu* 'cause/trigger' that seem to indicate some change, are taken into account.

Aside from these problems, I observe that, in Nitta's classification, two classes, (A) "the middle of action" and (B) "resultative", are interchangeable, if some context such as an additional time frame is given.

(13)a. (Jiken-no atta hi-wa ano-renchu-wa) minna soto-de ason-de iru.
(incident occurred day-TOP that-fellows-TOP) all outside play-TE IRU
'On the day of the incident, all those fellows/suspects (turned out to have) played outside.'
   b. (jiken-no atta   hi-wa   ano kouen-de ippiki-no) shiroi
      (incident occurred day-TOP that park-at one-GEN) white
      inu-ga   buru-buru-to hurue-te   iru.
      dog-NOM tremblingly   tremble-TE IRU
      'On the day of the incident, one white dog (turned out to have) trembled violently in that park.'
(14) Tsuma-mo hutari-no   kodomo-mo ima nemutte   iru
     wife-also two-person-GEN children-also now fall-asleep-TE IRU
     -kara,   okosa-naide.
     -because wake-NEG
     'My wife and two children all together are asleep now, so don't wake them up'

In the examples in (13), which are taken from the "middle of an action" examples in (7), two sentences now indicate "holding of a resultative state". Likewise, in (14), which is taken from the "holding of a resultative state" example in (8), the sentence now indicates "middle of an action". Note that these examples in the two groups, (A) and (B), have something in common: some kind of an "existential state" is indicated, due to the meaning 'remain/exist' signaled by *-iru* in the *-te iru* form, although it may not explicitly be translated in the glosses. That is a contrast to the present/future marker *-u* or to the preterite/perfective marker *-ta*, neither of which has any indication of a state.[4] I state that the assumed past tense marker *-ta* will change the meaning of the sentences in (13) if it replaces *-te iru*. The marker *-ta* describes a past event as one bit of the whole, not as an array of distinct constituents, though the English glosses would have the same past forms like "played" and "trembled" for either *-te iru* or *-ta* markings.

In Group (C), Nitta's definition "experience/completion" seems to be parallel to one of the uses of the English present perfect (hereafter PrP for present perfect). Following McCawley (1971), Michaelis (1994) analyzes an existential reading as one of the primary uses of the English PrP and raises examples like (15).

(15) I've been to a Neil Young concert.

As Michaelis states, the denoted event could recur *at the present time* in terms of conventional implicature. Therefore, Neil Young should be alive at present. Although that is not exact, as I discuss later, the argument, nonetheless, applies to Nitta's Group (C).[5] In (9), the subject person *kare* 'he'" must be *of current relevance* to the speaker.

(16) [= (9)]
　　　Kare-wa gan-no　　　shinyaku-o　　　hakken-shite　　　iru.
　　　he-TOP cancer-GEN new-drug-ACC discovery-do-TE IRU
　　　'(It is true that/I tell you) He has discovered a new drug against cancer.'

Likewise, in the following example (17), the "boss" must be alive or the speaker's main attention, at least.

(17) The boss has fired my colleague.

The existence of the "boss" is represented since he is still imprinted as the main attention in the speaker's mind at the time of the utterance.

　　　Now I reformulate Nitta's classification for V-*te iru*. Nitta states that Group (C) mainly indicates the completion of an activity. Thus, Group (C) indicates the existence of a state, with *iru*, after the completion of an activity, which can be subdivided into and contained in the tentative definition of -*te iru* that I have claimed: *existentiality of a state after the initiation of an act*, whether the act is complete or not. On the other hand, (A) and (B) are interchangeable concerning their meanings and, therefore, are disqualified from being inherent meanings. Note that, for both groups, my definition of -*te iru* applies, as argued in the examples, (7) – (14). Based on this observation, I take Group (C) as a subclass of the proposed definitive meaning denoting the existentiality of a state after the activation of an act.

　　　In fact, Hashimoto (1969: 349) points out that -*te iru* represents a *remaining (or resultant) state after some activity* denoted by the preceding verb, based on the core meaning of *-ta* as the completion of an act and also on an existential meaning denoted by the second element *iru*. Hashimoto states that *-te* and *-ta* share the same kind of the 'completion' meaning in modern Japanese.

(18) a. Shit*te*   *iru*.
       know-TE IRU
       '(I) already know (it).'
    b. Kabe-ni   kake*ta*   boushi
       wall-LOC hang-TA hat
       'a hat that (someone) hung on the wall'
    c. Sono ko-wa   oya-ni   ni*ta*. (= ni*te iru*)
       that child-TOP parent-to resemble-TA
       'The child resembles his parent.'
    d. Ara, koko-ni at*ta*.
       My, here   exist-TA
       'My! Here it is (= Oh, I've found (it) here).'

In (18a), the utterance indicates that the speaker is in the state of holding the knowledge of something, i.e., is familiar with some fact or information that the hearer also is familiar with. Note that verb *shiru* 'know' usually denotes an inchoative meaning such as 'come to know' and does not really represent stative.[6] The verb will denote a state as a result of it being combined with *-te iru*. Therefore, in (18a), according to Hashimoto, some preceding context of the completed act is relevant: the speaker had come to know a fact about the topic in conversation at one time before the hearer referred to it in the current discourse context. Therefore, the state of the speaker's awareness of it is represented in (18a). As I discussed in section 3.1 of chapter 3, temporal particle *-ta* may represent the perfective in subordinate clause such as the HIR. The particle *-ta* in (18b) also denotes the perfective meaning of the state after the act of hanging is over. Teramura (1984: 120–1) and Kindaichi (1988: 114–5) point out that *-ta* denotes both perfective and past meanings and that the decision of which is denoted in an utterance is understood by both speaker and addressee in discourse. Example (18c) illustrates that point. If *-ta* were taken as past-tense marker in (18c), simply on the ground that it is in the main (simple) clause, it would then be a puzzle to have such a paraphrase of *nita* in the parenthesis: the assumed past *-ta* is interchangeable in such a case with *-te iru* that represents the current existence/relevance of a state after a preceding act. Therefore, in this utterance, *-ta* must be understood as perfective marker. *Sono* 'the/that' suggests that some context is shared by the speaker and hearer in discourse: some chronological or parental information on the child's family. In (18d), a similar process of interpretation applies. Here, *-ta* represents perfective, not past. The confirmation of there being what was once lost is now made in (18d). In the speaker's mind, some expectation of the existence of it has been held during the search. Thus, the utterance tells that the speaker's holding of the expectation is over with the finding.

Hashimoto (1969: 210) further states that *-te* is derived from a classical perfective auxiliary *-tsu*. The auxiliary *-tsu* was used in classical Japanese and represented the completion of an act denoted by its preceding verb. Crucially, in what Kindaichi (1950, 1976) called the "*Dai-Yonshu* Verb"(= Verb of Class 4), the verbs can only be used with the *-te iru* form and indicate **state**, not continuation of an act: *sobiete-iru* 'in a state of towering/soaring'; *suite iru* 'be fond of.'[7] Thus, the "existential state" seems to be the only unique meaning that can be endorsed as a fundamental, invariable meaning of *-te iru*.

Matsushita (1930: 180–4), Sakuma (1966: 153–7), Teramura (1984: 127–9), and Shirota (1997: 207–9) arguably belong in the second group as to their insights into the fundamental meaning of *-te iru* as the *existential state after the preceding act*. Matsushita (1930: 184) argues against the "completion" as simply the primary meaning of *-te iru* and claims that the form *-te iru* denotes the result after the preceding activity in examples such as "*Yu-ga waite-iru* 'Water is boiled hot.'" Following Matsushita, Sakuma (1966: 156) makes the claim that, with the expression *-te iru*, an activity is already practiced and a state after that stays existent up to the present. He calls this the "existential expression". According to Sakuma, this class of expressions does not require any consensus of an explicit time frame between speaker and hearer. Teramura (1984: 125–46) extensively discusses the uses of *-te iru* and examines some of the traditionally held classifications, as I have mentioned above in (3) and (4). He (1984: 126–9) concludes that *-te iru* form mainly means that the result of a foregoing act is still existent at present. He (1984: 126) also points out that the "present routine act" and the adjectival use, which are often cited as main uses of *-te iru*, are immaterial to the classification of eventualities each verb denotes: i.e., the two meanings can emerge across the board. That suggests that classified uses of *-te* *iru* based on the eventualities of verbs are not satisfactory, since the meanings Teramura observes do persist across the board. He finally takes the "present routine act" as a generically represented core meaning that I have mentioned above. The examples of the "present routine act" are shown below.

(19) Examples of "present routine act" [Teramura 1984: 126, (23) and (24)]
    a. Chichi-wa konogoro rokuji-niwa okite iru.
       father-TOP recently six-o'clock-at get-up-TE IRU
       '*lit.*, My father recently gets up at six o'clock.'
    b. Chichi-wa saikin asa sanjuppun-hodo jyoggingu-o shite
       father-TOP recently morning 30 minutes-about jogging-ACC do-TE
       iru.
       IRU
       '*lit.*, My father recently goes jogging for about thirty minutes in the morning.'

Even with these cases, the existence of a state is invariably denoted as the result of some act that is already initiated. After repeated acts that are triggered by *konogoro* 'recently' and *saikin* 'recently,' the habitual states result. The father holds to his habitual state of getting up at six o'clock, as in (19a), or jogging for thirty minutes in the morning, as in (19b).

With the facts and discussion of data, together with the literature introduced above, I have claimed that the form *-te iru* uniquely denotes the existence of a state after the preceding act. I have shown that, as its derived meanings, *-te iru* can indicate either a terminated event or an on-going event, depending on the participants' shared understanding of a given discourse. Therefore, the representation of events with *-te iru* must involve discourse-semantic/pragmatic level of representation. In the next section 4.3, I will first compare parallel uses I observe between *-te iru* and the English present perfect. In 4.4, I will illustrate the aspectual representation of the existential *-te iru* with boundaries of time-intervals, as viewed from discourse-semantic/pragmatic representation.

4.3 Further arguments for the -*te iru* form as existential: comparison with the English present perfect

In the previous section, I have argued that:

(i) the aspectual form -*te iru* denotes "the existence of a state after the activation of an act" as its invariable meaning because of the combined form, -*te iru*,

(ii) depending on the kind of eventuality a preceding verb has, the meaning of the predicate Verb-*te iru* can vary between an on-going and a terminated event, and

(iii) the meaning that results from (ii) can take on an interchangeable meaning, with the addition of a tense operator such as a time adverb depending on the discourse context. In this section, I discuss further arguments for them. I will first examine the meaning of the English present perfect in comparison with that of -*te iru*.

In discussing the existential Present Perfect (hereafter PrP) in English, Michaelis (1994: 122) contrasts its unspecified time frame with the specific past time of the simple past tense, as in (20).

(20)a. I went to Paris.
    b. I've been to Paris.   [Michaelis 1994: 122 (13)]

Michaelis claims that (20a) evokes a specific past time interval and would require a past time adverb if the sentence is uttered as a *discourse-initial* assertion. In contrast, she argues that (20b) does not evoke an identifiable past interval. Instead, the addressee need only envision a general time span, whose upper boundary is the present time (and speech time), within which the denoted event in question took place. She classifies the uses of English PrP into three: existential, resultative, and continuative. (20b) is analyzed by Michaelis as **existential**. Although such an exact time reference is not always likely to be involved in an example such as (20a), it is nonetheless important to us to see the contrast between the two, (20a) and (20b). The point is that in the existential reading with (20b), no particular time reference is relevant to the speaker's mind and the sentence can be *discourse-initial* as existential.

The same kind of taxonomy in English PrP in fact applies in general to the readings of sentences with -*te iru* that I discussed: existential/resultative, together with continuative. The Japanese examples corresponding to (20) are shown in (21).

(21) a. Watashi-wa Pari-ni it<u>ta</u>.
I-TOP   Paris-to went
'I went to Paris.'

b. Watashi-wa Pari-ni it<u>te iru</u>.
I-TOP   Paris-to go-TE IRU
'I have been to Paris.'

In (21a), the speaker refers to his past experience that happened at a particular time. Therefore, some reference pertaining to the past time needs to be sought by the addressee. In contrast, in (21b), the speaker and addressee seem to assume the understanding of some past time/time interval without searching for a temporal reference for that. If a result after the speaker's experience is embodied, that can be termed as resultative. If not, there is still an existential reading in which his experience is relevant to the current discourse where the speaker resides. In (21b), it is not possible to identify a reference time or event time per se, due at least partly to the stative nature of *iru*, the second unit of the *-te iru*. It seems plausible to associate the Japanese example in (21b) with the English PrP example in (20b) in light of their identical reading: existential.

If the association of existentiality in the English PrP with a meaning of *-te iru* is right, I will be able to state that in Verb-*te iru* the upper boundary, i.e. the right boundary, as I termed it in the preceding chapter, is always the speaker's **speech time**, just as it is in the English PrP. However, this is not exact in discussing complex clauses. In example (22) repeated here from the previous chapter, *-te iru* in the subordinate HIR clause indicates the **event time** of the act represented by the main clause, with contiguity required between the two events.

(22) [= (16a) in Chapter 3]
John-wa [[Mary-ga   hako-o   tukut<u>te-iru</u>]-no]-o   kowasita.
-TOP   -NOM box-ACC make-remain-N-ACC broke
'Mary was making a box, and John broke it.'

In this respect, *-te iru* in HIR is bound by a temporal element of the main clause. No boundary in time interval is specified in the event denoted by the HIR clause. If there is invariably an existential reading in -*te iru* in HIR, as I have argued above, the existential reading gives only a temporal variable that is not bound. The variable must be bound by some temporal referent in discourse. However, the event of the main clause indicates a specific time reference because of the tense marking. Therefore, as I have argued in the previous chapter, the time of the main predicate is associated with that of the HIR predicate, given the "contiguity of time" requirement with the particle -*no*.

There are differences between the English PrP and Japanese -*te iru* form. First, as Michaelis argues, the English PrP cannot have an adverb like 'quickly' when the sentence is meant for a resultative reading.

(23) *The committee has <u>quickly</u> rejected my proposal.

In contrast, the Japanese counterpart seems to accept the adverb.

(24) Iinkai-wa <u>sugu-ni</u> watashi-no teian-o kyozetsu-shite iru.
    Committee-TOP quickly my proposal-ACC reject-do-TE IRU
    'The committee has quickly rejected my proposal.'

Second, the English PrP cannot indicate an on-going process, whereas the -*te iru* form can with *ima* '(just) now'.

(25)a. John-wa ima hashitte iru.
    John-TOP now run-remain.
    'John is running now.'
  b. ?John has now run. ≠ John is running now.

In fact, this difference can be accounted for once we review what I have argued for before. As I have mentioned in the previous section, in -*te iru*, the first unit -*te* indicates the activation of an act and the second unit *iru* stands for 'remain' or 'exist'. The aspectual marker as a whole denotes the existence of a "state after the activation of an act." If the preceding verb is a verb of process/activity such as 'run', there is no end point in time in the described act. Therefore, in (25a), "a state after the activation of an act" means the state after the beginning of running. That is, the subject person is still running. In this respect, denoted acts are two-fold in Japanese -*te iru*: the act by the preceding verb in Verb-*te iru* and the state denoted by *iru*. The act involved in 'have run' is just one kind of monolithic activity, *i.e.* to run, in any time frame given. In the English example (25b), the adverb 'now' conflicts with 'has run' in binding a time frame of an already initiated act without an endpoint, if the sentence is interpreted as ongoing. So, the kind of eventuality represented by the form 'have/has (X-ed)' is directly reflected in the determination of acceptability of the English example (25b). In addition, the kind of eventualities indicated by predicates in the English PrP examples can be directly coerced by tense operators such as time adverbials. Laurence Horn (p.c.) points out that the examples in (23) and (25b) will be clearer with the additions of 'once again' to (23) and of 'so he is going to shower' in (25b). The eventualities with the predicates shift with the adverbials: achievement to accomplishment with 'reject' in (23); and process to accomplishment with 'run' in (25b). In contrast, in -*te iru*, the determining element is the second unit *iru*, which indicates a generic state, but it accepts a preceding act denoted with any variety of eventualities of verbs except certain idiosyncratic ones. The second unit *iru* embeds the eventuality of the first verbal unit of the complex predicate and thus the sentence is acceptable with the addition of the adverbials.[8] Consequently, the difference occurs in (25). This combined nature of the constitution of -*te iru* is crucial in the discussion of a fundamental meaning of the -*te iru* form. This is one important and crucial difference in how the English existential PrP and the Verb-*te iru* form in Japanese are used.

Michaelis (1994: 149) argues that, when a serialization of two clauses occurs with '*and then*' in the English PrP, the only available reading is the existential one. As I already discussed above, the complex predicate Verb-*te iru* is analyzed as two-fold: a state existent after the activation of an act denoted by the first verb. Therefore, there is a serialization of the two acts involved inherently within the complex predicate. Along the same lines, Michaelis gives examples of the English PrP such as (26).

(26)a. I have (??now) cleaned the house <u>and then</u> fed the dog.
    b. I have cleaned the house and fed the dog.
    c. I have [[clean the house] and then [feed the dog]]-ed
        [Michaelis 1994: 149 (73) with slight modifications of symbols]

Although sentence (26b) with 'and' is ambiguous between existential and resultative readings, sentence (26a) with 'and then' has an existential reading only, which is not compatible with 'now' used for a resultative reading. The existential reading should have the interpretation of conjoined predications, as indicated in (26c). This is true of *-te iru*, as in the above example (24), in which the rejection of a proposal is enacted, and, after that, some state remains relevant to the speaker and hearer. That is, the existential fact of the rejection is likely to be a focus of the following context.

Another argument for the existentiality of the meaning of *-te iru* has to do with its *a priori* existential interpretation over a resultative one. As Michaelis (1994: 138) argues, the kind of an entity described by an NP and the discourse context can also affect the well-formedness of an utterance.

(27)a. #Einstein has visited Princeton.
    b. How can you say that Princeton is a cultural backwater? Einstein has visited Princeton.   [with a narrow-focus accent on the subject]
                                                [Michaelis 1994: 138]

McCawley (1971) quotes this classic example and states that the example (27a) is a priori anomalous on an existential reading, but that this anomalous sentence can be acceptable. It will be acceptable, once the person is highlighted as a symbolic famous figure whose significance still exists in the minds of participants in conversation, as illustrated in (27b).[9] Thus, in the above context, the existential reading of the PrP is evoked. The Japanese counterpart in (28a), however, seems to be transparent in the contrast of well-formedness shown in the above (27a) and (27b).

(28)a. Einstein-wa   Princeton-o   otozure-te iru.
      Einstein-TOP Princeton-ACC visit-TE   IRU
      'Einstein has visited Princeton.'
    b. Jiro-wa   kesa-kara   Tokyo-e it-te iru.
      Jiro-TOP this-morning-from Tokyo-to go-TE IRU
      'Jiro has been to Tokyo since this morning.'
                              [the predicates as "resultative" in Nitta 1997: 236]

It turns out that example (28a) is well-formed without further context.

Michaelis (p. 127) argues that, in discussing the distinction between existential and resultative readings of the English PrP, *recency* of the event with respect to speech time is not relevant to the existential reading, whereas it is of great relevance to the resultative reading.

(29) Have you seen my slippers? [Michaelis, p.127, (20)]

In (29), Michaelis states that the questioner does not intend an existential understanding, i.e. an interpretation which might cause the hearer to mention sightings of one or more pairs of slippers in the distant past. Michaelis claims that, instead, the questioner presumably intends a resultative understanding: he is inquiring about particular slippers which currently affects the hearer's ability to locate the slippers. The only relevant response is the one which concerns the questioner's current quandary. If I apply this argument to *-te iru*, the Japanese counterpart (28a) is correctly proven to denote the existential meaning, since it is acceptable without the *recency* of an event.

According to Nitta (1997: 236), however, the class of verb such as *iku* 'go' in (28b) would belong to "resultative," since Nitta classifies the example (28b) into the category of "resultant state." In addition, since the designated resultative predicate *itte iru* 'go-TE IRU' can be used as a paraphrase of *otozurete iru* 'visit-TE IRU' in (28a), the predicate *otozurete iru* 'visit-TE IRU' would consequently indicate a "resultant state."

(30) Einstein-wa   Princeton-ni   itte iru.
    Einstein-TOP Princeton-LOC be in-TE IRU
    'Einstein has been in Princeton.'
                [= (28a) Einstein-wa Princeton-o otozurete iru]

Unfortunately, Nitta's analysis poses a problem here in (30): Michaelis's example that she analyzes as "existential" falls under the "resultant" state in Nitta. Furthermore, the following example seems to denote an existential meaning with *-te iru*.

(31)a. Kare-wa shinyaku-o   **hak**ken-shite iru.
       he-TOP new-drug-ACC discovery-do-TE IRU
       'He has discovered a new drug.'

b. Einstein-wa   toki-no   soutaisei-o   **hakken**-shite iru.
Einstein-TOP time-GEN relativity-ACC discovery-do-TE IRU
'Einstein has discovered the relativity of time.'
[the predicate *hakken-suru* as "existential" by Nitta]

Since the verb *hakken-suru* 'discover' is "existential" in Nitta's classification, as in (31a), the same verb in the example (31b) would also fall under "existential." It will then be contradictory to argue that one identical historical figure Einstein who lived in the past can be analyzed either existential, as in the case of "Einstein's discovery," or resultative, as in the case of "Einstein's visit." Therefore, such an analysis by which existential and resultative are separated cannot be supported in the case of the sentences with *-te iru*. More importantly, sentences with Verb-*te iru* in Japanese is not relevant to the condition "recency of the event with respect to speech time," even if the recency condition is valid as to the English resultative examples. The examples in Japanese are all well-formed without further context for highlighting historical facts, as shown in (28a), (30), and (31b). Therefore, it seems reasonable to confirm here that all the Japanese examples above denote existentiality as an invariable meaning, due to a state indicated by *iru*.

Grounded on the comparison between the English (existential) PrP and *-te iru* form in this section, together with the claim shared by Hashimoto, Matsushita, Sakuma, and Teramura, as I examined in the previous section, I conclude that my claim of the fundamental meaning of *-te iru* is supported. The core meaning is now defined as:

(32) The core meaning of "(Verb) *-te iru*": the existentiality of a state that is relevant after the activation of an act denoted by the preceding verb.

In the next section, drawing on the argument I have just made, I will show how the core lexical meaning of Verb-*te iru* can be interpreted in the context of event representation, as I discussed in chapter 3.

4.4 A system of reasoning processes for the temporal interpretation of the Verb-*te iru*

I now demonstrate how the temporal interpretation of Verb-*te iru* predicate will be obtained in discourse. I will show that the predicate represents certain constrained aspectual meanings interactively with different eventualities that the first verbal units indicate. The task here is to illuminate, as part of the system of discourse structure, how the interactive reasoning process can be described for the temporal interpretation. In 4.4.1, I will first discuss the basic reasoning of temporal interpretation in simplex clauses with Verb-*te iru*. In 4.4.2, I will then apply it to the interpretation of the HIR complex-clause construction with Verb-*te iru*.

4.4.1 Matching of events for the temporal contiguity in discourse: a system of interpretation for the Verb-*te iru* predicate

Before I discuss the temporal/aspectual interpretation of the Verb-*te iru* predicate, let me point out the following. In considering the ending time-point of an act indicated by (the eventualities of) a predicate, *termination* and *culmination* must be separated as distinct concepts for defining aspectual meanings of Japanese temporal markers such as -*te iru*. As I mentioned in footnote 2 of section 4.2.2, a number of verbs indicate only the inception of the denoted activities. Another example of the same kind is given in (33).

(33)a. David-wa Larry-to   *kit*te-mo *kir*enai   naka-da.
        -TOP   -with cut-even cut-able-NEG term-ASSRT-CPLA
     '*lit.*, David cannot be cut off from Larry even if he is cut off from him.'
     'David is on unbreakable terms with Larry.'
  b. Mochi-o   kudamono-naihu-de kitta-ga, kirenakatta.
     Rice-cake-ACC fruit-knife-with cut-but   cut-able-NEG-PST
     '*lit.*, (I) cut rice cake with a fruit-knife but was not able to cut it.'
     'I tried to cut rice cake with a fruit-knife but was not able to do that.'

Although the verb *kiru* 'cut' appears to be a middle verb in (33a) and is used as part of an idiomatic phrase *kitte-mo kirenai naka* '(be) in very close relation (with someone/each other)', the two examples, nonetheless, show the nature of the issue. In general, verbs of this class do not indicate the culmination of the denoted act: for example, in (33), the act of cutting with *kiru* does not refer to the ending time-point as to whether the denoted act is completed or not, i.e. culminated or not. Instead, only the inception is indicated with *kiru* 'cut' in Japanese. Therefore, it is not contradictory in Japanese to state, with *kiru*, what in the English literal paraphrases of (33a, b) would be contradictory. On the other hand, I observe the group of verbs that clearly represent the culmination or the completion phase of the denoted act: *kau* 'buy,' *tomaru* 'stop (vi.),' *nogareru* 'escape', and so on. This kind of aspectual difference does not seem to be relevant to the syntactic level of representation. Furthermore, in (34), we will need to identify the temporal meaning of a denoted act at some semantic or discourse level, where tense or the time adverb binds and forces the end of the act.

(34) a. Kate-wa   ima   shousetsu-o kaite   iru.
         -TOP now   novel-ACC   write-TE IRU
      'Kate is writing/in the middle of writing a novel.'
   b. Kate-wa sannen-mae   shousetsu-o kaite   iru.
      -TOP   3-years-before novel-ACC   write-TE IRU
      '(I tell you,) Kate has an experience of writing a novel three years ago.
          [(1) She did not finish the writing or (2) she finished the writing]'

The paraphrases of the two examples in (34) do not sound natural, but I need to maintain this manner of paraphrasing *-te iru* expressions so that the aspectual meanings will not be lost. In (34a), the act of writing a novel is in progress with *ima* 'now', whereas in (34b) it is not specifically represented; that is, the writing may have been either in progress or done at the time of the reference, i.e., at one time three years ago. The utterance in (34b) represents a state in which the event of 'Kate's writing of a novel' is interpreted as extending long after the initiation. Thus, the past-time adverb *sannen mae* 'three years ago' forces the interpretation of the **termination** of the reference of aspectual phases that the act denotes. Therefore, in discourse, either of the aspectual interpretations remains plausible, as shown in the two paraphrases of (34b). Given the phenomena, I need to use a term different from "culmination" which refers to the inherent meanings that cover the overall picture of an activity denoted by (the eventualities of) a verb. Here lies the ground for employing term "termination", by which I mean a force of overriding the time interval indicated by the eventuality of the predicate. The additional time adverb such as *sannen mae* 'three years ago' in (34b) obviates the reference to the boundaries of the time interval with 'writing a novel' in discourse. Thus, in (34b) with the force of the past adverb *sannen mae*, the additional "termination" meaning is yielded, with the endpoint being put in: that the writing may have been done at the time of the reference, i.e., at one time three years ago. This secondary interpretation of the predicate *Verb-te iru* in (34b) is accountable only with the culmination/termination distinction, as I have introduced. I will hereafter use the two temporal concepts, *culmination* and *termination* distinctively with each other, based on the observation above.

I now discuss the system of temporal interpretation with Verb-*te iru* predicates. I first illustrate it with examples of **Process/Activity** verbs, as in (35).

(35) a. John-wa   [arui]-te iru.
       -TOP walk-TE IRU
       '*lit.*, John is in the state of walking.'
   b. John-wa   [ima arui]-te   iru.
       -TOP now walk-TE IRU
       '*lit.*, John is now in the state of walking.'

In considering the representation of a time-interval, as I discussed in chapter 3, the eventuality of a verb comes as an inherent meaning of the temporal interpretation. In both of the two examples in (35), verb *aruku* 'walk' expresses a continued activity of walking, and does not indicate culmination in itself. As I have argued in the previous sections in chapter 4, -*te iru* denotes the existentiality of a state that comes after the activation of an act. Existential readings evoke variables of referents, but the variables are unbound, as I argued in chapter 3 and also in section 4.3 with example (22) of the current chapter. As a result, the variable needs to be bound by some other temporal element. Because the second unit *iru*, i.e. the main predicate unit, refers to the present time, 'now', the act of the verb *aruku* 'walk' preceding -*te iru*, is interpreted as occurring just before 'now'. The existential variable is thus duly bound temporally by the main tense indication and by the temporal orders of complex predicate. However, there is no culmination with the act by walking, and, in the event representation, no right boundary (i.e. end point of an act) of the time-interval is relevant. Therefore, the continued state of walking after the initiation is interpreted in (35a) with 'walk-TE IRU'. In (35b), which is identical to (35a) except for the time-adverb *ima* 'now', the same kind of system for temporal interpretation works. The main tense indicates 'now' with -*te iru*, thereby binding an existential variable. However, because of the time adverb *ima* 'now', the predicate with *-te* indicates another time reference. Note that in Japanese, *ima* can mean either 'now, at present' or 'just now', i.e. very recently, as in (36).

(36) Tomodati-wa <u>ima</u> kaet*ta*. soshitara kare-ni denwa-ga haitta.
friend-TOP now went back. And then he-to phone-NOM came-in
'The friend went home <u>just now</u>. And then, I made a call to him.'

With the presence of the past tense indicated by *-ta*, the present-time adverb *ima* is acceptable. Thus, in (35b), *ima* can represent a certain period of time span up to the time close to the speech time. The adverb *ima* takes narrow scope, which means that it indicates a temporal point of the act by 'walk' in the first predicate unit. The temporal interpretation now involves an ordering with the two temporal indicators, 'now' by the main tense and the time close to 'now' by *ima*. Just after the initiation of 'walking' at a point in time close to 'now', an existential state emerges, which is an inherent meaning of *-te iru*. The eventualities of 'walk' do not involve any culmination but indicate duration/continuation. As a result, the continued state of walk is interpreted after the activation of the act. In this case, I observe that some matching process is involved in the interpretation concerning the compatibility of the time references between the two temporal indicators. This **matching** process involves the measurement of compatibility in the discourse context.[10] This is observed more clearly in (37).

(37) a. John-wa   imawa eki-made   arui-te iru.
         -TOP now   railway-station-up-to walk-TE IRU
    #'[In-progress state reading:] John is now in a state that comes after getting to the station now.'
    '[Resultant state reading:] John is now at the railway station after he walked there.'
  b. John-wa   sannen mae   eki-made   arui-te iru.
         -TOP 3-years-before railway-station-up-to walk-TE IRU
    'John has an experience of having reached the station on foot three years ago.'

In (37a), the utterance is **un**acceptable with an "In-progress" reading, since the relevant events have precedence relations with each other by the eventualities of the complex predicate *eki-made aruite iru*, whereas the two temporal indications, by *imawa* 'now' and by the present tense of the main predicate, point to one time-point 'now.' To be specific, with a goal argument *eki-made* 'up to the railway station', the first predicate unit indicates the eventualities of **Accomplishment/Achievement**, which indicates culmination. Thus, the activity of 'getting to the railway station on foot' preferably is finished at a time a little before the present time, while some existential state with *iru* 'exist' represents the present time (because of its present tense), thereby indicating the resultant state. In the In-progress reading, in contrast, 'walking to the station' would continue without culmination and without a right boundary of its time interval, and thus the current state that is indicated by *iru* 'exist' is still 'walking to the station', which would contradict the indicated precedence relations by the eventualities and by the time-gap between the two acts, 'walking to the station' and '(a state) existing,' in V_1-*te iru*$_2$. The only matching, **by default**, lies in a reading in which some state exists just after the completion of the act, John's getting to the station. Therefore, the resultant reading in which John is now at the station after his walking (there) is inferred. This matching is possible only in the reading with some kind of *default measurement* of plausible event relations.

In interpreting in the way described above, there is no determining factor in the available syntactic structure in (37a), nor in any lexical information available for identifying the compatibility of the two temporal indicators. Nevertheless, the interpretation process leads to different temporal readings between (35b) and (37a) with the same complex verb *aruite iru*. Therefore, determination of the compatibility of two events must involve some kind of reasoning for matching competing temporal readings in the discourse.[11] This discourse process is highlighted also in (37b). In (37b), the main tense indicates 'now' with *iru*, whereas the predicate *ekimade aruite* 'get to the railway station on foot' is bound by the past-time adverb *sannen mae* 'three years before'. There is a good **gap in time passage** between the two temporal indicators; by default, the act of John's getting to the station is interpreted as completed or terminated, just before an existential state that is 'now', due to the culmination indicated by the verb's eventualities and the time gap that I have just described. The examination of the time gap must involve discourse context information, together with the interpretation of the termination of the described act by the force of a time adverb. In the context, (37b) can only be interpreted as resultant through the matching grounded on the inferred default meanings. In the case of verbs in the pure **Achievement** class, the time gap that I mentioned above will not be material, since the eventualities involve a momentary act, which inherently leads to the instant culmination. Hence the predicate V-*te iru* indicates a Resultant state with an Achievement verb.

Note, once again, that the two utterances (37a) and (37b) indicate distinct temporal references with time adverbs, *imawa* in (37a) and *sannen mae* in (37b), and yet the utterances denote the same Resultant state reading. This interpretation would not be available solely in terms of syntactic structure.

I will now show that the same system of temporal interpretation applies, with a typical **Accomplishment** class verb, as in (38) with Verb-*te iru*.

(38)a. Tomoya-wa essei-o kai-te iru.
      -TOP   essay-ACC write-TE IRU
      'Tomoya is in the middle stage of writing an essay.'
      or 'Tomoya has an experience of writing an essay before.'
   b. Tomoya-wa sannen mae essei-o kai-te iru.
      -TOP   3-years-before essay-ACC write-TE IRU
      'Tomoya has an experience of writing an essay three years ago.'

In (38a), the main tense indicates 'now', whereas the first predicate before -*te* does not indicate any temporal reference. An existential variable evoked by -*te iru* is bound by the main tense. The eventualities of the verb 'write' with an internal argument 'an essay' denote culmination and duration of the act. Because of the duration, "one time-point after the activation of an act" can be interpreted as either one time-point in the middle or the terminal point (right boundary) of the time-interval of the durative act. Therefore, through the matching process in discourse, the act of writing an essay is either still In-progress just after the activation or already culminated after the activation. An existential state is therefore interpreted either as the middle stage of Tomoya's writing of an essay or as the Resultant state after Tomoya's writing. This explains the paraphrases in (38a). In (38b), as well as the indication of 'now' by the main tense, the time adverb *sannen mae* 'three years before' indicates another time reference, resulting in the time gap. Through the matching process, the time gap is interpreted as long enough to favor the completion of writing an essay by Tomoya, based on the culmination indicated by the eventualities of the predicate. The time gap precludes other readings through the matching process for temporal interpretation: that is, the time gap forces the termination of the essay writing. Thus, this process accounts for the paraphrase in (38b), *i.e.* the only possibility of a Resultant state reading.

In understanding the nature of the system of temporal interpretation, it is crucial to notice that ambiguities inevitably occur in *-te iru* predicates, on the one hand, and two distinct time adverbs can lead to the same aspectual meaning, as in the case of (37a) and (37b), on the other hand. This clearly explains the involvement of an essential interpretation process in discourse such as "matching" processes in temporal ordering, given the eventualities and time-intervals. I have shown how the basic system of temporal interpretation works for simplex clauses with Verb-*te iru* in distinct eventualities.[12] In the next section 4.4.2, I will further apply the matching process to the interpretation of the HIR with Verb-*te iru*.

4.4.2 The matching process for temporal interpretation of the Verb-*te iru* in the HIR construction

In the previous section, I have shown as part of a discourse representation system the process of temporal interpretation with the Verb-*te iru* predicate in a simplex sentence type. I will now apply the matching process to the context of a complex clause type, i.e. the HIR construction that I have examined in the previous chapters.

In the following examples, a contrast turns out to be the result of the temporal compatibility difference between two events.

(39) a. [[Mary-ga ringo-o tabe**te iru**]-no]-o John-ga totta.
-NOM apple-ACC eat-TE IRU-N-ACC -NOM took
'Mary was eating an apple, which John took.'
b. #[[Mary-ga ringo-o tabe**ta**]-no]-o John-ga totta.
-NOM apple-ACC eat-TA-N-ACC -NOM took
?'Mary ate an apple, which John took.'

In (39a), the first unit *ringo-o tabete* 'eating an apple' of the first complex predicate indicates the eventuality of Accomplishment. An existential variable is evoked by *-te iru*, as already discussed in the earlier section, and thus an existential state emerges just after the activation of Mary's eating of an apple.

There is no time gap here, as we have seen in (37b) and (38b) in the previous section. Therefore, grounded on the duration and culmination of the act, the clause in the HIR is expected to indicate either an In-progress or Resultant state. However, the tense indication with *iru* is not available, since the HIR clause is untensed, as discussed in earlier chapters. Consequently, the HIR clause is temporally bound by the main clause tense, which is the past in (39a).

Another relevant process here is the **default reasoning** of the matching of temporal orders between the two events in a complex clause construction such as the HIR constructions, given the untensed status of the predicate in the HIR clause. Therefore, the matching is necessarily involved in (39) for the temporal ordering between the two events. Because what the second event, represented in the main clause, indicates is to take something away from Mary and also because the eating of an apple by Mary in the first event is durative with culmination, the first event is by default, or preferably, interpreted as In-progress when the second event occurs. If the first event were already terminated, that would result in **no** reasonable **match**: after an apple is already eaten by Mary, nothing is left for John to take. The same reasoning of the matching process explains the unacceptability of example (39b). As I have already discussed in chapter 3, *-ta* in the HIR clause does not indicate tense but an aspectual meaning such as completion. Therefore, only the culmination meaning is available in (39b). With this aspectual marker *-ta* in the HIR, there is no available interpretation process relevant to determine a time gap, as is the case with *-te iru* in a simplex clause. Consequently, in (39b) the HIR clause simply indicates the culmination of eating an apple, thereby leading to the unacceptability of the whole utterance: through the matching, it is reasoned that, after the completion of eating an apple, nothing should be left for John to take. This contrast between the two examples in (39) clearly indicates the involvement of particular interpretation processes in discourse, since the only difference between the two examples is the aspectual markings for In-progress vs. Resultant, which syntactically have no significance in identifying the well-formedness of those utterances.

I have shown in this subsection that the temporal interpretation with aspectual markers, *-te iru* and *-ta*, in the HIR involves the reasoning process of "default matching," through which the ordering compatibility between two events is determined. In the next chapter, the overall picture of the discourse interpretation with the HIR construction, including the matching process, will be shown in a wider perspective of the discourse representation system. Note, however, that this kind of process in question is not strictly grounded on lexical knowledge. For instance, Achievement class verbs can be analyzed as having left and right time-interval boundaries, *i.e.* as durative. In certain cases, the following predicates can be deemed as durative: *win the race*; *arrive at an airport*; and so on. The reasoning process of the matching in this respect is **dynamic** or defeasible in another term, depending on the discourse context that a speaker and a hearer share. Therefore, in the next chapter, I will develop the dynamic process of matching and discuss a model of default measurement of plausible event relations in the general framework of discourse representation theories, as proposed in the recent literature on default interpretation.

Endnotes

1. As Seiichi Makino (personal communication) points out, there is some subtle but meaningful difference between the *-te iru* construction and *-koto-ga aru* construction.

    (a) Yoogisha-wa sono manshon-ni hati-do-mo ashi-o hakon-*de iru*.
    suspect-TOP that apartment-to eight-times-Intensifr foot-ACC carry-DE IRU
    'The suspect has been to that apartment as many as eight times.'
    (b) Yoogisha-wa sono manshon-ni hati-do-mo ashi-o hakno-*da koto*
    suspect-TOP that apartment-to eight-times-Intensifr foot-ACC carry-PST thing
    -*ga*   *aru*.
    -NOM exist
    'The suspect came to that apartment as many as eight times.'

    Makino states that it is likely that a detective utters the sentence (a) with *-te iru*, if he is really involved in investigating the suspect's whereabouts. This example seems to illustrate the involvement of some connoted meaning with *-te iru*, although I do not discuss the *-koto-ga aru* construction.

2. See Hasegawa (1996a, b) for thorough discussions of the taxonomy of *-te*.
3. By 'existentiality', I mean the semantic property of an existential presupposition, as in 'there is …' construction, following Milsark's (1977) term. I will later illustrate the invariable meaning of this existentiality with Verb-*te iru*, together with the subject marker *-ga*.
4. This form *-u* has been controversial concerning its indication of *present tense*.

    (1) Rainen-wa kanaraz*u* ie-o tater*u*.
    Next-year-TOP certainly home-ACC build
    '(I) will certainly build my home next year.'

Example (1) clearly refers to the future with -*u* because of the future time adverb.

(2)a. #Kodomo-ga   ima kouen-de asob*u*. Hohoemashii koukei-da.
     children-NOM now park-at   play   amusing   scene-Assrtn
     Intended: 'Children play in the park now. That is an amusing scene.'
  b. Kodomo-ga ima kouen-de ason-*de-iru*. Hohoemashii koukei-da.
     'Children are now playing in the park.   That is an amusing scene.' [with V-*te iru*]
  c. Kodomo-ga {itsumo/ashitamo} kouen-de asobu.
     'Children play in the park {always/tomorrow-as well}.'

In (2a), the sentence is unnatural when a present-tine adverb like *ima* '(just) now' is added. Therefore, -*u* does not seem to stand for the present, although it does stand for some unspecified future, as in (2c), together with (1) above. In fact, it can be argued that Japanese does not have an independent future or present marker morphologically. In fact, Suzuki (1979: 15) claims that Japanese has only two tense forms of what he calls *present-future* and *past*: the former is indicated by -*u* and the latter -*ta*. I share this idea with Suzuki and assume that, while I maintain my claim in the preceding chapter that -*ta* indicates either past or perfective depending on discourse context, -*u* indicates unspecified time after speech time. In this respect, let me quickly mention, with examples in (3), that the time adverb *ima* '(just) now' can indicate both speech time and a time before that, but it always indicates a brief moment.

(3)a. Jiro-wa   ima keeki-zukuri-ga   owatta.
     Jiro-TOP now cake-making-NOM done/finished.
     'Jiro (just) now finished making cake.
  b. #Jiro-wa ima hon-o   yonda.
     Jiro-TOP now book-ACC read-PST
     'Jiro (just) now read a book/books.'
  c. Jiro-wa   ima hon-o   yonde-iru.
     Jiro-TOP now book-ACC read-Imprf
     'Jiro is now reading a book.'

5 As Laurence Horn (personal communication) points out, the kind of meaning derived by 'have been to …' can be changed, as in:

I've been to an Elvis concert, but I've never heard anything like that.

In this example, the musician is already dead (or I may say 'has been dead'), unlike the case of (15) with Neil Young. As I discuss briefly, the point is that the kind of meanings Nitta classifies with verbs (plus -*te iru*) is not of one kind. Certainly some of the meanings with V-*te iru* also depend on the context, and I will illustrate that point with more examples. In some examples, only in the speaker's mind, the existence of the subject matter is of current relevance. Thus, the existence of a state, rather than the actual life or death, is left out as the remaining core meanings in those examples.

6   I do not discuss this but point out that, in the same vein, there are a good number of verbs in Japanese that are inchoative, although they appear to be stative, according to the approximate translation in English. Ikegami extensively discussed the phenomena of inchoative natures of certain Japanese verbs in his papers.

(1)a.   Kare-ni iku-you settoku-shita ga,   kare-wa ikanakatta.
         He-to to go   persuade-do-PST but he-TOP go-NEG-Pst
    b. *I persuaded him to go, but he wouldn't go.   [Ikegami 1982: 97]

Ikegami (1982: 97) argues that, in (1a), the weight of the description is on the act only, whereas the English counterpart (1b) contains the achievement of the persuasion effort, i.e., his going there, as part of the intended meaning of the verb *persuade*. Although the acceptability of (1b) seems dependent on the context and therefore should be marked with '#' or '?,' the English counterpart (1b) nonetheless seems to be inclined to the final phase of the persuasion act: the achievement of the persuasion, although the achievement may soon be overturned by an additional situation. Laurence Horn (personal communication) raises the following example.

(1b') I persuaded him to go. He changed his mind, and got run over by a truck.

In (1b'), the first sentence is more acceptable than the one in (1b). The additional context goes with the achievement of the persuasion, which contrasts with the case of the persuasion verb examples in Japanese. Ikegami also gives other well-quoted examples with verbs that show the same contrast as the one in (1). *Wakasu* 'boil', *kiru* 'cut', *kakeru* 'lock' and others show the same kind of contrast with the English counterparts: the Japanese counterparts do not indicate the final completed phases of the acts. They seem to be inchoative. Kuno (1973: 140, fn. 3) mentions the presence of many [-stative] counterparts of English [+stative] verbs. Similar phenomena of transitive/intransitive pairs are observed in Morita 1994: 294–51.

7   See Teramura 1984: 124–6 for some more idiosyncratic verbs of this kind, i.e. the verbs that can only take *-te iru* form.
8   Suzuki (1979: 7–8) lists the kind of predicates that are incompatible with *-te iru*. Existential verbs, *iru* 'exist (of a person)' and *aru* 'exist (of a thing)', cannot occur with *-te iru*, probably for tautological meanings. *Iru* 'need', *soutou-suru* 'be equivalent' and *atai-suru* 'be comparable' cannot occur with *-te iru*. Suzuki gives more examples, but they seem acceptable to me: for example, "...-*sugiru*" type verbs, "...-*eru*" type verbs. Teramura (1984: 124) raises some of the first examples above. The examples, at any rate, seem to be limited in number.
9   Similarly, Laurence Horn (p.c.) points out that the passive counterpart of the infelicitous (27a) turns out felicitous.

Princeton has been visited by Einstein.

The speaker who is proud of Princeton is likely to utter the example, with the historical moment associated with the current state of the city or the university there.

10 Similar notions have been proposed in the context of aspectual interpretation with the English imperfective. In discussing the well-known imperfective paradox, Asher (1992) calls the imperfective, as in progressives, a "default" option associated with a "complete event". Landman (1992) uses the similar notion of "reasonable option" in discussing the progressive. Glasbey (1998) uses "natural regularity," following Barwise and Seligman (1994). The notion of 'default' matching is further discussed in connection with *-te iru* in Ishikawa (2006).

11 This kind of default interpretation process for plausible relations between events will be developed in detail in the next chapter. Lexical default interpretation and discourse default will be distinguished as distinct levels of processes there, since the eventualities of *eki-made aruku* can be read out in the lexicon, as seen in the discussion of Pustejovsky (1991, 1995), but the temporal interpretation of the whole utterances of (37a, b) cannot.

12 I have not shown how the past tense examples with Verb-*te iru*, that is, the form Verb-*te ita* can be interpreted. As I earlier mentioned, *-ta* in a main predicate can indicate a modal meaning, the mechanism of which is still in controversy. That is beyond the scope of this thesis. However, let me note that my purpose of discussing the form *-te iru* is to explicate the temporal interpretation of the HIR clause, which is untensed. Therefore, the past tense form *-te ita* is immaterial in the current discussion. No time adverb occurs in the HIR clause, either. Thus, whether *-te iru* or *-te ita* occurs in the HIR, it is always bound by tense in the main predicate.

Chapter 5

Resolving the underspecified meanings: default reasoning in discourse interpretation

5.1 Introduction

In chapter 4, I argued that the temporal interpretation in the HIR involves a certain reasoning process which I call *matching*, through which the temporal ordering compatibility between two events is determined, grounded on two aspectual indications, In-progress and Resultant states. In this chapter, I will discuss this process from a wider perspective in order to explicate an overall discourse interpretation for underspecified constructions such as the HIR. I will develop a model of default measurement of plausible event relations that accommodates matching within the general framework of a discourse representation theory.

I will first discuss the nature of default reasoning in interpretation, examining past approaches to it, and will argue that the defaults in lexicon must be kept separate from those in discourse throughout the discourse interpretation process. I will then introduce a theory of discourse representation that is equipped with such default reasoning. I will claim that the theory can accommodate a potential model for the representation of underspecified unit sequences such as the HIR. With a brief overview of the theory, I will show that the discourse event relations between events can be explicitly accounted for and that they will constrain in a systematic way the inferences of plausible default readings, which are derived from the lexical and discourse information. Explicit types of discourse event relations and their constraints will be illustrated. Finally, I will discuss how such interpretation processes as default reasoning with the HIR can be operated in the introduced model.

Throughout the discussion in this chapter, my primary goal will be to explore a potential model for a default interpretation process which underspecified utterances such as the HIR in (1) are subject to. Therefore, although I draw on a specific theory of discourse representation, I will not comprehensively describe the model of the theory, nor show the complete logico-semantic formulae of (semantic) representation that the theory will eventually be equipped with. Those are beyond the scope of the present discussion and must be left for future research.

5.2 Two distinct defaults: lexical and discourse

As I have discussed in chapter 4, the potential ambiguity of the *-te iru* form between two aspectual readings, In-progress and Resultant states, is resolved in the HIR. That is achieved through the interpretation process of **matching**, and one of the two possible default event relations is excluded, as in (1)

(1) [[Mary-ga ringo-o   tabe**te iru**]-no]-o John-ga   totta.
     -NOM   apple-ACC eat-TE IRU-N-ACC   -NOM took
     'Mary was eating an apple, which John took.'

The plausible reasoning for the felicitous utterance is: nothing can be eaten by John after Mary finishes eating it. Thus, only an In-progress state reading obtains and the Resultant state that the Verb-*te iru* predicate is expected to indicate is excluded in the HIR. As stated in chapter 4, this reasoning process has to do with the **default** measurement of plausible event relations in discourse. Note that there is no tense indication in the HIR and the complement head noun *no* lacks semantic content. As a result, during the interpretation process of the utterance in (1), no explicit propositional meaning such as the English translation "Mary was eating an apple, which John took" obtains. The reasoning for matching invariably follows, in order to determine the temporal relation between the two events.

In chapter 3 the temporal organization between the two events is interpreted in terms of the time intervals that those events indicate as a basis for contiguity/non-contiguity determination. Therefore, for the integration of the temporal interpretation processes, I will discuss the nature of defaults in the interpretation of event relations, and develop two kinds of defaults that are evoked at different levels of the event interpretation process.

5.2.1 Lexical defaults versus discourse defaults
The notion of 'default' has been discussed in different linguistic circles: Minsky (1977); Landman (1992); Pelletier & Asher (1997); Veltman (1996); Briscoe et al. (1990); Poesio (1993); etc. Recently, Pustejovsky (1991, 1995) has developed a comprehensive lexical semantic theory that seems to be relevant to lexical default meanings. The examples are the following.

(2)a.   Mary enjoyed the book.   [Pustejovsky 1991: 424, 33a]
   b.   Mary enjoyed reading the book.   [Pustejovsky 1991: 425]

In (2a), the predicate of the object *the book* is underspecified, and the sentence can be read as (2b). Pustejovsky refers to the phenomena as logical metonymy (Pustejovsky 1991: 425; 1995: 54) and discusses it in terms of his lexical semantic theory. He claims that logical metonymy such as in the underspecified example in (2a) can be accounted for in the specific lexical values encoded in his lexical system, which resolves the underspecification in (2a) into the meaning expressed in (2b). Pustejovsky's (1991, 1995) system of lexical structures specifies the kinds of events that can be associated with the entity of nouns such as *book* in (2). Each lexical entry represents a complex of semantic roles and values encoded in the lexicon. Putstejovsky terms such essential role representations of a word entry **Qualia Structure**, a brief outline of which is shown in (3).

(3)   Qualia Structure
     Constitutive: the relation between an object and its constitutive parts.
     Formal: that which distinguishes it within a large domain.
     Telic: its purpose and function.
     Agentive: factors involved in its origin or "bringing it about."
                                            [Pustejovsky 1995: 76 and 85–6]

The **telic** role carries information on the purpose and function of a lexical entry. For example, the following sentence will be accounted for in terms of the telic roles of the words in the qualia structure.

(4) ?Mary enjoyed the pebble.

In (4), the noun *pebble* that involves an **unconventional** telic role value such as *enjoying* is odd, according to the information on *enjoy* and *pebble* encoded in the telic roles of the lexical system. There does not seem to be a common telic role value shared between the two entries. The entry *enjoy* should be associated with the kind of event that the entry of *pebble* represents in the lexical system, but *pebble* does not seem to indicate any entity relevant to any such event as enjoying in the indicated telic roles: the purpose or goal of enjoying doing something is much less likely to have anything to do with doing something with a pebble. Thus, the pieces of information available in the qualia structure result in the oddity or indeterminacy of (4), as expected.

However, against expectations, such a sentence as (4) will not be blocked by the grammar, but, rather, will only result in a semantic representation that will be pragmatically odd or underspecified, unless context provides a more specific interpretation. As Lascarides & Copestake 1998 (hereafter L&C 1998) argue, the lexical-semantic information for (4) should contain a very general **act-on-predicate** as a **default** value. This predicate denotes a generalized action value such as "do something." Therefore, the underspecified predicate in (4) would be interpreted as *do the pebble* as a default.

However, the default information will be defeated as odd in discourse, unless a specific predicate is involved in a further context; no event or entity associated with *enjoying* can be identified with *do the pebble* in discourse or in our knowledge base. Thus, the default results in a pragmatic **mismatch** between lexical and discourse information. This indicates that the oddity or indeterminacy of such sentences as in (4) does not directly result from the lexical default; rather, it results from the defeated lexical default through the discourse pragmatic reasoning. Crucially, the lexical default remains in the lexicon, and therefore cannot directly compete with information that is represented at the discourse level, unless an independent principle or rule is involved and the default is associated with the discourse representation.

More importantly, Pustejovsky's lexical semantic system concerning the qualia structure faces exceptional cases, although the problem with the first case could be resolved ad-hoc, as observed in the following with verbs such as *enjoy* in English and *tanoshimu* 'enjoy' or *najimu* 'get familiar' in Japanese.

(5)a. The high school student enjoyed a/the new dictionary.
   b. ?The high school student enjoyed reading a/the new dictionary.
   c. Sono koukousei-ga   atarashii jisho-o   tanoshinda.
       That high school-student-NOM new   dictionary-ACC enjoyed
       'The high school student enjoyed a/the new dictionary.'
   d. ?Sono koukousei-ga   atarashii jisho-o
       That high school-student-NOM new   dictionary-ACC
       yomu-no-o   tanoshinda
       reading-ACC enjoyed
       'The high school student enjoyed reading a/the dictionary.'

Unlike the above example in (5a), the telic role of the verb *enjoy*, i.e. *(to) read*, seems not to fit *dictionary* in (5b); the combination sounds odd as a default. Similarly in (5d), the telic role of the identical verb *tanoshimu* 'enjoy,' i.e. *yomu* 'read,' seems not to fit *jisho*, the Japanese word for 'dictionary,' in (5d); the sentence (5d) even sounds anomalous as a default, unlike (5c). In spite of the common values of the lexical semantic information shared between the two entries, 'book' and 'dictionary', the difference in acceptability arises between (5a) and (5b) [that is in contrast to (2b) with the predicate *read*] and also between (5c) and (5d) with *yomu* 'read' in Japanese examples. As previously suggested, such a telic role as 'read' can be a **default** value and defeasible/cancelable; as such, the degree of oddity of the utterance in (5b) would somehow be accountable. In fact, Briscoe et al. 1990 claim that such cases are allowed for in the lexical system by using a *default inheritance hierarchy* in lexicon. The entries *book* and *dictionary* can be related to each other because both are under the same general hierarchy of *book*, on the one hand, but are differentiated by different telic role values and different hierarchical statuses in the *inheritance structure*, on the other hand. For the purpose of background information for this approach, part of the representation of the lexical entry for *autobiography* is given below.

(6) part of the Lexical Entry for *autobiography*:

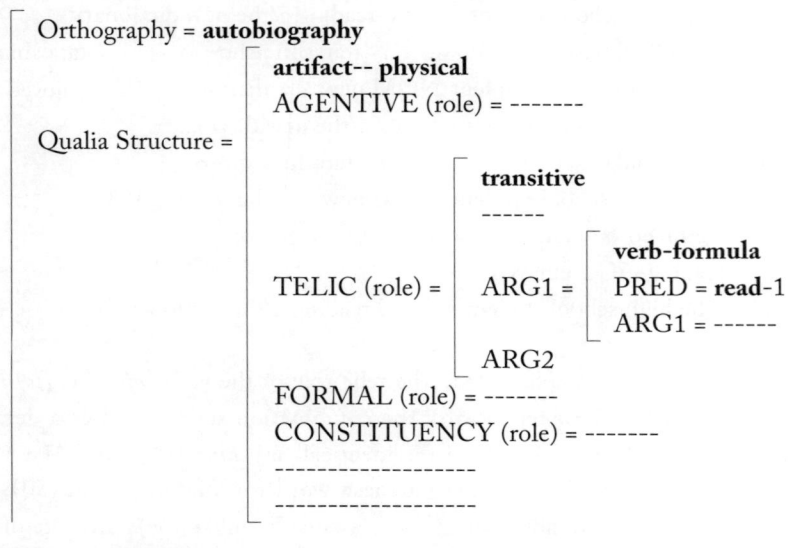

$$\begin{bmatrix} \text{Orthography} = \textbf{autobiography} \\ \text{Qualia Structure} = \begin{bmatrix} \textbf{artifact-- physical} \\ \text{AGENTIVE (role)} = \text{-------} \\ \text{TELIC (role)} = \begin{bmatrix} \textbf{transitive} \\ \text{------} \\ \text{ARG1} = \begin{bmatrix} \textbf{verb-formula} \\ \text{PRED} = \textbf{read}\text{-}1 \\ \text{ARG1} = \text{------} \end{bmatrix} \\ \text{ARG2} \end{bmatrix} \\ \text{FORMAL (role)} = \text{-------} \\ \text{CONSTITUENCY (role)} = \text{-------} \\ \text{-------------------} \\ \text{-------------------} \end{bmatrix} \end{bmatrix}$$

[Copestake 1993: 225 The details are partly omitted and the omissions are marked with broken lines.]

In diagram (6), the telic role of *autobiography* is specified as *read*. The hyponymy and its relevant information between words of the same type will be represented in an inheritance structure such as (7).

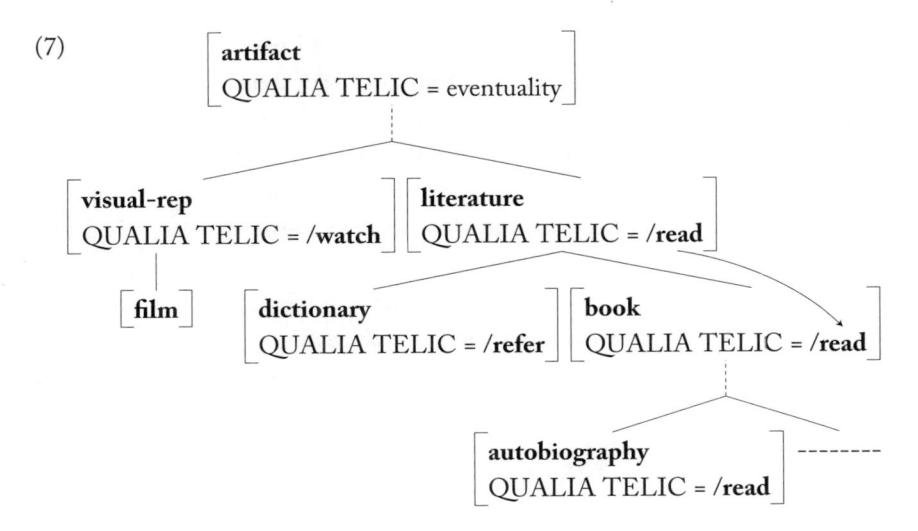

(7)
$$\begin{bmatrix} \text{artifact} \\ \text{QUALIA TELIC = eventuality} \end{bmatrix}$$

$$\begin{bmatrix} \text{visual-rep} \\ \text{QUALIA TELIC = /watch} \end{bmatrix} \quad \begin{bmatrix} \text{literature} \\ \text{QUALIA TELIC = /read} \end{bmatrix}$$

$$\begin{bmatrix} \text{film} \end{bmatrix} \quad \begin{bmatrix} \text{dictionary} \\ \text{QUALIA TELIC = /refer} \end{bmatrix} \quad \begin{bmatrix} \text{book} \\ \text{QUALIA TELIC = /read} \end{bmatrix}$$

$$\begin{bmatrix} \text{autobiography} \\ \text{QUALIA TELIC = /read} \end{bmatrix}$$

[L & C 1998: 400, (27), with some additions]

In (7), the telic role of *(to) read* of *literature* is inherited by *book*, as marked with an arrow in the diagram. Likewise, the same telic role is inherited by *autobiography* in the lower hierarchy. However, the purpose of *dictionary* is to ***refer to***, rather than to *read*. Thus, although *dictionary* is under *literature* in the hierarchy, lower entries must override the inherited information from the upper one. This clearly indicates the default nature of the telic role in the lexical information. Given the above, Briscoe et al. (1990) argue that the inheritance of the telic role must be **canceled** by more specific information about the purpose of the *dictionary*.[1] The modified value could then be inherited in the lexicon. The incorporation of lexical defaults into the inheritance hierarchy would work for particular ad-hoc cases such as the above example, except that such additional value inheritance will eventually lead to overloading the lexicon. However, as long as the repair by Briscoe et al. stays within the lexical semantic domain, that alone does not account for the next examples in (8).

(8) a. My goat eats anything. He really <u>enjoyed</u> the <u>book</u>.
    b. The goat enjoyed <u>eating</u> the book.
    c. ?The goat enjoyed reading the book.

[L & C 1998: 392, 9 with partial modification]

The second sentence in (8a) can only mean (8b) and not (8c). Furthermore, if one assumes, for (8c)'s account, that additional lexical information on goats' inability to read is given in the lexicon, such information should also be default and in fact turns out to be cancelable, i.e., defeasible; in a fable, a goat **can read**. As L & C (1998) argue, under the assumption that such information is encoded in the lexicon, it seems difficult to resolve a conflict between the assumed two lexical defaults, i.e. information like 'Goats cannot read,' on the one hand, and information like 'Goats can read,' on the other hand, even in a revised lexical approach. Apparently, two defaults conflict with each other without a guiding principle or system for resolution.[2] Likewise, in the following examples with verbs like *oboeru* (or *narau*), the same kind of problem arises with reasoning between competing defaults.

(9) a. Ano keikan-wa hana-ga kiku. Sono kusuri-o suguni oboeta.
that policeman-TOP nose-NOM sharp that drug-ACC soon learned
'*lit*.: That policeman has a sharp nose. He soon [learned and] identified the drug.'
b. That policeman soon learned to recognize the smell of the drug.
c. That policeman soon got the habit of taking drug.

In (9a), given only the lexical semantic information in the lexicon and without a previous context for the first utterance, the second utterance would be interpreted as follows: a preferred telic role of *kusuri* 'drug' would be something like 'to cure [someone of disease]'; it would not be 'to smell.' Although the preferred reading with the second sentence in (9a) is (9b), 'to smell a drug for probing a crime' would be an exceptional telic (purpose) role, if any, in the qualia structure for a 'drug.' Instead, the underspecified subevent of *oboeru* 'learn' would be to 'take [a drug]', derived from the qualia agentive role where the agent performs an act of 'taking [a drug],' and so (9c) would be derived, instead of (9b), grounded on such a lexical default. However, against the reading grounded on the encoded lexical semantic information on *kusuri* 'drug,' the second sentence can only mean (9b), not (9c). Crucially in (9a), additional lexical information is not plausible for resolving the interpretation fallacy, unlike the earlier examples: in the lexical system alone, the property of having a sharp nose is not likely to work to cancel the lexical semantic information for 'to take a drug/drugs' either in terms of the qualia structure roles or of the inheritance hierarchy. The felicitous sequence in (9a) can only be accounted for if a discourse interpretation system overrides the lexical defaults by prioritizing the relevant discourse defaults in a coherent manner. That is, in (9a), the preferred default, 'to smell a drug for probing a crime,' could only survive systematically if it were prioritized at the level of the discourse representation over the lexical default.

Given the unresolvable conflict of information within the lexical system, it seems clear that some independent guiding principle or system is needed to separate lexical (default) information from discourse information and then link them together. Such a system must also prioritize discourse defaults over lexical ones. Thus, the observation in this section directs one to discuss the resolution of conflicting defaults in discourse.

5.2.2 Defaults in discourse representation

In the preceding section, I argue that once defaults conflict with each other it is not clear how the interpretation will be reached solely by means of the available lexical system, and they seem to require some guiding principle or system in discourse.

As far as conflicting defaults are concerned, if they are lexical, they might be claimed to be managed in reasoning processes with cancellation of the inheritance of values or properties, but the lexical default cannot directly compete with discourse level information, which overrides them in the interpretation processes, as discussed in the previous section. Therefore, it is unclear how the lexical system, as it is, could have a link with discourse representation especially in the case of underspecified utterances, such as those shown earlier.

In fact, the underspecified utterances have been discussed within a framework that one may see as a potential model for the system of discourse default interpretation: Asher (1993), Lascarides & Asher (1993), Asher & Lascarides (1998a)[hereafter A & L 1998a], Asher & Lascarides (1998b) [hereafter A & L 1998b], and L & C (1998), which was previously mentioned, among others. L & C (1998) specifically discuss how such a problem with pure lexical approaches can be resolved concerning the underspecified utterances such as (2) and (8) above. I will briefly sketch their general framework.

5.2.2.1 SDRT: a theory of discourse structure that constrains conflicting defaults

The framework for discourse representation I mentioned in the previous section is referred to as Segmented Discourse Representation Theory (hereafter SDRT). The theory has to do with the representation of information updates in discourse, whether the process of interpretation involves the update of a word meaning or that of a sentential meaning, i.e., a proposition/event. This means that the process is involved in the (minimal) incremental change of information between two parts, the preceding context and a new context. Such a change in the content of the sequence of utterances is represented in a segmented discourse structure (SDRS) in SDRT.[3]

In example (10), the interpretation of the meaning of *enjoy the book* in the second utterance depends on the first utterance.

(10) [= (8a)] My goat eats anything. He really enjoyed the book.

The lexically derived default telic role with *book*, that is, 'to read,' is defeated by the preceding context including information such as *My goat eats*, and thus part of the logical form/meaning in the second utterance will be replaced with one that represents part of the content of the preceding context. Therefore, SDRT attempts to represent the content that a speaker would intend to convey incrementally. There are two components in SDRT. The first component is a formal logic language equipped with defeasible logic that can accommodate default meanings. An SDRS, as noted earlier, is a representational component of the theory and represents the utterance's semantic content and information change/update in discourse. The SDRS is labeled and recursive, and sequences of utterances can be represented and combined with labels under certain conditions of discourse event relations. The second component is a discourse-pragmatic system for building a text or a dialog in which the SDRSs are aligned in an orderly fashion. This second component, referred to as *Discourse in Commonsense Entailment* (hereafter DICE) is a pragmatically motivated logic which specifies how SDRSs connect together in terms of certain discourse event relations, principles, and rules. It accommodates the notion of defeasibility and subsumes a weak conditional scheme in the following manner:

(11) If P, then normally Q. [P > Q in A & L 1998a: 92][4]

All rules are in this defeasible format in DICE and are referred to as axioms. They function as a linking system for reasoning/computing discourse relations between fragments of the utterance representation, i.e. SDRSs. The axioms and rules involve information in three parts: first, τ, an existing built SDRS; second, α, the content of an utterance that is available in τ; and third, β, the content of another utterance that is to be attached to α under the conditions of a discourse event relation. Therefore, combined with the above scheme, the axioms look like the following:

(12) If <τ, α, β> & some relevant information, then <u>normally</u> a discourse relation R (α, β).[5]

Illustrated below is the system with an example.

(13) a. Mary enjoyed the book. [= (2a)]
  b. SDRS of (13a)

e (= event e), e', x, y
mary (x)   enjoy (e, x, e')   book (y)   act-on-pred (e', x, y)   *read (e', x, y)

The content of the meaning of (13a) can be represented in SDRT as an SDRS in (13b). If sentence (13a) is interpreted, lexical information is accessed and included among the conditions for identifying the referent variables x and y that are evoked by *Mary* and *the book* respectively. This is a simplified diagram and elements as temporal representation are omitted here. The notation "*" indicates that the condition marked with "*" is derived from defaults in the lexicon. The condition in an SDRS is roughly the content of a proposition or propositions. The condition for identifying the referents can therefore be defeated later through the interpretation process. It may turn out that the referent for *Mary* is a goat so that the canonical lexical information, 'reading,' of the telic role of *the book* is not compatible with the event of Mary's enjoying the book.

(14) a. Mary enjoyed the book.
  b. The goat in fact ate the whole library.

Thus, depending on the further discourse update, the telic role of *the book* in (13a), i.e. 'reading' can be overridden by 'eating,' due to the updated information including the referent of *the goat* in the utterance in (14b). One question is how the meaningful units of a set of utterances can be connected to each other so that the underspecification of utterances, as in (13a), can be interpreted. SDRT is equipped with a component that deals with patterned discourse event relations called **rhetorical relations** between utterance meanings. In the case of (14a) and (14b), one of the specific rhetorical relations constrains their relational meanings. *Elaboration* is reasoned as a relevant relation between the two events indicated by the sequence of the utterances.

(15) Elaboration: $<\tau, \alpha, \beta>$ & Subtype (α, β), then normally Elaboration (α, β)
Axiom on Elaboration: *Must* (Elaboration (α, β), then $\alpha \Downarrow \beta$)

[$\Downarrow$ means '... is a topic for .....']

The two utterances could share a topic; it is reasoned that such agents as *Mary* and *the goat* are topic candidates for the sequence of an enjoying and eating event, and *Mary* and *the goat* are associated with each other. However, as it stands, *the book* is lower in the hierarchy than *the library* in the inheritance hierarchy information, with both sharing the telic roles such as 'reading', as discussed earlier in (7). Therefore, in the newly-given discourse context, Mary's enjoying of the book is reasoned as a subset or a subtype event of the goat's eating of the whole library. *Mary* is now identified as a *goat*. Although this contradicts the interpretation of (16a) [= (14a)] as (16b), the definition and axiom of (15) are met and Elaboration is selected among other event relations between the two events in (14). The discourse update information is given priority and the lexical default "enjoy reading the book" in (16b) is defeated.

(16) a. [= (14a)] Mary enjoyed the book.
b. Mary enjoyed reading the book.
c. Mary enjoyed eating the book.

Here an axiom works for the resolution requiring the prioritization of discourse defaults over others, and the following rule works as a constraint for the systematic reasoning in the discourse structure.

(17) A discourse default is prioritized over lexical information in SDRS as long as the discourse is coherent.[6]

Although the explicit distinction between lexical and discourse default is my own development, a discourse default is clearly **prioritized** over lexical defaults, so that, based on the updated discourse, "Goats don't read" is obtained in the discourse interpretation, assisted by the world knowledge in knowledge base (KB). When interpreting the act of 'enjoying' as either 'reading' or 'eating' results in a conflict between the discourse defaults, a general principle called the Specificity Principle works for the resolution of those conflicting defaults.

(18) Specificity Principle:
A more specific reasoning is given priority, as long as Discourse Coherence is maintained.[7]   [Based on L & C 1998: 400, (26)]

This is a brief outline of SDRT, with some modification, and the development of the priority constraint in (17) is added here. Some of the formal semantic representations have been omitted. Nevertheless, this outline suggests that, equipped with the system of rules of discourse relations and of constraints called axioms, SDRT has the potential to provide a specific account of the interpretations of underspecified utterances.

Note that the representation of an E-card (Event File card) discussed in chapter 3 is akin to the box representation of the SDRS introduced here, except that each referent is indicated here as a variable, not as a number. Along theses lines, Kadmon (2001) discusses the commonality between the file card approaches and the approaches of discourse representation theories in general. Yet no system is developed in the E-card approach to interpret a series of events for systematic event relations by accommodating defeasible default information. With this in mind, if the interpretation of a series of events becomes a focus, SDRT can be taken as an evolved approach to the kind of event representation that discourse semantic analyses should seek. Nevertheless, I maintain that the basic temporal ordering relation between events is identified in terms of time intervals, as discussed in chapter 3. Therefore, the time interval will be part of my system with SDRT throughout the remainder of this book, although I omit the detailed diagrams demonstrated in chapter 3.

I will now demonstrate how each component of the system works with the others in SDRT to interpret a sequence of underspecified utterances with conflicting defaults.

5.2.2.2 Discourse event relations: linking defaults to discourse interpretation

In the theory under discussion, an SDRS connects multiple different SDRSs together, using certain rhetorical relations which I call *discourse (event) relations*, as in (19).

(19) **Narration**: <τ, α, β> & event ($e_α$) & event ($e_β$), then normally Narration (α, β)
Axiom on Narration: *Must* (Narration (α, β), then $e_α$ precedes $e_β$)
[$e_α$ and $e_β$ refer to the events of α and β respectively.]
Distinct Common Topic: *Must* (Narration (α, β), then ∃γ (γ ⇓ α & γ ⇓ β & ¬α ⇓ β & ¬β ⇓ α))   ["⇓" means '… is a topic for …']
Elaboration: <τ, α, β> & Subtype (α, β), then normally Elaboration (α, β)
Axiom on Elaboration: *Must* (Elaboration (α, β), then α ⇓ β)
["⇓" means '… is a topic for …']
[(15) is repeated here. Based on A & L 1998a: 93 and L & C 1998: 406]

Narration states that if one is attaching β to α with a discourse (event) relation, then normally, that relation is Narration. Narration is deemed one default discourse relation among other discourse event relations.[8] *Axiom on Narration* states that when *Narration (α, β)* holds, then indefeasibly, α's event precedes β's. *Distinct Common Topic* stipulates that α and β must have a distinct common topic γ. Narration, together with the Axiom on Narration and Distinct Common Topic, captures the intuition that the textual order of events normally matches their temporal order, and the propositions have a distinct common topic. I will account for the Narration relation in further detail later.

Through defaults, a discourse event relation is computed and the relation in turn connects SDRSs together to form a bigger SDRS. When lexical defaults lead to bad discourse, the constraint (17) works for a coherent relation between the sequences of events, and the lexical default information may be overridden by the discourse default information.

Now, I return to example (10). The only default relation that would apply to (10) would be Narration. However, Narration (α, β) can hold only if a distinct common topic can be found for α and β.

(20)   [= (10)]
   a. My goat eats anything.
   b. He really <u>enjoyed</u> the <u>book</u>.

If the event of enjoying is unrelated to eating, the topic will not be shared on any obvious common ground of the two utterances. The verb of an 'act-on predicate' that is derived from the lexical qualia structure would be something like "(the goat) did things." Since it does not explain the topic in a particular proposition, the discourse is not sufficiently coherent or is at best weak. This kind of weak coherence is avoided via the coherence constraint, as in (17). Therefore, if particular discourse segments occur, as in (20) with *he*, an accessible antecedent must be identified in the previous SDRS representing the first utterance. Then, the axioms and principles narrow the antecedent candidate down to *a goat* as a common topic for Narration. As a result, instead of the lexical default meaning 'reading' with *enjoy*, another interpretation, "(the goat's) eating (of the book)", is obtained by default for the 'act-on-predicate'.

In another pair of examples, I show some of the significance of the discourse event relations in the system I have discussed.

(21) <u>Max stood up.</u>$_A$ <u>John greeted him.</u>$_B$
                           [Lascarides, Copestake, & Briscoe 1996: 20a]
(22) <u>Max fell.</u>$_A$ <u>John pushed him.</u>$_B$
                           [Asher 1999: (2) with change of proper names]

In (21) and (22), two relationally similar sets of utterances can indicate different relations in discourse. This relational difference cannot be accounted for in either pure lexical semantic approaches or in past inference-based analyses such as the accommodation approach by Lewis (1979), which I will further discuss in 5.3.2. The standing-up and greeting events in (21) and the falling and pushing events in (22) do not seem to be related to each other in lexical qualia structure for their ordering relations. In contrast, in the system under discussion, each set is distinguished from the other through the different discourse relations. That is, for (21) and (22), each discourse relation links a set of the two labeled SDRSs, A and B, differently from the other set. The two SDRSs of the two events in each case are labeled as SDRS-1 and SDRS-2. In (21), the corresponding discourse relation between the two events, e_1 and e_2, indicated by the sequence of the two utterances is predicted as **Narration**. The formula in the whole SDRS for (21) is something like the following:

(23) SDRS-1: Stand (e_1, Max) & Greet (e_2, John, Max) & Narration (SDRS-1, SDRS-2) [Asher 1999: 4, partially modified]

The relation *Narration (SDRS-1, SDRS-2)* must be constrained by the rules called axioms. Narration requires the satisfaction of the following axioms in their general formulae, which are repeated below in (24).

(24)a. Narration: If <τ, α, β> & event ($e_α$) & event ($e_β$), then normally Narration (α, β)
 b. Axiom on Temporal Consequence of Narration: If Narration (α, β), then indefeasibly $e_α$ precedes $e_β$.
 c. Axiom on Distinct Common Topic: If (Narration (α, β), then indefeasibly ∃γ (γ is a topic for α) & (γ is a topic for β) & ¬(α is a topic for β) & ¬(β is a topic for α)
[Based on A & L 1998a: 93 and L & C 1998: 406]

Narration states that if one is attaching a context β to a context α with a discourse relation, then normally, that relation is Narration. The axiom in (24b) states that, when Narration (α, β) holds, α's event must precedes β's. Distinct Common Topic in (24c) states that α and β must have a common topic γ.

In (21), only when the axioms are met, is the discourse relation *Narration* **discourse-coherent** and selected as the sequence relation between the two events. *Narration* entails that the textual order of the events matches the temporal order, given the lexical semantic and world knowledge information. In (21), the two events are episodic, i.e. eventive, not stative, and, therefore, they can be in a precedence relation because of the indicated time intervals. According to the given textual order in discourse and world knowledge, the default reading is the one in which Max's standing precedes John's greeting of Max. The lexical semantic information on qualia structure does not conflict with the default reading concerning the agent and the purpose/telic roles of 'standing' and 'greeting': the goal of John's greeting is accessible since the agent Max who stands exists there for the greeting to happen. Therefore, the qualia information works as part of the compositional meaning of the two-event sequence. Note that the lexical semantic information including qualia structure is checked for a two-event relation at the discourse interpretation when the two events are being fully associated sequentially. The lexical qualia information is thus defeasible as a background in the discourse interpretation processes.

However, if a conflict occurs, relevant principles such as the Specificity Principle (18) for discourse coherence interact with DICE to constrain the plausible discourse relations and lexical semantic contents of the sequence of events. In (21), the second axiom of Narration is met; in the sequence, the topic is *Max*. In contrast, in (22) the discourse relation between the two events is predicted as **Explanation** (SDRS-1, SDRS-2), i.e. *Explanation* (α, β).[9] The explanation SDRS-2 (or β) serves as an answer to the question why the event in SDRS-1 happened. It is reasoned that the eventuality of Max's falling must come after John's pushing him, grounded on the fact that John's pushing Max is an achievement as a momentary act with a terminal point in the time interval, and through world knowledge, after falling down to the ground Max cannot normally be pushed. These inferences are in accord with the temporal consequence of *Explanation*: SDRS-2 explains SDRS-1. Thus, coherence is obtained and the discourse relation of the sequence in (22) is by default Explanation. The purpose of examples (21) and (22) is to demonstrate that the discourse event relations at issue specify and constrain the semantic consequences, i.e., the ordering and spatial compatibilities, between the events expressed in the sequence of utterances. These consequences involve temporal and spatial effects, the effects on lexical choice, etc.

Furthermore, as Asher 2001 discusses, discourse event relations can have truth-conditional effects as well.

(25) [= (22)] Max fell.$_A$ John pushed him.$_B$
(26) A-1: John failed his exams.
    B: No, he didn't. He got 60 %.
    A-2: I mean John Smith.

The discourse relation between the two utterances A and B in (25) is **Explanation**, as discussed. In (26), A and B **correct** their mutual misunderstandings, through the negation and pronoun *he* in B's utterance, as well as the updated name *John Smith* in A-2's utterance. While discourse relations like *Explanation* in (25) semantically **entail** that the proposition represented in the first utterance is **true**, the discourse relation of *Correction* in (26) does not. As a result, the difference of entailment is obtained. Otherwise, the first utterances of (25) and (26) would be both analyzed solely as assertions and an additional and more significant relational difference could be lost. Thus, the discourse relations have empirical consequences for the contents of logical semantic representation, so that they constrain the semantic contents of SDRSs.

It is necessary to note that the HIR examples under question involve some processes of interpretation that require certain inferences and default measurement of plausible event relations, due to the lack of tense indication and the lack of semantic content with the nominal head *-no* in the HIR clause. Therefore, the interpretation of the HIR should depend more on the system for the identification of a discourse sequence relation than that of regular tensed clauses.

5.3 Interpreting the underspecification without a presupposition trigger: a case for default matching

Thus far, I have discussed interpretation with conflicting defaults in the case of underspecification. In the previous chapters, in discussing the interpretation of the HIR, I have consistently analyzed the HIR as an underspecified construction, in that interpretation requires a process of identifying a missing link between the two events in the bi-clausal construction. In chapter 4, I stated that such an interpretation process involves a certain kind of inference-based reasoning process like default reasoning. In the following section, I will develop in detail the default reasoning process of "Matching" proposed in Chapter 4 for the resolution of the interpretation of the underspecification.

5.3.1 Identifying the missing antecedent of a discourse referent: *Bridging* as a subsumed process in SDRT

Different approaches to the interpretation of underspecification have been discussed in the literature: (Clark 1977; Sperber & Wilson 1986; van der Sandt 1992; Hobbs et al. 1979, 1993; Chierchia 1995; etc.). In particular, a certain inference process called ***bridging*** seems relevant to the current discussion of discourse interpretation (Clark 1977; Sperber & Wilson 1986; Hobbs et al. 1993; Matsui 1995; A & L 1998a).

Bridging is understood to be a process of inferences through which two objects or events in a text are related in a particular way that is not explicitly stated, and yet the relation is an essential part of the content of the text. By 'essential', it is meant that without this information the lack of connection between the sentences would result in the uninterpretable **incoherence** of the text. Discussion of bridging inferences has typically concentrated on definite descriptions, with some presupposition trigger in a prior context. Unlike anaphora, however, the connection is not always confined to that of identity. As Clark (1977: 414–9) and others have discussed, a taxonomy of relations has been proposed for linking one proposition to the other in discourse: set membership; necessary parts; probable parts; inducible parts; reasons; causes; consequences; etc. (27) is an example of bridging.

(27) a. I've just arrived.
    b. The camel is outside and needs water.

I assume that these two sentences are uttered as a sequence. There is some **presupposition** evoked concerning the definite description, *the camel*, in the second utterance. The prior context in the first utterance, however, does not seem to indicate an antecedent of a definite description in the second. An inference should help identify the plausible referent by associating part of the information available in the first utterance with the potential referent of *the camel* in question. Bridging inference is so called to cover such phenomena as that in (27). Although the taxonomy of relations is useful, to some degree, to narrow down the nature of the bridging inferences, this alone does not suffice for the exploration of an explicit system of interpretation. Certainly it is not likely that the inference that the subject "I" arrived by a camel is achieved solely through lexical semantic information, for the lexicon would overgenerate word meanings with one lexical entry indicating multiply different possible meanings. Some discourse interpretation system should come into play for a plausible chain of reasoning in a case like (27). Bridging itself, on the other hand, does not point to any explicit approach to the interaction of lexical information with the semantic content of utterances. Therefore, some more explicit and comprehensive approach to the underspecified utterances in discourse is needed to subsume bridging, and thereby it is equipped with some taxonomy of discourse relations, as Clark stated. SDRT, as discussed, seems to have a potential for approaching the problems with underspecification comprehensively. Given this, I will apply the core part of SDRT, a theory of discourse representation, to such examples as (27).

In interpreting the examples in (27), SDRT works like this: in discourse, with the aid of common world knowledge, a hearer may infer that camels in general can be used as *transport*. Then the hearer can interpret the relation between the two events as that of my arrival causing the camel to be outside, which yields discourse coherence. Therefore, it can be reasoned that the two events are connected via the discourse event relation of *Cause-Result*. According to the axiom, the relation of Cause-Result requires some **common topic**. In the example, transport can be a common topic, and "the camel" is interpreted as a mode of transport for "arriving." Crucially, lexical knowledge and world knowledge are utilized to combine the two events to interpret the underspecified relations in the bridging inference. ***Discourse coherence*** works as a general constraint on different relations between events. Thus, the bridging inference can be subsumed into the relational taxonomy in a more specific system like SDRT concerning the task of computing discourse event relations between semantic contents.

5.3.2 Default matching for interpretation without a presupposition trigger

In the previous section, I have discussed examples of underspecified relations between two utterances and argued that the bridging inferences involved in the interpretation can be subsumed in comprehensive theories such as SDRT. I will later apply the system of matching introduced in chapter 4 to the interpretation of the HIR and will further develop it, drawing on SDRT. However, before this application I will first discuss the question of how the interpretation of underspecification, without a trigger of presupposition for an antecedent reference, can be modeled in SDRT. The head *-no* of the HIR clause also lacks any obvious presupposition trigger for a referent.

When a presupposition trigger is available for a second utterance, for example *the camel* in (27) in section 5.3.1, an antecedent can be sought directly and narrowed down within the previous discourse information expressed in the first utterance of the sequence. When no presupposition trigger is available, however, some extra process would have to be involved in the interpretation process. As mentioned toward the end of chapter 4, I claim that a ***default matching*** process is inevitable for examining lexical default information across the different events at discourse level. The discussion as a whole will provide an important path toward modeling an interpretation of the HIR, which is regarded as an underspecified construction that lacks any presupposition trigger.

van der Sandt (1992) claims that presupposition is anaphoric in discussing the interpretations of definite descriptions. However, in the context of underspecification, it would be wrong to claim that definite descriptions necessarily involve presupposition that leads to an acceptable interpretation. It would also be wrong to claim that indefinites necessarily fail to be interpreted in the absence of a presupposition trigger. The following pair of examples illustrates this.

(28) a. Mr. A.: Did you hear about John?
  b. Mr. B.: No, what?
  c. Mr. A.: He had an accident.
    ??The car hit him. / A car hit him.
(29) Jack was going to commit suicide. He got a rope.   [A & L 1998a]

In (28c), the classic accommodation approach to presupposition would make no distinction between *the car* and *a car* or would predict that (28c) with *the car* as a subject is acceptable. As the examples show, however, it turns out that the presupposition of *the car* cannot be accommodated, in spite of the fact that *the car* could in theory be associated with *an accident* within which the relevant person, *John*, appears. It seems that, in (28), the utterance with *the car* lacks discourse coherence and, as a result, a specific connection between the events cannot be determined. In (29), on the other hand, no presupposition is evoked in the pre-context when "a rope" occurs, since it is an indefinite noun phrase. (29) is nevertheless acceptable as a sequence of utterances. It seems that the events indicated in (29) somehow are linked together through some relational reasoning that results in coherence of the discourse **without any presupposition trigger** for an antecedent. Indefinites, as in (28c) and (29), are regarded as non-anaphoric in presupposition-based approaches. Such accommodation approaches therefore make wrong predictions and cannot specifically analyze how the underspecified indefinites in (28c) and (29) are accepted in discourse. In (29), it seems that without a trigger for presupposition *a rope* is interpreted as being associated with the event of *committing suicide* indicated in the pre-context. When a presupposition trigger is available with the second utterance, for example *the camel* in (27), an antecedent would be sought in the previous discourse through bridging inferences, with the definite NP *the camel* as a trigger for such a process. When no presupposition trigger is available, however, I claim that the default reasoning process of *default matching* is involved, across the lexical default information that belongs to the separate events in the discourse. This is an extension of what I discussed as the matching process in chapter 4, and I will elaborate it later on to cover the general case in which no presupposition trigger is available for sequences of utterances, as in the case with the HIR.

Included in my argument thus far, the interpretation of the sequence of utterances must be maximally discourse coherent, as described in section 5.2.2.1. Under these conditions, without a presupposition trigger, the sequence of utterances must be connected in the interpretation through the available lexical information across the sequence of events that are to be connected: the lexical information is the only resource for the goal of attaining coherence in the situation. Thus, default matching is involved in connecting two events.

The default matching goes as follows. First, *a rope* is lexically encoded as an **instrument** for some act in its lexical qualia structure, while *suicide* carries some information about a method like 'hanging' for achieving its goal, as part of lexical inheritance structure. Second, across the events, based on these bits of information, it is reasoned that *suicide* 'by default' involves some means or instrument to achieve its goal: hanging with *a rope* is **part of** the *suicide* event. Hanging with a rope can be interpreted as a default telic value of suicide. Note that this is an extended default (i.e. defeasible) telic value, and that all these bits of information cannot be encoded in the lexicon, which would result in an overload of the lexical system. Instead, such information ought to be derived from the process of default matching at the level of discourse interpretation. This default matching is then supported in DICE by discourse-pragmatic reasoning: hanging with a rope is 'normally' part of Jack's **plan** relevant to committing suicide.[10] Based on the relation between the whole plan (i.e. suicide) and its part (i.e. a rope as a means), **Elaboration** is obtained as the discourse relation connecting the two events represented in the two semantic representations of SDRSs. This relation is essential to the coherence of the discourse with the sequence of events in (29). Crucially, without the link of a discourse relation, there would be no obvious connection between the two events, resulting in discourse incoherence. Instead, the matching of a sequence of events is defeasibly worked out in discourse through given lexical information such as qualia structure. For maximal coherence, the reasoning process of default matching fills the gap of information between information obtained through the lexical contents separate among each lexical entries, on the one hand, and information obtained through the context-dependent interpretation process in discourse. The process of the matching occurs, prior to the overall interpretation between the two event representations in SDRSs.

Similarly, another bridging phenomenon is observed in the utterances in (30).

(30)a. John took engine E1 from Avon to Dansville.
   b. He picked up a boxcar and took it to Broxburn.
[A & L 1998a: 94, (12); A & L 1998b: 249, (14)]

Once again in this case, the pair of utterances is without any presupposition trigger, with the indefinite noun phrase *a boxcar*. In the current approach, the two events represented in a sequence of utterances in (30) must be connected to observe maximal coherence in discourse. Then, a discourse relation must also be obtained through pragmatic formulae in DICE. Therefore, given the lexical information, default matching must be involved, prior to an overall reasoning process for the event relations. For example, the lexical compatibility between *engine* given in the prior discourse and the indefinite, *a boxcar*, must be examined, under the condition that no presupposition trigger obtains with *a boxcar*.

The default matching goes as follows: in its qualia structure, *engine* carries the lexical information that it is a piece of equipment of a car for moving or driving, while *a boxcar* is encoded as part of transport for moving and storing. Through matching, the *engine* can either be inferred to be part of the *boxcar*, as being in the boxcar, or being not related to the boxcar, although they all have something to with moving. The boxcar may be equipped with the engine. However, in qualia information, the telic value of a boxcar is for freight or as a container, and it is much bigger than a regular car, by default. Given this and also given that the events must be connected for discourse coherence, the relation between them can be 'in.' Then the engine would be *in* the boxcar. For example, the *engine* could be left on the floor as a load inside the boxcar. Once information that the engine is for an automobile is given further, the matching is enhanced through further processes like the following. The goal point of the picking-up event is by default Dansville, given the lexical background information on the goal of *taking ... to Dansville* in the precedence relation with *picking up*. The object that is *picked up* is also in Dansville. As a result, it is reasoned that the boxcar is in Dansville when the event of taking the engine is complete and comes to its goal, i.e. Dansville. Therefore, it can be inferred that the engine is carried ***in*** the boxcar as a load. However, with the given lexical information, the matching may result in wrong reasoning, depending on whether or not a particular piece of information is further specified. In which case, other knowledge sources may interact with the lexical defaults: world knowledge enhances information on the function and size of a boxcar: it is by default bigger than a regular car. This is as far as the default matching can go with the compatibility measurement of the given lexical information across the events. Information obtained during the default matching will be added to the later reasoning for the overall interpretation of the event sequence.

For maximal discourse coherence, the two events must be connected. It is inferred that the textual order is normally equivalent to the temporal order, and that the taking of the engine from Avon to Dansville occurs before the boxcar is picked up. This goes well with the temporal **precedence** relation axiom on Narration. As seen in (24c), the other axiom on Narration that the two events must share a **common topic**, is met, since *John* can be a topic on the grounds that the only antecedent to *he* is *John* in the previous discourse, and also that *a boxcar* in the new context can now be related to the *engine* in the previous discourse, which is background information obtained through ***default matching***. Thus, Narration is obtained as a link to the process of DICE. With the default matching working as the background reasoning process for the compatibility of lexical defaults, coherence constraint allows one to infer a particular way of identifying a discourse relation between the two events in (30). Furthermore, the resolution of the underspecified content is determined by the way the newly-asserted content attaches to the previous discourse context.

5.4 Default matching to interpret the HIR in discourse

In the previous sections, I have claimed: when no presupposition trigger is available, a *default matching* process is involved in examining lexical default information across the different events in discourse. This occurs under the condition that the sequence of utterances must be connected, as the current approach assumes in the light of the discourse coherence principle. Before the overall interpretation process for the whole sequence of events, lexical information is the only resource for the reasoning of the event relation that could lead to successful information update. Without it, the events would eventually result in discourse incoherence unless their viable connection is provided prior to the across-the-board update interpretation process. In fact, the same default reasoning of the matching process applies to the bi-clausal HIR construction, since it is analyzed as a case of underspecification. As discussed in earlier chapters, a *-no* nominal lacks referentiality and does not indicate a particular referent by itself. I have therefore argued that, without any presupposition trigger, the reference of the nominal entity is inferred in the discourse event representation of the HIR construction, with the aid of the temporal contiguity relationship between the events expressed by the two clauses. I have concluded that the HIR indicates that the first event is contiguously connected to the second event, with either an *In-progress* or a *Resultant* state denoted by the HIR predicate. In chapter 4, however, I have stated that, in the HIR construction, the possible ambiguity, i.e. which of the two states will be relevant for two-event relations, does not seem to occur in contrast to some other bi-clausal construction. This is because, as previously argued, through the interpretation process of matching, one of the two possible default event relations is excluded, as in (31).

(31) [[Mary-ga   ringo-o   tabe**te iru**]-no]-o John-ga   totta.
    -NOM apple-ACC eat-TE IRU-N-ACC   -NOM took
  'Mary was eating an apple, which John took.'

The kind of reasoning involved in the utterance is: nothing can be eaten by *John* after *Mary* finishes eating it. Thus, only an In-progress state reading obtains. This reasoning process has to do with the default measurement of compatible lexical defaults in their plausible relations. However, I have not provided an overall process for matching with the HIR. Given the discussion of the detailed default matching with the English examples in the earlier sections of this chapter, it is now possible to incorporate the discussion in an interpretation of the HIR.

5.4.1 Discourse relations between the two events in the HIR

As previously argued, the two events in the HIR are interpreted as temporally contiguous with one another, with the preceding event either in-progress or resultant when the second event occurs. I have also argued that the events expressed by the sequence of utterances must be connected under the condition of discourse coherence. Therefore, given the contiguity of the two events represented in the HIR construction, it can be reasoned, by default, that the textual order of the utterances corresponds with the temporal order of the two events expressed by the utterances, so that the event relations can be Narration, as long as the second axiom specifying the involvement of a common topic is met. In fact, as discussed in chapter 3, the argument, i.e. the object, of the main predicate is interpreted as that of the subordinate clause, i.e. the HIR clause. Unless further information comes in, it is therefore a shared common topic between the two events. There are grounds for this assertion. Observe the following.

(32) a. [[Mary-ga   ringo-o   tabe**te iru**]-no]-o John-ga   totta.
           -NOM apple-ACC eat-TE IRU-N-ACC   -NOM took
       'Mary was eating an apple, which John took.'
    b. #[[Mary-wa   ringo-o   tabe**te iru**]-no]-o John-ga   totta.
           -TOP apple-ACC eat-TE IRU-N-ACC   -NOM took
       'Mary was eating an apple, which John took.'
    c. #[[Mary-wa   ringo-o   tabe**te iru**]-no]-o John-wa   totta.
           -TOP apple-ACC eat-TE IRU-N-ACC   -TOP took
       'Mary was eating an apple, which John took.'

As discussed in chapters 2 and 3, the particle -*wa* is often analyzed as contrastive, not as topic, when it occurs in the subordinate clause. Therefore, in the infelicitous (32b) and (32c), one might argue that the contrastive -*wa* cannot occur exceptionally in the HIR, following the standard analysis. However, there is a contrast in the acceptability of the contrastive -*wa* between the HIR and some other construction, as the example in (33) illustrates.

(33) John {-ga/-wa}   kyuyoude   kitaku-shita **tokoro**,   Mary
         {-NOM/-wa} for-urgent-matter returned home in-the-place, Mary

{-ga/-wa}   utiake banashi-o   hajimeta.
{–NOM/-wa} secret story-ACC started
'When John came home for an urgent matter, Mary started to talk about her secret.'

In (33), any combination of -*ga* and -*wa* is acceptable either in the main clause or in the subordinate clause, whereas in the HIR example in (32), -*wa* is not possible across the board in the subordinate clause. The problem is now clear for the following reasons. First, as seen in (33), the utterance is acceptable even when no clear contrast is described. Example (33) indicates that two occurrences of -*wa* are also acceptable. Therefore, -*wa* does not always have to be contrastive when it appears in the subordinate clause. Second, the HIR would be an exception, since no -*wa* occurs in the subordinate HIR clause, as shown in (32). Instead, it seems reasonable that in the subordinate HIR, -*wa* is not possible because the common topic between the two events is inferred through the indefinite contiguity-indicating -*no* in discourse. Therefore, in (32a), *ringo* 'apple' is identified as a common topic between the two events, i.e. Mary's eating and John's taking, through reasoning processes, grounded in the contiguity of the two events and in the lexical semantic information across the two events. Since the common topic works, the event relation of *Contrast* is precluded, and the contrastive use of -*wa* is not viable. Furthermore, in (32b) and (32c), *Mary* as a topic would result in discourse incoherence. Two separate topics cannot occur within one sequence of events, since a shared common topic is maintained in a sequence like the HIR examples in (32). It is clearly reasoned that *Mary* cannot be part of the 'John's taking' event. This is well accounted for if the topic is analyzed as underspecified with the nominal -*no* after it is evoked in the previous discourse. However, with the new information of the second event denoted by the main clause, the referent turns specific. Given this, it seems plausible to infer by default that the underspecified entity evoked by the nominal -*no* is a common topic in the discourse. Thus, the involvement of a common topic is reasoned with the HIR utterances.

Now that temporal contiguity and a common topic are acknowledged in the HIR utterances in (32a), the plausible discourse relation is interpreted as Narration, with the two axioms of Narration being met. Note that this reasoning is defeasible, and therefore for maximal discourse coherence, the compatibility reasoning of the lexical defaults, i.e. default matching, must be further checked in the interpretation process of the overall discourse update.

The **default matching** with the HIR in (31) [= (32a)] is as follows. In qualia information, the telic roles of *ringo* 'apple' seem to contain 'consumed' or 'food' and those of *taberu* 'to eat' contain 'consumption' or 'to ingest'. *Toru* 'to take' requires an object to take, and it has a telic role of 'possession.' Through a compatibility check, it is reasoned that before the eating activity is complete, possession by the act of taking is plausible. Eating contiguously precedes taking. Furthermore, in qualia information, the consumption verb 'to eat' indicates Accomplishment, with the durational interval of the act, whereas the possession verb 'to take' in (31) indicates Achievement as a momentary act. Thus, unless the 'taking' occurs during the given interval of 'eating' for consumption, the object of the 'taking' cannot be obtained. Consequently, only an In-progress state reading is plausible.

Note that the HIR clause is untensed and the nominal head *-no* in the HIR clause does not indicate an explicit semantic content. Therefore, the temporal ordering cannot be determined solely by the comparison of the main predicate *totta* 'took' with the untensed predicate *taberu* 'to eat' [and '*tabete iru*']. In addition, the object of 'taking' is not explicitly indicated by the head *-no* of the object complement (HIR) clause. Thus, the above reasoning process across lexical default information, together with discourse defaults, is vital to the interpretation of the HIR construction, as in the examples in (31).

Finally, through default matching, it is reasoned that the events must overlap, i.e. the eating event is in-progress when the taking event begins. In (31), this is the plausible combination of the two acts, eating and taking, which results in discourse coherence. Grounded in such reasoning processes as this, the discourse event relation *Narration* will be obtained with further reasoning, as I have previously discussed. The common topic of eating and taking will also reasonably be identified as 'apple'. In this way, successful default matching leads to maximal coherence.

5.4.2 Apparent exceptional examples as more grounds for the involvement of default matching

In the next example of the HIR construction, the same reasoning of default matching should apply. However, ambiguity arises as to the identity of the agent(s) of the main predicate, as Kuroda (1992) discusses.

(34) [Keikan-ga dorobo-to hashi-de momiatte iru]-no-ga
[Policeman-NOM burglar-against bridge-on fight-Prgrssv]-N-NOM
ayamatte   kawa-ni otita.
by-mistake river-to fell
'A policeman was fighting a burglar on a bridge, {and/but} {he/they} fell
into the river.'   [Modified from Kuroda 1992: 155, (32)]

The English translation is awkward, but the ambiguity is highlighted through the use of slashes and braces. The participant(s) in the event denoted by *(kawa-ni) oti-ta* 'fell (into the river)' can be: a policeman, both a policeman and a burglar, or a burglar, although the last is the least likely reading. If the positions of *keikan* and *dorobo* were reversed, that would reverse the likelihood of the readings. In pointing out the ambiguity, Kuroda (1992) states that some pragmatic factors affect the readings, and he uses the term "direct relevance" for the events of the participant interpretation. I assume that his intuition is correct, and yet I need to investigate this particular case further in order to make that intuition part of a system. I argue that the problem with example (34) is not the problem of vagueness, but rather of the multiple compatibilities of lexical information observed across the two events. This multiplicity affects the reasoning of a plausible event relationship. In fact, depending on the reasoning processes of default matching, the discourse event relation can be analyzed as either *Narration* or some other relation. As long as the common topic is inferred to be the policeman, the discourse rhetorical relation is analyzed as Narration, meeting the two axioms of a common topic and of temporal contiguity indicated by *-no*. If the burglar or both two are reasoned as the agent(s) of the main predicate, the discourse event relation would be *Result*, since there is no common topic.[11] The burglar can be an agent (although it is a less likely case), since the comitative *-to* can be interpreted as coordination in some cases, for example: 'The policeman and burglar had a fight and ...'

This kind of ambiguity is accounted for if lexical information comes into play as an essential resource for the identification of event relations and is checked across the events for compatibility. Here lies another grounds for the involvement of default matching. By default, the policeman should be interpreted as the participant in the predicates of both the main and HIR clauses, partly due to the fact that it is the only argument in the preceding context, as well as the temporal contiguity of the two events derived from the lexical meaning of -*no*. The sequencing of events therefore ought to result in *Narration*. However, in (34), more than one person can be reasoned as participants in the event of the preceding discourse context indicated by the first clause. Such a reading is supported by the lexical information with the second predicate as well as the first. In the event sequence, the auxiliary *au* 'do (something) with each other' in *momi<u>au</u>* 'to fight,' together with the verb *otiru* 'to fall,' can select more than one human participant, and the 'fighting' event accommodates this. The policeman and the burglar are both human, and the predicate *momiau* 'to fight each other' indicates Accomplishment with some duration, whereas the predicate *otiru* 'to fall down' is an Achievement as a momentary act. It is then plausible to reason that they fight each other for a while because of the *duration* of the 'fighting' and that, as a result, one or both could fall into the river with further context. No contradiction occurs when any such participant candidates are selected, given the lexical information across the events. This is the source of ambiguity. The indeterminacy remains in the reasoning of default matching, and as a result the discourse event relation will not be identified as Narration, due to the lack of a common topic. The resolution of the ambiguity with (34) depends on a later stage of discourse information updates including new contextual information. Such indeterminacy of the participant identification at the stage of default matching is passed on to and reflected in the overall discourse reasoning: ambiguity about the participants in (34). Otherwise, the ambiguity would be left a mystery and one would have to follow the intuitive term of some kind of *direct relevance* to the content of the event with the HIR, as in Kuroda's (1992: 146–7) relevancy condition.

As further support for the involvement of default matching in the interpretation of the HIR, I will give two similar examples in which an aspectual shift occurs with the same predicate in the subordinate clauses, depending on the contiguity compatibility of the two events in a sequence, as seen in (35a) and (35b).

(35)a. [Tue-tuki jiisan-ga eki-made **aruite iru**]-no-o,
cane-thrust old-man-NOM station-to walk-TE IRU]-N-ACC,
chocho-ga yobitometa.
mayor-NOM call-stop-Pst

'An old man with a cane **was walking** to the station, and the mayor called (him) and stopped him.'
b. [Tue-tuki   jiisan-ga   eki-made **aruite   iru**]-no-o,
cane-thrust old-man-NOM station-to walk-TE IRU]-N-ACC,
chocho-ga   shosan-shita.
mayor-NOM praise-Pst
'An old man with a cane (iteratively/usually) **walks** to the station, and the mayor (once) praised him.'

In (35a), an in-progress reading is obtained with the subordinate clause, whereas in (35b) an iterative/habitual reading is obtained with the same subordinate clause as in (35a). In addition, in (35b), the acceptability could also change, depending on how the mayor perceives an old man with a cane. Only when the man's walking to the station is interpreted as iterative/habitual (35b) is felicitous, although it can still be regarded as resultant since the old man's walking is praised by the mayor only after it is achieved. In contrast, when the walking to the station is a single culminated event, (35b) becomes less acceptable. The utterance is even less acceptable if the mayor witnesses the old man completing his walk to the station and his arrival there. Note that the tense indication with the subordinate predicates in both examples in (35a) and (35b) is in the same neutral form, *eki-made aruite-ir**u***. No difference is indicated. This seems to suggest that the indicated aspectual meaning differences between iterative/habitual and in-progress acts can only be interpreted through a reasoning process across the two events. When no presupposition trigger is available, as in the HIR, the default matching of the across-the-board compatibility measurement of lexical information is expected to be the only means for a successful reasoning process.

The reasoning of the default matching involves the following processes. In (35b) through lexical qualia information, it is reasoned that the act of *shosan-suru* 'praise' normally takes place after the 'walking to the station' event in question is over, since the goal or telic role of 'praising' requires some marked property, *i.e.* change, or achievement for evaluation. 'Praising' cannot be achieved without it. The two events, the old man's walking to the station and the mayor's praising, therefore, involve some time gap between them. However, the contiguity meaning derived from *-no* seems to coerce the temporal relation between the two events in (35b). In addition, as discussed in chapter 4, the neutral form *-te iru* indicates some existence of a current state that comes after an act is initiated. The predicate therefore cannot indicate a simple past act such as 'walked to the station.' Thus, the iterative/habitual reading is obtained. As shown in the illustration of the event representation (36), the act of walking to the station is in effect stativized as resultant and the contiguity of the two events is obtained.

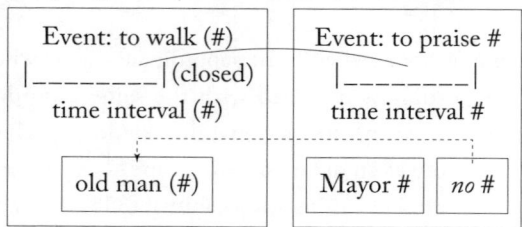

(36) [← (35b)] 'An old man walks to the station.' 'Mayor praised him.'

Event: to walk (#)	Event: to praise #
|_____|(closed)	|_____|
time interval (#)	time interval #
old man (#)	Mayor # *no* #

In contrast, in (35a), *yobitomeru* 'call and stop (him)' in the main predicate requires, as a telic role, something in progress: '(an old man) walking to the station' is in progress. This accords with the contiguity indicated by *-no*; no coercion for an aspectual shift would occur.

As mentioned in the last section of chapter 4, the discourse interpretation process with the HIR involves a dynamic reasoning for the temporal interpretation: the in-progress aspect of the old man's walking to the station in (35) can be shifted to the stative iteration/habit, as in (35b) in spite of the identical expressions of the HIR clause between (35a) and (35b): *Tue-tuki jiisan-ga eki-made arui-te iru.* Due to this dynamic nature of characterizing the HIR, the interpretation inevitably involves the compatibility measurements of lexical information across the indicated events, given the lack of a presupposition trigger. Default matching thus works as a background process for default identification of event relations, which will then be passed on to the overall pragmatic linking mechanism of DICE in discourse representation.

5.5 Summary of the chapter

I have presented at least partially a system for resolving underspecification in discourse, drawing on one version of SDRT theory as an extension of the approaches to presupposition. The theory is a discourse-semantic model of discourse representation, and is equipped with DICE, a pragmatic reasoning link between logico-semantic representation and discourse contextual information, which accounts for default information that depends on discourse information updates. Drawing on the theory, I have argued, first, that, in resolving the underspecification, two kinds of defaults, i.e. lexical defaults and discourse defaults, are involved in discourse. Discourse defaults override or are prioritized over lexical defaults. Second, a particular default reasoning process of default matching is involved when no presupposition trigger is accessible during the resolution of the underspecification. The default matching involves compatibility checking of lexical information across the sequence of events that the utterances indicate. This matching process yields grounds for further stages of default interpretation processes in identifying plausible event relations. I have demonstrated such cases with examples of logical metonymy and a sequence of English utterances, and then with those of the HIR, a bi-clausal construction in Japanese. In the matching process, lexical semantic information turns out to be an essential resource for measuring compatibility of event relations, given the inaccessibility of anaphora or presupposition. Third, discourse event relations are shown to be vital clues to the resolution of conflicting bits of overall default reasoning processes. Fourth, I have argued that *accommodation* and *bridging* can be dispensed with by means of a more general mechanism of discourse-semantic linking such as the one I have presented in this chapter.

Endnotes

1 As Larry Horn (personal communication) points out, this is similar to the non-monotonic inference like the following. "Birds fly. Tweety is a bird. Therefore Tweety flies." is overridden when the premise "Tweety is a penguin" is added. The logic of *modus ponens* is defeated because of the update. This is accommodated in DICE and is called 'Defeasible Modus Ponens.'

2 The Japanese counterpart of 'enjoy' also faces the same kind of conflict, as seen below.

Watashi-no yagi-wa   nandemo teberu. (Ano yagi-wa)   hon-o   mankitu-shita.
my   goat-TOP anything eat   (that goat-TOP) book-ACC enjoyed
'My goat eats anything. {That/the goat} enjoyed the book.'

The predicate *mankitu-suru* indicates the meaning close to that of 'enjoy.' As in (8), two pieces of default information will conflict: 'Goats can read' and 'Goats cannot read.'

3   The theory was first developed by Asher (1993) among others (the predecessor as its archetype was proposed as Discourse Representation Theory (DRT) in Kamp (1981) and Kamp & Reyle (1993).
4   In fact, the notion of defeasibility has been recognized in the literature as 'normality' or similar terms concerning the discussion of discourse constraints: Minsky (1977); Landman (1992); Veltman (1996); Pelletier & Asher (1997). Therefore, the condition like (11) above goes along the line of those in the literature. In A & L (1998a), (11) takes the form of "A > B."
5   There are additional functions that I will not introduce because of the irrelevancy and complexity, but, with the additional functions, the defeasible logic language of DICE is allowed to check information about the contents of utterances. See the details in A & L (1998a, b) and L & C (1998).
6   Although the principle of discourse coherence is not defined here, I draw on the literature on SDRT such as A & L (1998a, b) and uphold the view that discourse information ought to be in accordance with the overall updated discourse context for coherence, as information gets updated. The generalization of (17) is presented first in Ishikawa (2003).
7   The original Specificity Principle in L & C (1998) goes as follows.

Specificity Principle: If both of the conflicting defaults have their antecedents verified, then the consequent of the default with the most specific antecedent is preferred.

8   Other examples of discourse (event) relations are Consequence, Background, Condition, Contrast, Parallel, etc. Details of the relations can be found in Asher (1993).
9   In de Swart and Molendijk (1999, 30), the relation of Explanation generally corresponds to the sequence of two events in which the first event is an effect of the second event. So, the second event precedes the first. However, the details of this type of discourse relation require more research.
10 Grosz and Sidner (1986) discuss a system of how connections between utterances in discourse serve to constrain the world knowledge. They define a close relationship between the discourse segmentation of dialogues and the intentional structure of an *underlying plan*. Incorporating their framework, Poesio (1993) further argues that focus affects the denotation of definite descriptions. This accords with the intuition that the uniqueness constraint on definite is closely related to the notion of saliency, which I will discuss in the next chapter.
11 See the detail of (Cause-)Result relation in Asher (1993).

Chapter 6

Ga and information structure of the HIR

6.1 Introduction

In this chapter, I will address the issues of the particle *-ga* that is essential to the HIR clause. In this connection, I will only examine the subject marker *-ga* in its theta-marked position in a sentence. In previous chapters I have discussed the fact that the HIR clause appears to allow only the particle *-ga* in the subject position. No occurrence of *-wa* is acceptable there, as recapitulated in (1).

(1)a. [[Mary-ga   ringo-o   tabe<u>te iru</u>]-no]-o John-ga   totta.
            -NOM   apple-ACC eat-TE IRU-N-ACC   -NOM   took
       'Mary was eating an apple, which John took.'
   b. #[[Mary-<u>wa</u>   ringo-o   tabe<u>te iru</u>]-no]-o John-ga   totta.
            -TOP   apple-ACC eat-TE IRU-N-ACC   -NOM   took
       'Mary was eating an apple, which John took.'
   c. #[[Mary-<u>wa</u>   ringo-o   tabe<u>te iru</u>]-no]-o John-wa   totta.
            -TOP   apple-ACC eat-TE IRU-N-ACC   -TOP   took
       'Mary was eating an apple, which John took.'   [Chapter 5, (32)]

In chapter 5, I argue that, in the subordinate HIR, *-wa* is not possible because the *common topic* between the two events is inferred through the indefinite contiguity-indicating *-no* in discourse. That is, in (1a), *ringo* 'apple' is identified as a shared common topic between the two events, i.e. Mary's eating and John's taking, through the reasoning process grounded in the temporal contiguity of the two events and in default matching of the given lexical semantic information across the two events. Since the common topic works in discourse, no additional topic is available, since there is only one topic within a sequence of discourse events. Therefore, the topic marker *-wa* is not viable. Drawing on Grosz & Sidner (1986), Hobbs (1979), Vallduvi (1992), Asher (1993) and Birner & Ward (1998), I assume that in discourse there is one primary theme, topic, or, in Vallduvi's term, 'link,' between adjacent events that must be connected to one another, although more than one occurrence of *-wa* is possible as a secondary or tertiary within a sentence. In addition, in the HIR examples like (1) because of the involvement of the common topic, the event relation of *Contrast* is excluded among others, since the event relation of Contrast is not expected to have a common topic by definition, as discussed in chapter 5. Consequently, the contrastive use of *-wa* is not viable. I have given grounds for this uniqueness of the HIR based on the unavailability of *-wa*. Interestingly, the following example of a different bi-clausal construction, *tokoro*-clause construction, yields an acceptability contrast concerning the so-called contrastive *-wa*.

(2) John {-ga/-wa} kyuyoude kitaku-shita tokoro,
{-NOM/-WA} for-urgent-matter returned home in-the-place,
Mary {-ga/-wa} utiake banashi-o hajimeta.
Mary {-NOM/-WA} secret story-ACC started
'When John came home for an urgent matter, Mary started to talk about her secret.' [Chapter 5, (33)]

In (2), any combination of *-ga* and *-wa* is acceptable in either the main clause or the subordinate clause, while, in the HIR example in (1), *-wa* is not possible in the subordinate clause, also not for contrastive use.[1] Only the *-ga* marking is allowed in the subordinate HIR clause subject. In chapter 5, I concluded that, when the common topic interpretation is obtained in the HIR construction in the process of discourse representation, no use of *-wa*, topic or contrastive, is allowed.

In chapter 3 I also argued that only existential quantification is allowed in the subject NP of the HIR clause. However, a question arises concerning the nature of the existential particle *-ga* as the only option for the subject position in the HIR: does the particle indicate any inherent meaning that supports the existential nature of the HIR?[2] With this question in mind, I will pursue the following questions in connection with the discourse interpretation of the HIR. First, what core meaning does the particle -*ga* represent in the subject position from the discourse-semantic viewpoint, together with any additional derived meaning? Second, how is the core meaning, if any, involved in the discourse interpretation of the HIR construction? Although I give short outlines of past analyses of -*ga*, I will not pursue a comprehensive discussion of all the functions of -*ga* in the subject position; that would be beyond the scope of this chapter. Rather, I will make an effort to pursue the core nature of the subject marker -*ga* insofar as it is relevant to the characterization of the HIR construction.

In section 6.2 I will briefly describe past analyses of the particle -*ga* in the subject position and pin down one relevant lexical-semantic meaning. In section 6.3 I will further pursue one core meaning that seems most relevant to the HIR. Then I will examine the examples of two categories that have been claimed to describe the function(s) of -*ga* in section 6.4, and analyze the system of prosodic highlighting involved in those examples with the particle -*ga*. Finally, I will present one central meaning of the particle. In section 6.5 I will illustrate the discourse-pragmatic system of Gricean principles that in fact is closely related to the assumed second function of the subject marker -*ga*. In section 6.6 I will associate the characterization of -*ga* with the HIR, as discussed in earlier sections.

Overall, I will establish one core function of the subject marker -*ga* that accounts for the basic nature of the HIR in discourse representation. I will show that prosodic forces and the phenomenon of focus, assumed to be part of the second property of -*ga*, are actually separate from that core property. Finally, I will demonstrate that the properties of -*ga* is reducible to one core meaning that is rooted in the property of the HIR as a whole.

6.2 Analyses of the subject marker -*ga*

In the literature, it has been argued that the particle -*ga* in a subject position indicates two distinctive meanings.[3] For example,

(3)a. Neutral Description (ND):
      John-g<u>a</u>   kita.
         -NOM came
      'John came.'

b. Exhaustive Listing (EL):
John-ga   gakusei desu.
-NOM student Copular/Politeness
'John and only John is a student. It is John who is a student.'

[Kuno 1973: 51; also 1984]

There are also some scholars who argue that the Exhaustive Listing (hereafter EL) reading in (3b) should be derived from the Neutral Description (hereafter ND), for example, Ando (1980); Makino (1987); Miyagawa (1987); Iwasaki (2002) among others.[4] Others, especially Shibatani (1990: 271) and Heycock (1994), analyze the EL as derived from a discourse pragmatic force, which I will discuss in 6.5. In addition, there are semantic or discourse notions that have been associated with or assumed to be associable with the NP-*ga* in the subject position: grammatical subject, indefinite, new (discourse-new) information, focus, and so on. I will later analyze those terms only in connection with the interpretation of the HIR. I will first discuss the ND with -*ga* in (3a) which should cover a majority of sentences with -*ga* as the subject marker. In the following discussion, I will refer to the distinction between old and new information, and, drawing on Chafe (1976), Lambrecht (1987, 1994, 1996), Vallduvi (1992), Birner & Ward (1998) among others, I assume that there is a need to package information on focus and presupposition so that hearers can identify which part of the utterance represents an actual contribution to the information state at the time of the utterance, and which part represents what is already subsumed in this information state. Concerning notions included in *information structure* such as focus, presupposition, old/ new information, I basically adopt Chafe (1976), Lambrecht (1987, 1994, 1996), Vallduvi (1992), Vallduvi & Engdahl (1995), and Birner & Ward (1998). As one will see later in the chapter, the same propositional content is expressed by two different intonational and/or morpho-syntactic structures such as particles -*ga* and -*wa*. I will argue that the other meaning, EL, is a result of the influence of three distinctive general forces: semantic, discourse pragmatic, and intonational forces.

Returning to example (3), it is often argued typically in an ND example, that the Japanese NP-*ga* denotes a part of the whole propositional meaning of the sentence in which it appears, whereas what the NP-*wa* phrase denotes can be outside the propositional content. The following contrast highlights the proposition-internal nature of the NP-*ga*, in comparison with the NP-

wa, which has to do with the meaning outside the proposition unit, seems to represent a topic for the overall utterance sequence.

(4)a. Taro-wa (…) [iti-wa no   minarenu tori-ga
       -TOP one-CLSSFIER-GEN unknown bird-**NOM**
       higashi-ni mukatte tobitatu] tokoro-o   mita.
       east-to   heading Fly   Place/scene-ACC saw
       'As for Taro, he saw an unknown bird fly to the east.'
   b. #Taro-ga (…) [iti-wa no   minarenu tori-wa
       -**NOM** one-CLSSFIER-GEN unknown bird-**TOP**
       higashi-ni mukatte tobitatu] tokoro-o   mita.
       east-to   heading fly   Place/scene-ACC saw
       Intended: 'Taro saw an unknown bird fly to the east.'

In (4a), the main subject is marked with *-wa* and the embedded clause subject is marked with *-ga*. The scene that Taro witnessed is represented with *-ga* in the embedded clause as one proposition such as one bird flying to the east, while the given witness, Taro, is represented with *-wa* in the main clause. In the infelicitous (4b), the same scene is represented with *-wa* in the embedded clause as a proposition, while the given witness with *-ga* is in the position outside the clause of the description of the scene. Along these lines, Iwasaki (2002: 218) refers to the example of ND with *-ga* as a topicless sentence, and states that the speaker reports information by presenting it as an unanalyzed whole rather than breaking it up into a topic and a comment, as with a *-wa* sentence. As long as the scene is something to be introduced in the utterance in (4), *-ga* cannot be outside the description of it, i.e., the propositional content. Instead, *-ga* functions as the grammatical subject of a proposition. In this sense, the subject marker *-ga* stays within the proposition, whereas the topic marker *-wa* is outside the proposition.

Another relevant example (5) is the classic case of the start of a folk narrative.

(5) Mukashi mukashi arutokoroni   ojiisan-to   obaasan-ga   sunde
    old-days old-days certain place-at old man-and old woman-NOM lived
    imashita. Ojiisan-<u>wa</u>   yama-ni shibakari-ni,   obaasan-<u>wa</u>
    -existed   Oldman-TOP mountain-to get firewood old woman-TOP
    kawa-ni sentaku-ni ikimashita. ......
    river-to washing-to go-POL-PST
    'Once upon a time, in a certain place there lived an old man and an old woman. He went to the mountain to get firewood, and she went to the river to do the washing.'

What is observed in (5) is the division of labor between *-ga* and *-wa*: when a new discourse begins (here as narrative), where *-ga* is used for the introduction of an entity of an NP, then the introduced entity is repeated in the form of the NP-*wa*. Therefore, it seems reasonable that in the beginning of the narrative, an event or a state is introduced as a whole with *-ga* in (5), and then the main topic of the tale is sorted and repeated with the topic marker *-wa*. The first segment with *-ga* can be analyzed as ND and the second with *-wa* as a topic-comment sentence. As Iwasaki (2002: 225) mentions, this line of analysis is closely related to the notion of *judgment* discussed in Kuroda (1972, 1992) who follows Brentano and Marty. The notion is associated with the type difference between sentences that contain *-ga* or *-wa*, as in (6).

(6)a.   Inu-<u>ga</u>   aruite-iru. [Thetic Judgment]
        Dog-NOM walk-TE IRU/Nonpast
        'There is a/the dog walking by.'
   b.   Inu-<u>wa</u>   aruite-iru. [Categorical Judgment]
        Dog-TOP walk-TE IRU/Nonpast
        'The dog(, it) is walking.'   [Iwasaki 2002: 225–6, (27), (28)]

As Iwasaki (2002: 225) discusses, in (6a) the speaker verbalizes his perception of a dog's walking as one entire scene, an unanalyzed whole, in discourse, whereas in (6b) the process of predication is represented by the speaker with its topic-comment structure. The former type is called *thetic judgment*, as in (6a), and the latter *categorical judgment*, as in (6b). The speaker's intervention in the propositional content is indicated in an utterance like (6b) with *-wa*. This is illustrated in the following examples.

(7)a.   Nijyu-nin   kurai-ga   onaji tooan   ni natta.
      Twenty-persons about-NOM same answer-sheet to became
      'About twenty people's answers came out identical.'
  b. Nijyu-nin   kurai-wa   onaji tooan   ni natta.
      Twenty-persons about-TOP same answer-sheet to became
      '[As far as I know] as many as/at least about twenty people's answers came out identical.'

As seen in the translation of (7b), an additional meaning can be read in the sentence with the subject plus -*wa*, whereas the whole sentence in (7a) describes a scene without an indication of the speaker's assessment of the number, as if the situation were described by an omnipresent being. With -*wa*, the addressee assumes that the speaker has assessed and acknowledged the referent in the utterance, whereas, with -*ga*, the speaker is not involved in such an assessment of the referent in the utterance. The contrast illustrates that the particle -*ga* marks the grammatical subject but clearly lacks the marking of the speaker's assessment of the propositional content in discourse.

Similarly, Makino (1987: 296–7) argues that the particle -*ga* is **speaker-oriented**, whereas -*wa* is **listener-oriented**. This seems to accord with my argument: the listener-orientation with -*wa* corresponds with discourse orientation including both speaker and addressee, whereas the speaker-orientation with -*ga* corresponds with the lack of marking of the speaker's assessment, since the speaker gives no clue to the addressee. This type of contrast seems conspicuous in Japanese, as discussed in Makino (1987).

However, it would be misleading to state that the core function of the particle -*ga* is as the grammatical subject of a proposition. As already seen in (5), -*ga* appears when a new discourse begins and propositional content is introduced as a whole. In the following example, however, the particle appears without complete propositional content, and the content needs to be recovered in interpretation.

(8)a.   Hon-ga ..., hon-ga...!
      book-NOM book-NOM
      'A/The book, a/the book ... (is missing / is on fire / is in the air, and so on.)'

b. #Hon-wa ..., hon-wa ...!
   book-TOP book-TOP

In discourse, this type of incomplete sentence as an utterance is abundant. If one assumes in (8a) that the NP-*ga* is merely the grammatical subject of a proposition, the felicity of the utterance in contrast to the infelicity of (8b) with -*wa* would be a mystery. Instead, I assume that there is some additional function or meaning that -*ga* is inherently equipped with in discourse and that explains the contrast. Earlier I claimed that newly-introduced propositional content is presented with -*ga*. In fact, something to be presented must provide new information in discourse. Concerning the information structure, the old-new distinction seems significant in (8). The infelicity of (8b), in contrast, suggests that the acknowledged old information is not enough to be the whole component of an utterance in discourse. Since the topic marker -*wa* is the marking of the speaker's assessment of an entity indicated by the subject NP, the subject plus -*wa* cannot be new information in itself in discourse.[5] Note that the term 'new information' is not equivalent to new information **in discourse**. If (8a) represents the meaning in (9), *hon* 'book' does not always represent a new entity to the speaker at the time of the utterance.

(9) Hon-ga nai.
     '(The/A) book is missing',

Therefore, the particle -*ga* in the subject position is not necessarily tied to an indefinite reference, given the fact that Japanese is not equipped with any articles such as *the/a(an)*. The English translation in (9) illustrates this. The speaker could have a particular book in mind and could say:

(10) Hon-ga.
     book-NOM
     'The book (that I should have with me here is missing).'

In this case, 'book' is a newly introduced entity in a discourse context consisting of a speaker and an addressee. Prince (1992) uses terms such as 'discourse-new' and 'discourse-old' in this connection, and I will adopt the 'discourse-new' for the function of -*ga* because of the above discussion with (9) and (10).[6]

The following provide supportive examples for the argument that the marking of new information is one important function of -*ga*.

(11) a. ?Taro-ga   itu   kimashita?
     Taro-NOM when come-Pst
     'Intended: When did Taro come (here)?'
   b. ?Taro-ga   dokoni tatte imasu?
     Taro-NOM where stand-exist-Polite
     'Intended: Where does Taro stand (now)?' or 'Where is he?'
(12) a. Itu Taro-ga kimashita?
     'When did Taro come (here)?'
   b. Dokoni Taro-ga tatte imasu?
     'Where does Taro stand (now)?' or 'Where is he?'
                    [Kuno 1973b: 215–6, (34)–(37) with partial modification]

The (a) and (b) sentences in both (11) and (12) have identical vocabulary. The only difference is the ordering of the subject NP-*ga* and the Wh-elements. In both (11a) and (11b), the subject NP-*ga* appears before the Wh-elements and the sentences indicate lower acceptability than examples (12a) and (12b), where the Wh-elements appear before the subject NP-*ga*. Kuno (1973b: 215–6) argues that with the use of an Wh-element, the speaker assumes that the remaining part of the sentence signifies old information, since the Wh-element seeks new information in the question sentence in which it appears. Therefore, when the subject NP-*ga* instead of the Wh-element appears in the sentence-initial position, a priority conflict occurs in my terms, although Kuno uses the expression "the occurrence of subordinate-like character" (p. 216) with the Wh-element, which has to do with focusing for seeking new information. There is some priority preference for the relative position in an utterance between the -*ga*-marked subject and the Wh-element. As Kuno argues, the acceptability contrast is accounted for only in the light of focus and old/new information, based on the following facts: first, the fact that, in (11), the old informational value of what remains other than the NP-*ga* contains the Wh-element that is expected to be in focus and seeks 'new' information; second, the fact that the only difference between (11) and (12) is the ordering of the Wh-elements and the subject NP-*ga*. That is to say, on the one hand, new information must be carried by subject NPs in the examples above with the use of -*ga*, and, on the other hand, the Wh-element is in focus because of the overall function of the utterance as a question.[7] As a result, there is a competition in the sentence-initial position for the status of 'newness,' unless extra prosodic or discourse-pragmatic forces are brought in. This causes the conflict that I mentioned in (11). Example (12) legitimatizes the sentence-initial Wh-elements in that the overall function of the utterances as question is primary. With *-wa* in place of *-ga* in (11), such a conflict would not occur.

A similar argument could apply to the following examples.

(13) a. Nante koto-da.
What-CNNCTVE thing-Copula
'What the heck!'
b. Yatta.
Do(Cllq.)-Prfct
'Oh, my!' or 'Hurray!' (about something that is just done, successful or disastrous)
c. Naanda.
What-Copula
'[with some disappointment or surprise] For crying out loud, is that it?'

Literal translations are not possible for these examples in (13), and I use free translations instead. These sentences are incomplete, since they lack full-fledged predicates and identifiable subjects on the surface. Yet they are acceptable. Even a generic demonstrative pronominal phrase such as *are/sore-wa* 'that-TOP' would not be possible as ellipted subjects. Nevertheless, they clearly convey new information concerning the speaker's (emotional) assessment of a certain event or change of state. Otherwise, they would be uninterpretable informationally, as in (8b). The point of these examples is that any utterance must represent something as informationally new, and, when it comes to an utterance with *-ga*, the subject marker indicates discourse-new information, together with being part of a subject, as seen in (8a). Similarly, the following examples support the involvement of the subject marker *-ga* in conveying new information.

(14) a. Oto{-ga/#-wa} suru.
sound-NOM/#-TOP do
'*lit.*, A sound does.' or 'A sound rings.'

b. Henna nioi{-ga/#-wa} suru.
     strange smell-NOM/#-TOP do
     '*lit.,* Strange smell does' or 'Something smells odd.'
  c. Ama-mori{-ga/#-wa} suru.
     rain-leak-NOM/#-TOP do
     '(There is) some leakage with the rain.'

As the contrast between the two particles demonstrates, the sentences in (14) are felicitous only with *-ga*. The particle selection between *-ga* and *-wa* is the only difference that is responsible for the felicity/infelicity of the examples in (14). As is well-known, the predicates *suru* of the above examples are light verbs. The light verbs lack semantic content, and the other part of the sentence, i.e. the subject NP-*ga*, must represent the semantic content. Thus, it is clear that new information is conveyed with the NP-*ga* phrases, since those NP-*ga* phrases are the only semantic contents of the sentences. In contrast, the NP-*wa* phrases are infelicitous in (14). This contrast also demonstrates that the particle *-ga* itself marks new information.

Another semantic factor arises from the function of *-ga* as the introduction of (discourse-) new information. As mentioned earlier, Kuroda (1972, 1992) and others argue that a sentence with the subject marker *-ga* can be analyzed as marking a thetic judgment, thereby **introducing** an indivisible propositional content as a whole. McNally (1998: 295–7) basically follows this cognitive explication and further argues that the NPs in thetic sentences are not referential and that they do not denote entities. Rather, she claims that a thetic sentence constitutes a description of an event and is licensed indirectly via the existence of an eventuality to support its truth. Ladusaw (1994) points out that a thetic sentence simply affirms the **existence of an eventuality**, and further claims that a property-denotation cannot be the basis of a thetic judgment. As a result, that eventuality necessarily contains a dog as a participant, as in (6a) recapitulated in (15a) below.

(15)a. Inu-ga   aruite-iru. [Thetic Judgment]
       Dog-NOM walk-TE-IRU/Nonpast
       'There is a dog walking by.'

b. Inu-<u>wa</u>   aruite-iru. [Categorical Judgment]
   Dog-TOP walk-TE-IRU/Nonpast
   'The dog(, it) is walking.' [Iwasaki 2002: 225–6, (27), (28)]

The same line of argument is observed in Iwasaki (2002) as well. The relevance of McNally's (1998) argument to the current discussion lies in her argument for the introduction of new information by -*ga* which was clarified in the preceding paragraph. If one incorporates her analysis into the current discussion, it will show that the function of -*ga* as a way of introducing new information has to do with the existential nature of the kind of sentence accompanying the subject marker -*ga*. This in turn will support one of my basic arguments in earlier chapters for the existential interpretation of the HIR. However, instead of returning to that particular argument, I will now provide my argument for the existential nature of -*ga* (and of the sentence containing it) with supportive data.

(16) a. Aru   hito-ga   kita.
       some/a certain person-NOM came
       'A/one person came.'
     b. #Aru   hito-wa   kita.
       Some/a certain person-TOP came
       'A/one person came.' [Miyagawa 1987: 199, (32)]

As the grammaticality contrast between (16a) and (16b) shows, existential quantification is viable only with -*ga*. As Miyagawa argues, in (16b) with -*wa*, the speaker and the hearer share knowledge of (a set of) individuals. Consequently, the presentation of the already shared knowledge is informationally infelicitous. In other words, the combination of *aru* 'some' with *hito-wa* 'person-TOP' is contradictory since the indefinite entity newly introduced is regarded as something that has already been introduced in discourse. The indefinite 'some person' ought not to denote a person who is already in the earlier discourse context. In contrast, in (16a) with -*ga*, the sentence is felicitous, which suggests that the existential quantification indicated by *aru* 'some' is in accordance with the function of -*ga* as existential in the sentence that contains it. Therefore, it seems reasonable that the sentence in (16a) represents the new entity of an eventuality that is existentially introduced with -*ga*. I have so far discussed some of the concepts that have been frequently discussed in connection with the function(s) of -*ga*, and have clarified the involvement of the **existentiality**, a term used in Milsark (1977: 28), in the interpretation of a -*ga* sentence. I will further examine one core meaning that seems most relevant to the HIR in the next section 6.3. In section 6.4 I will discuss another alleged meaning, EL, that has been studied as one of the two categories of functions of -*ga* and I will see if the category of EL can be explained in terms of the core meaning under discussion.

6.3 Existential individuation of -*ga*

As I have discussed in the previous section, existentiality is claimed to be one fundamental meaning of a -*ga* sentence. In this section, I will further analyze the nature of -*ga* in the subject position and elaborate its existentiality into some more particular property, which I will later argue is rooted in the overall HIR construction. When I observe the issue in question from the semantic viewpoint of genericity, further data seem to suggest the following. The sentence with -*ga* does not allow a generic reading, as opposed to the one with -*wa*, as observed in (17).

(17) Mori{#-wa/-ga}   akai. [Are-wa   kaji-ni tigai   nai.]
     forest{-TOP/NOM} red   that-TOP fire-to difference not-exist
     '{#Forest/the forest I see} is red. [That must be a fire.]'

In general an NP in Japanese is not accompanied by an article. Therefore, the NP indicating a kind or a category can in theory represent either a generic entity, a particular individual, or a particular individual group [as the sum]. When the NP appears with -*ga*, as in (17), however, the sentence only presents the existence of an individual forest or of the forests that are individually recognizable. In contrast, when the NP appears with -*wa*, the sentence is infelicitous, which suggests that the generic "kind" meaning with *mori-wa* 'forest-TOP' is not in accordance with the meaning of the predicate, *akai* 'red'. Whether there is a second sentence or not does not affect the readings that have just been explained, and the addition of the second is only for a better understanding of the example.[8] Therefore, based on the contrast in (17), it is arguable that the subject NP-*ga* represents some kind of individuation, although that may or may not be derived from the existential nature of -*ga*.

In fact, in the following examples (18) to (21), the individuation does seem inherent to -*ga*.

(18) Minna{-wa/#-ga}   benkyoo tanoshii?
     Everybody{-TOP/#-NOM} study   fun
     'Is study(ing) fun, everyone?' or 'Is everyone enjoying study?'

In (18), the sentence with -*ga* only presents the existence of an individual person or of persons who are individually separable, but that context is implausible with the vocative phrase *minna-ga* 'all-NOM' that the particle -*ga* is a part of. The vocative *minna* usually refers to everyone the speaker is addressing, thereby evoking a universal reading.[9] Thus, the utterance is infelicitous with -*ga* unless the particle is replaced with -*wa*, which can indicate any acknowledged students, one or many, allowing a universal reading for vocatives. The following example involves universal quantification.

(19) Shinbun-o   yomitai]   hito{-wa/#-ga},   koko-ni
     [newspaper-ACC read-want] person–TOP/#-NOM here
     arimasu.
     exist/Nonhuman
     'For those (of you) who want to read a newspaper, {here is (one) / there is (a newspaper).'   [Tateishi 1994: 131]

Tateishi (1994) refers to this kind of example as a *Conditional Topic* sentence. In (19), I observe that the particle is infelicitous in two respects. First, the subject NP with -*ga* cannot find an appropriate predicate because of incompatibility between the non-human feature that the predicate *aru* 'exist/<u>non</u>human' lexically represents and the human subject *hito* 'person.' Second, when the preceding phrase is interpreted semantically as a conditional, the referent will not be existentially bound. No individuation is relevant. Instead, universal quantification is associated with conditionals in logico-semantic traditions. Therefore, the utterance in (19) can be read: For all x, if x wants to read a newspaper, here is a newspaper. Given such a formula that has been one of the general premises in logico-semantic traditions, the infelicity of the sentence with -*ga* provides evidence for existential individuation with -*ga*. The universal quantification in (19) is not compatible with the individuation with -*ga*.[10]

The following example supports this argument. Example (20) shows that the 'conditional' topic sentence which Tateishi discusses turns out to be functionally vocative in discourse.

(20) Atui hito{-wa/#-ga}, reizooko-ni juusu-ga aru.
 hot person–TOP/#-NOM refrigerator-in juice-NOM exist
 'For those who feel hot, there is some juice in the refrigerator.'

In the first NP *atui hito-wa/-ga*, there is no plausible clausal structure that can be interpreted as conditional, as in (19). Therefore, the first NP in (20) is arguably analyzed solely as vocative. The utterance in (19) can also be interpreted as containing a vocative, and the second occurrence of the head NP, *shinbun* 'newspaper' in the embedded clause, is assumed to be ellipted in the main predicate, as the translation shows. In fact, Lambrecht (1996: 270–4) combines both topic and vocative phrases in the light of their high saliency, through which he develops the process of referent identification in discourse. Saliency has been used as a criterion for the accessibility of an entity that is referred to in discourse. The literature includes Gundel, Hedberg, & Zacharski (1993), Lambrecht (1987, 1994, 1996), and Prince (1992). Lambrecht (1996) discusses the identical position between the topic and vocative phrases in his presentation of information structure. The entity represented by a topic or vocative phrase is analyzed as equally salient in the preceding context. If Lambrecht is right about the parallelism between the vocative and topic phrases, the occurrences of the topic *-wa* in opposition to *-ga* in (18), (19) and (20) can be accounted for naturally: in those vocative phrases with *-wa*, the referents are universally quantified, i.e., individuation is excluded, since general information is given out in those utterances to everyone described in the modifying phrases: e.g. in (20), 'any person who feels hot,' but it does nto address one person who feels hot. The individuation with *-ga* seems to be even more clearly illustrated in (21).

(21) Otoko$_i${-ga/#-wa} sannin$_i$ tati-agatta.
 guy(s)–NOM/#-TOP three-persons stood-up
 'Three men stood up.' [*lit.*, 'Men stood up by three.']

The reason the occurrence of *-wa* results in infelicity is not clear, and yet a clear contrast obtains with *-ga* in (21). In this Numeral Quantifier Float example, the individuation indicated by the classifier *sannin* 'three persons' is in accordance with the NP-*ga* phrase, while the parallel example with the NP-*wa* phrase is ruled out. This seems to support the relevance of existential individuation to *-ga*. The ban on *-wa* in (21) may be due to the division of the whole topic phrase into *otoko* 'men' and *sannin* 'by three persons' in information structure: a topic must stay in one topic structure unit. No part of the topic structure can be separated from the rest and contained in any other structural unit. In essence, in all of the examples (18) to (21), one of the core meanings of the subject marker *-ga* is identified as existential individuation.

6.4 Exhaustive Listing (EL) as a reflection of prosodic highlighting

In the last section, I discussed one core meaning of the subject marker *-ga* that has something to do with presentational neutral description (ND) utterances. However, questions still remain regarding the other categorization of the dichotomy that has been discussed in the literature for the meaning of *-ga*: Exhaustive Listing (EL), as introduced in section 6.2. In this section, I will examine the assumed second meaning of *-ga*, EL, and break it down into separate levels of representation: discourse-pragmatic force, a semantic phenomenon, and prosodic forces. The dichotomy is recapitulated in (22).

(22) [= (3)]
    a. Neutral Description:
    John-ga   kita.
        -NOM came
    'John came.'
    b. Exhaustive Listing:
    John-ga   gakusei desu.
        -NOM student Copular/Politeness
    'John and only John is a student.' or 'It is John who is a student.'
                                                                 [Kuno 1973: 51]

In defining ND, Kuno (1973: 52–3) states that such predicates are limited to actions, existence, or temporary states, as opposed to property-denoting or characterizing predicates. However, as Kuno states, with an additional prosodic contrast, those sentences can be felicitous with characterizing predicates. Example (22b) is one such example, with an additional accent on the subject NP-*ga*. Kuno analyzes those examples as EL and separates them from the examples of ND. He calls the particle -*ga* in such examples a *Focus Particle*, and claims that the sentence is divided into a focus part and remaining presupposed part. The following examples also illustrate the involvement of prosodic factors. Capital letters for a phrase indicate that the additional accent is placed on it.

(23)a. With some accent on the subject:
 [Kind-reference NP subject]-*ga* + property-denoting predicate
 KEIKAN-ga   aikokuteki-da.
 policeman-NOM patriotic-Copula
 'Policemen are patriotic.' or 'It is policemen who are patriotic.'
 b. Without an accent on the subject:
 #Keikan-ga   aikokuteki-da.
 policeman-NOM patriotic-Copula
 Literal: '#Some policeman is patriotic.'

In (23a), with an explicit accent added onto the subject NP, the sentence is felicitous, meaning that policemen (as opposed to other people) are patriotic. In contrast, (23b) is infelicitous without such a prosodic contrast. Although Ando (1980), Shibatani (1990), Iwasaki (2002) and others also point out that the examples of EL involve some additional accent on the subject NP-*ga*, these prosodic additions do not seem to be confined to the type of examples such as (22b) and (23). As seen in (24), in the different types of examples containing either -*ga* or -*wa*, the prosodic highlighting of the subject NP can result in similar effects on the interpretation of the utterances.

(24)a. [Kind-NP Subject-ga] + eventive predicate
 KEIKAN-ga taiki-chu da.
 'Policemen are available.' or 'It is policemen who are available (there).'
 b. [Kind-NP Subject-wa] + property-denoting predicate
 KEIKAN-wa aikoku-teki da.
 'Policemen are patriotic.' or 'It is policemen who are patriotic.'

c. [Kind-NP Subject-<u>wa</u>] + eventive predicate
KEIKAN-wa taiki-chu da.
'Policemen are available.' or 'It is policemen who are available (there).'

In (24a), with an eventive predicate, *taiki-chu* 'available,' the preferred reading is such that no one other than policemen are available, which would fall under EL, although this example does not belong to EL, according to Kuno's account. Kuno limits the kinds of predicates in EL to property-denoting or characterizing predicates in spite of the same EL effect observed in the case of an eventive predicate, as in (24a). In (24b) and (24c), the discourse-new information seems to be *keikan* 'policemen,' unlike common topic sentences that can be produced without such added accents. The preferred readings of (24b) and (24c) are such that it is policemen who are patriotic/available.

The point is that, when subjects are marked with additional accents, any type of predicate, with either particle of *-ga* or *-wa* in the subject position, results in a focused meaning. I note that the use of the term 'focusing' here will be rather broad and can be replaced with prosodic emphasis as a generalized phenomenon. I will not discuss the structure of focus assignment, but the focus assignment in the current discussion here seems to coincide with prosodic prominence provided solely by the additional accent on a meaningful unit of an utterance, which is conspicuous in Japanese. If my observation based on the above data is correct, the assumed second meaning, EL, of the subject-*ga*, turns out to be no more than the consequence of a more general prosodic phenomenon, on the one hand, and of different kinds of predicates, on the other.

In fact, Milsark (1974, 1977), Ladusaw (1994/2000), and Herburger (1997) argue that weak NPs cannot co-occur with property-denoting or characterizing predicates. Only quantificational (strong) NPs may appear as the subjects of property-denoting predicates. The generalization along the lines of Milsark is illustrated in the following example.

(25) There is/are {a/some/several/few/Ø} wolf/wolves at the door.
[**non-quantificational** (weak)]
*There is/are {the/all/every/those/John's} wolf/wolves at the door.
[**quantificational** (strong)]

Similarly, a contrast obtains between non-quantificational and quantificational subject NPs that occur with a property-denoting predicate such as 'intelligent.'[11]

(26)a. *<u>A man</u> was intelligent.   [non-quantificational (weak)]
   b. <u>Everyone</u> was intelligent. [quantificational (strong)]

This is parallel to the contrast between -*ga* and -*wa*, as in (23b) and (24b). Under the generalization, non-quantificational NPs such as NP-*ga* cannot appear in a subject position with those predicates. Uttered without an additional accent, (23b) with -*ga* is infelicitous, while (24b) with -*wa* is felicitous without the accent. The generalization accords with my claimed existentiality or non-quantificational nature of -*ga*: unless some additional discourse context is given in the utterance, the particle -*ga* is not compatible with those predicates due to existentiality. Given this observation, I maintain that the infelicity with the assumed typical EL example such as (23b) is due to a general semantic factor: the incompatibility between a non-quantificational subject such as an NP-*ga* and a property-denoting predicate such as *aikokuteki-da* 'be patriotic.'

Note that the generalization I have just discussed is extended in the literature under the terms *stage-level* and *individual-level* predicates (hereafter SLP and ILP) instead of predicates of state description and of property denotation. Building on the Milsarkian generalization, Diesing (1988, 1992) proposes a hypothesis of direct mapping (called Mapping Hypothesis) in which the relative difference in interpretation between the two kinds of NPs (DPs) correlates with the difference in the structural positions. That is, the structural positions of NPs differ, depending on whether they occur with stage-level or individual-level predicates. NPs with stage-level predicates are base-generated within the VP domain, whereas NPs with individual-level predicates are outside the VP domain. As a result, quantifier raising may follow, depending on the kinds of NPs. However, the idea of this obligatory direct mapping causes problems. I point out part of the difficulty related to the nature of the EL. As discussed in (23a), without a prosodic addition, the sentence is infelicitous. According to the Mapping Hypothesis, ILPs must have strong subject NPs, and the strong NPs must undergo quantificational raising and be bound by an operator. Now in the case of (23b), the subject NP, *keikan* 'policeman/policemen,' denotes either a particular individual, an individual sum, or a generic profession, as previously described in relation to (17). Therefore, the NP can be interpreted as generic (strong) and the Mapping Hypothesis predicts that the whole sentence in (23b) should be acceptable, with a typical ILP *aikokuteki-da* 'patriotic.' Consequently, the infelicity of (23b) that occurs when the sentence is uttered without an extra accent on the NP cannot be accounted for. The hypothesis does not accommodate the properties of *-ga* outside of its function as a case marker. Heycock (1994: 168) shows that there are counterexamples to Diesing's (1988) prediction that the accented subjects of ILPs must be interpreted as being in narrow focus. Heycock states that focus projection for the subject is not determined only by the kinds of predicates. Other problems with the hypothesis in relation to the ILP/SLP distinction are discussed in Ladusaw (1994/2000), Herburger (1997), and Fernald (2000). In the current discussion, the Milsarkian generalization is fundamental enough to serve as a basis for elaboration of the proposed core meaning of *-ga*. As mentioned above, when *-ga* is analyzed solely as the case marker of a subject, the both possibilities of felicity and infelicity in sentences like (23) cannot be accounted for. Some more examination is required regarding the inherent properties of *-ga*. I will now discuss why the prosodic addition in discourse can save such infelicitous utterances as (23b).

Ando (1980) correctly points out that an EL reading is involved in the placement of focus in connection with an additional accent given to the relevant subject NP, although he does not take into account quantification of the subject NP that turns out to be fundamental to the EL reading. The focus is derived from prosodic highlighting by additional accents placed on a particular meaningful unit of an utterance. I term 'placement of focus' **focusing** in order to avoid any confusion; my discussion will not be related to any existing theory on focus structure. Focusing can be understood to divide a relevant propositional content into two components: a focused and a defocused part. As has been discussed in the literature, these components convey new information and presupposition respectively in discourse. Kuno (1973) and Ando (1980) point out the involvement of new information in the subject of the EL examples. I illustrate these phenomena as follows.

(27)a. [= (23)a.] With some accent on the subject:
[FOCUS KEIKAN-ga] aikoku-teki da.
policeman-NOM   patriotic Copula
'Policemen are patriotic.'

b. Evoked Presupposition: 'X is patriotic'
Asserted in focus: 'X = policemen'

'X' in (27b) is a variable that has to be identified with the presupposed proposition 'Some entity is patriotic' that is given in the preceding discourse. This presupposition coincides with discourse-old information. Importantly, the subject NP-*ga* does not represent a generic entity, and instead represents an existentially individuated entity through -*ga*'s core function. Discussing the thetic judgment observed in Japanese -*ga* examples, McNally (1998: 296) states that the introduction of a new discourse referent requires the existence of a particular sort of eventuality from the sentence in which the referent is introduced. If the sentence in (27a) were presented without prosodic highlighting, the sentence as a whole would represent new information, as previously discussed in the light of Iwasaki (2002). The sentence would be infelicitous due to the semantic incompatibility of the subject NP-ga with the predicate, as in the case of (23b). When the sentence is accompanied by the focusing of the subject, however, the defocused predicate component evokes a presupposition that represents the existence of a particular eventuality in connection with the preceding discourse context: some X is patriotic. Through this presupposition, some individual entity is necessarily contained in the eventuality of being patriotic which is mentioned in prior discourse. Some individual entity which is patriotic exists. In this regard, at the level of information structure the semantic property of 'property-denotation' which is indicated by the predicate *aikokuteki-da* 'be patriotic' is reduced to the presupposition with the particular eventuality. The entity existentially individuated by -*ga* is now focused and maintained in discourse. Consequently, the subject NP now represents new information.[12]

The important point is that, if EL is simply held as a distinctive use of -*ga*, the generalization that one of the uses of -*wa* is genericity would be lost. Both (23a) with -*ga* and (24b) with -*wa* indicate similar meanings, given the property-denoting predicate and the additional accent. Both -*wa* and -*ga* would be generic, since only quantificational (*e.g.* generic) subject NPs can co-occur with a property-denoting predicate, according to Milsark (1974, 1977) and Herburger (1997). Furthermore, -*ga* would have to be understood to be either generic or existential, but that would be contradictory. Two questions would arise: (1) if -*ga* is existential, why is the existential interpretation infelicitous with -*ga*, as in (23b)?; and (2) if -*ga* is generic, why is the generic interpretation infelicitous with it? In either case, the identical proposition would be expected, as long as the sentence is pronounced without an extra accent on the subject. Instead, if the so-called EL sentences like (23) is associated with the generalized notion of focusing, as mentioned above, the following generalization applies.

(28) a. One core meaning of -*ga*: existential individuation when -*ga* appears as a subject marker.
b. Focusing: prosodic prominence will be given by an additional accent to any meaningful unit of an utterance, so that discourse-new information will be conveyed in discourse.

A subject NP-*ga* can be focused even when it appears with a property-denoting predicate, thereby conveying new information such as *keikan-ga* 'policemen' in (23a), together with the presupposition such as X-*ga aikokuteki-da* 'X is patriotic' evoked by the defocused property-denoting predicate.

Note that a -*ga*-marked subject is not inherently focused, as seen in the following example.

(29) A: Mary-wa   John-yori se-ga   hikui desu-ka?
       Mary-TOP John-than back-ga low   be Qn
       'Is Mary shorter than John?' [free translation]
     B: Iie, Mary-wa   totemo se-ga   takai desu yo.
       no, Mary-TOP very   back-ga tall   be Assrtn
       'No, Mary is very tall.' [free translation]   [Heycock 1994: 165–6, (30)]

As Heycock (1994: 166) argues, the focus is the predicate, i.e. 'low' or 'tall,' and therefore the *ga*-marked subject is not the focus. Nonetheless, the subject *se-ga* is part of new information, *se-ga takai* '[Mary] is very tall,' concerning the topic, Mary. Therefore, -*ga* is not inherently a focus marker but instead introduces an existentially individuated entity, and marks it as a subject, which is newly presented as part of propositional content.

In summary, the subject NP-*ga* in EL is prosodically prominent as a result of focusing, and the focusing is the reflection of semantic incompatibility of the -*ga* subject with the property-denoting predicate. EL is now reduced to a result of different levels of phenomena: first, the lexical-semantic property of

-*ga* as existential individuation; second, the semantic incompatibility of NP-*ga* with a property-denoting predicate; third, the additional prosodic phenomenon of focusing of NP-*ga* that leads to the division into focus and presupposition components.

Therefore, the particle *-ga* is not simply a case-marker but represents something more lexical: existential individuation (for discourse-new presentation of a whole proposition). Another point is that the apparent idiosyncrasy of EL examples with extra accents is accountable through a more general prosodic property, namely focusing, which applies to *-wa*-marked subjects as well, as observed in (24).

In this section I have argued that EL is not the second core meaning but that it is a reflection of complex phenomena. In the next section, as the final stage in pinning down the nature of *-ga*, I will discuss one more twist and present the fourth factor of the EL reading in connection with a question of why the preferred reading of EL obtains, instead of one simple reading.

6.5 Implicature of preferred readings of EL examples

In this section, I will analyze examples of EL from the viewpoint of discourse pragmatics. In the preceding section, I discussed the preferred reading of the EL examples. The other reading is viable depending on the context that limits the domain set of the reference entities of the subject NP.

(30)a. [from (3b) and (23a)] KEIKAN-ga aikoku-teki da.
                                policeman-NOM patriotic Copula
    'Policemen are patriotic.': 'Policemen [as opposed to others] are patriotic.'
    or 'Policemen are really patriotic [with no other jobs excluded].'
  b. SORA{-ga/wa} aoi.
     Sky   {-NOM/-TOP} blue
     Preferred Reading: 'The sky [as opposed to others] is blue.'
     The other: 'The sky is especially blue [with nothing excluded].'
  c. SORA{-ga/-wa} aoi. Umi-mo aoi. Keredo, ho-wa
     Sky{-NOM/-TOP} blue sea also blue but   the/a sail-CNTRST
     aokunai.
     blue-not

'The sky is really blue. The sea is really blue as well. But the/a sail is not.'

(30a) illustrates the other reading as well as the preferred EL reading when the focusing occurs with an extra accent on the subject. The same is true of (30b) in which either -*ga* or -*wa* maintains the second potential reading with nothing excluded, i.e., in a non-exhaustive way. Here I do not take into account the distinction between the sky at a particular place and the sky in general. Note, however, that the preferred reading of EL can be canceled. The example in (30c) illustrates this point. In (30c), an additional context is given and 'the sea' is also described as blue, together with 'the/a sail' being described as not blue, so 'the sky' is not the only entity that is really blue. The only difference between -*ga* and -*wa* in the example is that -*ga* requires some kind of individuation, while -*wa* points to a generic entity in that the subject NP is a kind-referring expression. The point here is that, in the assumed EL examples such as (30), the exhaustive import is cancelable and the other non-exhaustive reading can replace it if the domain information for the reference of the subject NP is added in discourse context. Either reading turns out to be cancelable; the remaining one is the propositional content plus the meaning evoked by focusing, i.e. discourse-new information. Therefore, the closest translation of (30a) will be: It is policemen who are patriotic [in some particular context].

A similar case is illustrated in (31).

(31) A: INU-<u>ga</u>   kashikoi.
       Dog-NOM clever
       'It is dogs which are clever.'
   B-1: Soo-da-ne.
       So-Copula-isn't it
       'That's right.'
   B-2: Demo, sono ehon-dewa   hoka-ni iruka-mo   ne.
       but   that picture-book-in else-to dolphin-also isn't-it
       'But <u>in that picture book</u>, dolphins are [clever] as well.'

The particular domain in which the set of referent entities is relevant is mentioned later with 'in that picture book' in the second utterance by B. Without assuming a context, the EL examples are necessarily ambiguous.[13]

In fact, Kuno (1973) and Miyagawa (1987: 209) point out that EL examples such as (23b) and (30) are awkward out of context. This awkwardness seems to correspond with the possibility that the reading can be canceled. Either reading of the EL examples is indeterminate. Therefore, an approach to the cancelable meanings is in order here.

In fact, Horn (1981) analyzes the cleft sentences in English and shows that their exhaustive import is cancelable and derived from a general pragmatic phenomenon, *conversational implicature* (hereafter C.I.). Along the same line, Shibatani (1990) argues that EL is an epiphenomenon in the meaning of *-ga-*marked subjects, since the EL reading is derived from the C.I. associated with a particular kind of sentence with an extra accent on the subject. Similarly, Heycock (1994: 158–9) points out that the same kind of implicature is derived from a narrow focus in the subject position in English examples.

C.I. has been analyzed in light of general pragmatic forces in Grice (1975), Levinson (1983) and others. The preferred reading in (30a) [=(23a)] is cancelable and can be analyzed as an example of C.I. There have also been constant efforts to boil down Gricean maxims and submaxims into more fundamental principles. Among those efforts, Horn (1984, 1993) has developed two competing principles concerning C.I., as in (32).

(32) ... The *Q Principle* is a lower-bounding hearer-based guarantee of the sufficiency of informative content ("Say as much as you can, modulo Quality and R") ... The *R Principle* is an upper-bounding correlate of the Law of Least Effort dictating minimization of form ("Say no more than you must, modulo Q").[14]

Now coming back to example (30a), C.I. tends to emerge as a preferred reading.[15] Because the speaker does not produce a more common, neutral accent on the subject NP-*ga*, the hearer might infer that the speaker is not in a position to abide by the R Principle, i.e. to utter a more straightforward statement without extra prosodic prominence. As a result, the hearer may infer an implicit meaning connoted by the additional, complex prosodic contrast, which will lead to prioritizing the Q Principle. Nothing in the structure of the sentence explicitly means that the described entity of the subject NP is the only relevant object of the event, 'being patriotic,' as indicated by the predicate. If the hearer considers such a possibility, however, he may infer that the simple introduction of an existential individual was not intended to be part of the new information, and that the speaker's extra effort was made in order to foreground the relevant entity as a unique one. Therefore, the preferred reading 'None other than policemen' can be inferred for the relevant entity with the subject NP-*ga*, thereby observing the Q Principle. The same line of argument is developed in the discussion of Japanese complex predicates in Ishikawa (2001).

Hence, the assumed category EL turns out to be the result of distinctive levels of interrelated phenomena: first, the lexical-semantic property of -*ga* as existential individuation; second, the semantic incompatibility of a non-quantificational NP-*ga* with a property-denoting predicate; third, the additional prosodic phenomenon of focusing of a subject NP-*ga* resulting in representing new information and presupposition; and fourth, as a preferred meaning, conversational implicature (C.I.) prioritizing the Q Principle.

Finally, I will associate the above characterization of -*ga* in the subject position with the HIR.

6.6 The HIR to represent sequenced events

As should be evident from the previous discussion, the HIR clause represents an existential description of an event with a subject NP-*ga*. As a sentence of thetic judgment, the HIR clause presents a whole propositional content, i.e., an event with an episodic predicate, as already discussed in chapters 2 and 3. However, focusing which I discussed in the preceding section is not allowed in the HIR.

(33)a. #[[MARY-ga   ringo-o   tabete iru]-no]-o John-ga   totta.
           -NOM apple-ACC eat-TE IRU-N-ACC   -NOM took
     'MARY was eating an apple, which John took.'
   b. #[[Mary-ga   RINGO-o tabete iru]-no]-o John-ga   totta.
           -NOM apple-ACC eat-TE IRU-N-ACC   -NOM took
     'Mary was eating an APPLE, which John took.'
   c. [[Mary-ga   ringo-o   tabete iru]-no]-o John-ga   TOTTA.
           -NOM apple-ACC eat-TE IRU-N-ACC   -NOM took
     'Mary was eating an apple, which John TOOK.'

Except for (33c) in which the matrix clause predicate is focused, the examples in (33) are infelicitous, with each NP focused inside the HIR clause. As a result, unlike the alleged EL examples, the proposition cannot be divided into focus and presupposition components in the HIR clause. Instead, it is held as the presentation of the whole clausal content as new information, which is referred to as *global focus*. That is in contrast to *narrow focus* observed in the EL examples in the preceding section. As discussed earlier, this is characteristic of a thetic judgment, presenting and describing one entire event. This accounts for how the entire HIR construction is interpreted. Together with the second event indicated in the main clause, the entire construction represents a sequence of events in which the discourse (rhetorical) relation depends on the properties of two events. As McNally (1998) argues, the NPs in thetic sentences are not referential. Although the NP-*ga* existentially introduces an individuated entity, that entity is part of the whole propositional content. As a result, such NPs cannot be focused; otherwise, an entity indicated by the subject NPs will be separated from the remaining part of the proposition through division by focusing. Sequencing two events cannot be achieved without presenting/describing the events rather than the individual entities. In chapter 5, by means of SDRT representation, I argue that the indefinite nominal -*no* in the HIR indicates temporal contiguity of two events. However, as Ladusaw (2000: 236–7) argues, a thetic sentence is only relevant to a description. Descriptions cannot combine with non-description or predication that has to do with the basis for a categorical judgment to represent an individual object and a property directly. As a result, combining the descriptions directly with properties is impossible. I claim that, instead, the interpretation of the relation between the described event indicated in the HIR clause and the second event indicated in the main clause obtains somewhere else: i.e., through the reasoning process of default matching grounded in the available lexical information across the two events in discourse. Through these processes, individual entities subsumed in the event in the HIR clause can be identified as participants in the event.

All of these processes of discourse interpretation are concerned with the **sequencing of two events** indicated in the construction. The existential introduction of a new event in the HIR, together with the subject NP-*ga*, ensures that the interpretation of the HIR construction as a whole is directed toward such sequencing of the two events, without focusing on an entity that would be interpreted as narrow focus. With focusing, an individual entity would be highlighted and it would be separated from the remaining predication.

The HIR construction instead highlights the eventualities indicated in the two propositions, without focusing on an individual entity. This seems to be the overall function of the HIR construction in discourse interpretation. In this respect, the HIR construction is a background representation to highlight sequenced events without focusing on an entity that takes part in the event indicated in the HIR clause. The individual entity of the NP is only interpretable by way of the eventuality that the HIR indicates with the existential -*ga*.

6.7 Summary of the chapter

In this chapter, **first**, I have examined the nature of -*ga* in the subject position of a sentence and claimed that -*ga* existentially individuates an entity indicated by the subject, as opposed to describing a generic entity. The whole sentence with a subject NP-*ga* is the instantiation of a thetic judgment the basis of which is the presentation and description of a whole new proposition. The particle -*ga* is not simply a case marker but represents substantial lexical meaning as well. **Second**, what has been classified as the second meaning of -*ga*, i.e., EL, turns out to be the result of different phenomena. They are independent of each other by nature and analyzed as general properties observed in a wider perspective: (i) semantic factors concerning non-quantificational NPs and property-denoting predicates; (ii) a general prosodic phenomenon, focusing, on the -*ga*-marked subject of an EL example; and (iii) a discourse-pragmatic force, conversational implicature that tends to emerge with the EL examples through focusing or an extra accent. The particular effect of implicature with the EL examples prioritizes the Q-principle of the pragmatic system. **Third**, as a consequence of the above observations, -*ga* is not a focus marker in itself, although -*ga*-marked subjects represent new information as part of the whole propositional content. In addition, with focusing, the exhaustive import of EL that is assumed to arise with a particular construction with -*ga* is observed also in other constructions without -*ga* in the subject position. **Fourth**, the HIR construction subsuming the existential -*ga* highlights the eventualities to sequence the indicated events without focusing on the subject of the HIR clause. Without a tense indication, the reasoning process of *default matching* operates in the interpretation of the HIR to identify the temporal relations between the two events, grounded in the lexical information available across the events in discourse. All of these factors eventually work toward sequencing of the two events indicated in the bi-clausal HIR construction.

Endnotes

1. As Seiichi Makino (personal communication) points out, the degree of subordination has been discussed concerning a variety of complex clause constructions in Japanese: e.g. in Kuno (1973). This line of research could be either for or against the argument that I have made here, and 'the degree' could subsume, perhaps, the *tokoro* clause as a very loose subordination. This issue, however, has to be left open to future research.

2. If *-ga* is treated only as a functional element, the following questions seem to remain unanswered: first, why *-ga* and *-o* can be replaced with *-wa* or *-mo*, while other case markers including oblique *-ni* cannot; second, why *-ga* cannot be omitted, while *-wa* and *-o* can.

3. I will argue that *-ga* is not simply a nominative-case marker, as is assumed [cf. Heycock (1994)]. I will claim that the particle has some inherent lexical meaning. In addition, the particle can appear in a non-argument position, as in the following 'major subject' example:

   <u>Ima</u>-**ga**   asagata   turara-**ga** ookiku naru.
   Now-GA in-the-morning icicle-GA big   become
   'Icicles can become big in the morning now/around this time of the year.' [free translation][with a strong high-pitch accent on the first mora of the *-ga*-marked phrase, *ima-ga*.]

4. Iwasaki (2002) has a somewhat different view from this dichotomy and divides the use of *-ga* into the following two: exclamatory and presentational. The exclamatory meaning can be subsumed into the presentational one, with the discussion of a general prosodic mechanism of focusing, as I argue later. For a reference, Iwasaki's (2003: 219) examples for the Exclamatory is given below.

   Exclamatory: A! inu-ga   iru!
                Oh. Dog-NOM exist
                'Oh, there is a dog!'   [Iwasaki 2002: 229, (38)]

5. I do not discuss the overall characterization of *-wa*, but its generic use will be an important one. In this example, the NP with *-wa* carries old information.

6. As I mentioned earlier, 'discourse-new' and 'new' to the hearer are not equivalent. However, such notions are not categorical, and if something is new to the hearer it must be 'discourse-new.' Likewise, if something is already evoked in discourse it will be old to the hearer as well as 'discourse-old.' Otherwise, typically discourse-status and hearer-status are independent of each other. See Prince (1992) for details.

7   I do not assume that a subject NP-*ga* is inherently the focus here. I will discuss this issue later in 6.4.
8   In the example I assume that the utterances are read without any prosodic addition such as emphasis or focusing, which will be the main theme of my discussion in later sections of this chapter. The first sentence unit is pronounced with phrase-internal (pitch) accents but flatly with no additional supra-segmental intonation contour.
9   A typical universal quantifier such as *subete* cannot occur in this position here, although the basic lexical meaning is shared between *minna* and *subete*.
10 Seiichi Makino (personal communication) points out that a topic is often a conditional marker. One such example can be:

Kaki-<u>wa</u>   Hiroshima(-da).
oyster-TOP [the name of a city]-Copula
'{If you talk about oyster/Talking of oyster}, the one in Hiroshima is best/superior.'

11 This line of analysis is not without problems when it is extended. I refer readers to Abbott (2003), Herburger (1997), and Breivik (1983).
12 Examining French articles, de Swart (1996: 175–6) argues that an NP consisting of an indefinite article *de(s)* and a nominal can occur in a generic sentence, if it is **focal** and part of the matrix, because there it will get an **existential** reading. Although the NP-*ga* in Japanese does not always correspond with indefiniteness, the Japanese data of the assumed typical EL with property-denoting predicates here seems to be parallel to her data of French '*de(s)* N'.

Dans cette partie du Pacifique naissent souvent <u>des</u> ouragans violents.
'In this part of the Pacific arise often INDEF-PL storms/typhoons.'

In this example, 'storms/typhoons' is read existentially, with the whole sentence interpreted only as 'there arise storms/typhoons in this part of the Pacific', but not as 'storms/typhoons in general arise in this part of the Pacific.' Therefore, de Swart claims that indefinite NPs are uniformly interpreted as (dynamic) existential quantifiers. More specific discussions of existential subject are seen in regard to -*ga* in Ishikawa (2005, 2008).

13 Even with an episodic predicate, the same kind of cancelability occurs, with either a common noun, *shoonen* 'boy' or a proper noun, *John* 'John':

{SHOONEN/JOHN}-ga hashitte-iru.
'It is {a boy/John} who is running.' → 'Nobody other than {a boy/John} is running' or '{A boy/John} is running [with nobody excluded]'.

Therefore, the phenomena referred to as the category EL seem to be relevant to a more general discourse-pragmatic system.

14 In connection with the general discussion of C.I., "scalar implicatures" are discussed in detail in Horn's seminal work, as in Horn (1984, 1989). Reinhart (2006) examines

the scalar implicatures in the context of children's processing difficulty about such implicatures. Concerning another kind of implicature, "conventional implicature (CVI)," Potts (2005) develops his logical system of interpretation for CVI, which has something to do with Japanese deictic expressions such as *-no* in the HIR. However, this is beyond the scope of the current study.

15 Portner & Yabushita (1998: 148) also argue that implicature is involved in EL. However, they do not take into account its cancelability and instead seek to accommodate the implicature evoked in EL examples into logical representation directly. Their analysis therefore cannot be supported here. I consider separate levels for the meanings reletaed to EL, as discussed later.

Chapter 7

Final remarks

In this study, I have presented a model of representation of interpretation for an untensed, prenominal complement construction, HIR, in Japanese. First, I have examined the structure of this apparent relative clause construction, and claimed that in spite of its name, the subordinate clause, i.e. HIR, is in fact a prenominal complement clause. The HIR clause is untensed and furthermore the head nominal *-no* of the HIR clause lacks semantic content. The head nominal, however, turns out to require the two events to be contiguous. With the untensed status, the HIR construction necessarily has access to the discourse representation of event units indicated by the two clauses. The temporal ordering relation between the two events is identified through time intervals in the event representation in discourse, together with two aspectual properties involved in temporally combining the two events. However, because the HIR clause is untensed and the referent of the head nominal is not explicitly indicated, I have claimed that the whole interpretation process requires a specific reasoning process, which I call Default Matching. This matching process is achieved through the available lexical default information across the two events in discourse. I have shown that all the above observations can be presented within an integrative model of discourse representation, SDRT, which is equipped with a discourse-pragmatic system of combining sequences of events, together with a mechanism to determine discourse event relations. All of these processes of discourse interpretation are directed toward the sequencing of two events indicated in the HIR construction. By examining the properties of *-ga*, I have shown that the particle in the subject position existentially individuates an entity indicated by the subject, and the whole HIR clause is the instantiation of a thetic judgment of which the presentation and description of a whole new proposition is the basis. The particle *-ga* represents substantial lexical meaning in this respect. At the same time, since the whole HIR clause serves to present new propositional content, *-ga* cannot be a focus marker; otherwise the proposition would be divided into separate components. Through the thetic presentation, individual entities subsumed in the event can be identified as participants of the event, and the existential introduction of a new event in the HIR, together with the existential *-ga*, ensures that the interpretation of the HIR construction is directed toward sequencing of the two events. The HIR sets up an existential condition sufficient for the consequent event, which is contiguous with the first event, to occur.

BIBLIOGRAPHY

Abbott, B. 2003. Definiteness and indefiniteness. In Horn, L. and G. Ward, eds., *Handbook of Pragmatics*. Blackwell.

Akatsuka, N. 1978. Another look at *no, koto*, and *to*: epistemology and complementizer choice in Japanese. In Hinds, J. and I. Howard, eds., *Problems in Japanese Syntax and Semantics*. Tokyo: Kaitakusha.

Anderson, S. R. and E. L. Keenan. 1985. Deixis. In Shopen, T. ed., *Language Typology and Syntactic Description, Vol. III: Grammatical Categories and the Lexicon*. Cambridge University Press.

Ando, S. 1980. Nihongo no *wa* to *ga* no kinoo ni tuite. (Concerning the functions of *wa* and *ga* in Japanese) *Gengo* Vol. 9, No. 7. Tokyo: Taishukan.

Asher, N. 1992. Semantics for the progressive. *Linguistics and Philosophy* 15, 463–508.

Asher, N. 1993. *Refernce to Abstract Objects in Discourse*. Dordrecht: Kluwer Academic Publishers.

Asher, N. 1999. Discourse structure and the logic of conversation. Turner K., ed., *Current Research in the Semantics Pragmatics Interface*.

Asher, N. and A. Lascarides. 1995. Lexical disambiguation in a discourse context. *Journal of Semantics*, 12.1, 69–108.

Asher, N. and A. Lascarides. 1998a. Bridging. *Journal of Semantics* 15, 83–113.

Asher, N. and A. Lascarides. 1998b. The semantics and pragmatics of presupposition. *Journal of Semantics*, 15, 239–300.

Avrutin, S. 1994. *Psycholinguistic Investigations in the Theory of Reference*. Ph.D. dissertation, MIT, Cambridge, MA.

Avrutin, S. 1997a. Events as units of discourse representation in root infinitives. *Proceedings of MIT Workshop on Root Infinitives*.

Avrutin, S. 1997b. Development of the syntax-discourse interface. ms.

Avrutin, S. 1999. *Development of the Syntax-Discourse Interface*. Kluwer Academic Publishers.

Babyonyshev, M. and E. Gibson. 1999. The complexity of structures in Japanese. *Language* 75, 423–450.

Bach, Emmon. 1986. The algebra of events. *Linguistics and Philosophy* 9, 5–16. Reidel.

Barwise, J. and J. Seligman. 1994. The rights and wrongs of natural regularities. In Tomberlin, J., ed., *Philosophical Perspectives*.

Basilico, D. 1996. Head position and internally headed relative clauses. *Language* 72, No.3, 498–532.

Birner, B. J. and G. Ward. 1998. *Information Status and Noncanonical Word Order in English*. John Benjamins.

Breivik, L. E. 1983. On the use and non-use of existential *there*. *Lingua* 61, 353–368. North-Holland.

Briscoe, E., A. Copestake, and B. Boguraev. 1990. Enjoy the paper: lexical semantics via lexicology. *Proceedings of the 13th International Conference on Computational Linguistics*, Helsinki, 42–7.

Carlson, L. 1981. Aspect and quantification. In Tedeschi, P. and A. Zaenen, eds., *Syntax and Semantics Vol. 14, Tense and Aspect*. New York: Academic Press, 31–64.

Chafe, W. L. 1976. Givenness, contrastiveness, definiteness, subjects, topics, and point of view. In Li, C. N., ed., *Subject and Topic*, 25–55. Academic Press.

Chierchia, G. 1995. *Dynamics of Meaning*. University of Chicago Press.

Chomsky, N. 1981. *Lectures on Government and Binding*. Dordorecht: Foris.

Chomsky, N. 1986. *Barriers*. MIT Press.

Chomsky, N. 1991. Some notes on economy of derivation and representation. In Chomsky, N., 1995. MIT Press.

Chomsky, N. 1995. *The Minimalist Program*. MIT Press.

Chung, S. and A. Timberlake. 1985. Tense, aspect, and mood. In Shopen, T. ed., *Language Typology and Syntactic Description, Vol. III: Grammatical Categories and the Lexicon*. Cambridge University Press.

Clark, H. 1977. Bridging. In Johnson-Laird, P. N. and P. C. Wason, eds., *Thinking: Readings in Cognitive Science*, Cambridge University Press.

Cole, P. 1987. The structure of internally headed relative clauses. *Natural Language and Linguistic Theory* 5, 277–302.

Cole, P. and G. Hermon. 1994. Is there LF wh-movement? *Linguistic Inquiry* 25, 239–62.

Comrie, B. 1976. *Aspect*. Cambridge University Press.

Comrie, B. 1985. *Tense*. Cambridge University Press.

Copestake, A. 1993. Defaults in lexical representation. In Briscoe, E.J., A. Copestake, and V. de Paiva, eds., *Inheritance, Defaults and the Lexicon*, 223–45. Cambridge University Press.

Culy, C. 1990. Grammatical relations and verb forms in internally headed relative clauses. In *Grammatical Relations: A Cross-Theoretical Perspective*. Palo Alto: CSLI.

Davidson, D. 1967. The logical form of action sentences. In Rescher, N., ed., *The Logic of Decision and Action*. Pittsburgh: University of Pittsburgh Press.

Diesing, M. 1992. *Indefinites*. Cambridge: MIT Press.

Dowty, D. 1979. *Word Meaning and Montague Grammar*. Boston: D. Reidel.

Enc, M. 1987. Anchoring conditions for tense. *Linguistic Inquiry* 18, 633–657.

Fernald, T. B. 2000. *Predicates and Temporal Arguments*. Oxford University Press.

Fukui, N. 1988. LF extraction of *naze* 'why': some theoretical implications. ms. Cambridge: MIT.

Fukui, N. and T. Nishigauchi. 1992. Head-movement and case-marking in Japanese. *Journal of Japanese Linguistics* 14.

Giorgi, A. and F. Pianesi. 1996. From semantics to morphosyntax. ms.

Glasbey, S. 1998. Progressives, states, and backgrounding. In Rothstein, S., ed., *Events and Grammar*, 105–24.

Grice, P. 1975. Logic and conversation. In Cole, P. & J. L. Morgan, eds., *Syntax and Semantics*, 3: *Speech Acts*, 41–58. New York: Academic Press.

Grosz, B. and C. Sidner. 1986. Attention, intentions, and the structure of discourse. *Computational Linguistics*, 12, 175–204.

Gundel, J., N. Hedberg, and R. Zacharski. 1993. Cognitive status and the form of referring expressions in discourse. *Language*, 69, 274–307.
Gueron, J. and T. Hoekstra. 1995. The temporal interpretation of predication. In Cardinaletti, A. and T. Guasi, eds., *Syntax and Semantics*, 28. Academic Press.
Haegeman, L. 1994. *Introduction to Government and Binding Theory*. Cambridge, M.A.: Blackwell.
Harada, S-I. 1973. Counter equi-NP deletion. *Annual Bulletin of the Research Institute of Logopedics and Phoniatrics* 7, 113–47. University of Tokyo.
Hasegawa, Y. 1996a. *A Study of Japanese Clause Linkage: The Connective TE in Japanese*. CSLI and Kuroshio Publishers.
Hasegawa, Y. 1996b. The (non-vacuous) semantics of TE-linkage in Japanese. *Journal of Pragmatics*, 25, 763–90.
Hashimoto, S. 1969. *Jyoshi, Jyodoshi No Kenkyu*. Tokyo: Iwanami Shoten.
Heim, I. 1982. *The Semantics of Definite and Indefinite Noun Phrases*. Ph.D. dissertation, University of Massachusettes, Amherst.
Heim, I. 1983. File change semantics and the familiarity theory of definiteness. In Bauerle, R. et al., eds., *Meaning, Use, and Interpretation of Language*, 164–89. Walter de Gruyter.
Herburger, E. 1997. Focus and weak noun phrases. *Natural Language Semantics* 5: 53–78. Kluwer Academic Publishers.
Heycock, C. 1994. Focus projection in Japanese. *NELS* 24, 157–71.
Heycock, C. 1995. The internal structure of small clauses: new evidence from inversion. *NELS* 25, 223–38.
Higginbotham, J. 1983. The logic of perceptual reports: an extensional alternative to situation semantics. *Journal of Philosophy* 80, 100–27.
Higginbotham, J. 1985. On semantics. *Linguistic Inquiry* 16, 547–93.
Hinds, J., S. K. Maynard, and S. Iwasaki. 1987. *Perspectives on Topicalization: The Case of Japanese WA*. John Benjamins.
Hobbs, J. 1979. Coherence and coreference. *Cognitive Science* 3, 67–90.
Horie, K. 1993. Internally headed relative clauses in Korean and Japanese: where do the differences come from? In Kuno, S. et al., eds., *Harvard Studies in Korean Linguistics* 5.
Horn, L. R. 1981. Exhaustiveness and the semantics of clefts. *NELS* 11, 125–42.
Horn, L. R. 1984. Toward a new taxonomy for pragmatic inference: Q-based and R-based implicature. In Schiffrin, D. ed., *Meaning, Form, and Use in Context (GURT 84)*, 11–42. Washington: Georgetown University Press.
Horn, L. R. 1986. Presupposition, theme, and variations. *Papers from the Parasession on Pragmatics and Grammatical Theory*, CLS 22/2, 168–92.
Horn, L. R. 1989. *A Natural History of Negation*. The University of Chicago Press.
Horn, L. R. 1993. Economy and redundancy in a dualistic model of natural language. In Shore, S. and M. Vilkuna, eds., *SKY 1993 (1993 Yearbook of the Linguistic Association of Finland)*, 33–71.
Horn, L. R. 1997. Presupposition and implicature. In Lappin, S., ed., *The Handbook of Contemporary Semantics*. Blackwell.
Hoshi, K. 1995. The head-internal relative clause in Japanese: an empty head noun approach. In Akatsuka, N. and S. Iwasaki, eds., *Japanese/Korean Linguistics* 5. Stanford:

CSLI.
Hyams, N. 1996. The underspecification of functional categories in early grammar. In Clashen, H., ed., *Generative Perspective on Language Acquisition*. Amsterdam: John Benjamins.
Iida, M. 1987. Case-assignment by nominals in Japanese. In Iida, M., S. Wechsler, and D. Zec, eds., *Working Papers in Grammatical Theory and Discourse Structure*. Stanford: CSLI.
Ikegami, Y. 1982. Hyougen-kouzou-no hikaku. In Kunihiro, T., ed., *Nichieigo Hikaku Kouza* 4: *Hassou-to Hyougen*, 67–110. Tokyo: Taishukan Shoten.
Ishii, Y. 1988. Head-internal relative clauses in Japanese. *Proceedings of ESCOL* 8, 234–245.
Ishikawa, K. 1998. So-called head-internal relatives in Japanese and event representation. ms., Dept. of Linguistics, Yale University.
Ishikawa, K. 2000. Duplicated complex predicate involves Davidsonian event predicate. Presented at LSA (Linguistic Society of America), Chicago.
Ishikawa, K. 2001. Path and implicature in *Go* and *Come* complex predicates. In: *Imi to katachi-no intaafeisu* (Interface between meaning and form). Kuroshio Publishers.
Ishikawa, K. 2003. Danwa kaishaku riron-ni yoru kashou-hyouji-deno difouruto imi-kaishaku (Default interpretation of underspecified representation in discourse). *JELS* 20. English Linguistic Society of Japan.
Ishikawa, K. 2005. Focus-affected readings of weak NPs and information updating. *LACUS FORUM* 31. Linguistic Association of Canada & U.S.
Ishikawa, K. 2006. Discourse event-matching in the interpretation of Japanese auxiliary *-te iru*. Presented at LSA, Albuquerque.
Ishikawa, K. 2008. Overriding effects of focus on weak NPs in thetic sentences. *CLS* 40. Chicago Linguistic Society, University of Chicago.
Ito, J. 1986. Head-movement at LF and PF: the syntax of head-internal relatives in Japanese. In: Hasegawa, N. and Y. Kitagawa, eds., *University of Massachusetts Occasional Papers in Linguistics* 11, 109–138.
Iwasaki, S. 2002. *Japanese*. John Benjamins.
Josephs, L. 1976. Complementation. In Shibatani, M., ed., *Syntax and Semantics* 5: *Japanese Generative Grammar*, 307–369. New York: Academic Press.
Kabakciev, K. 1984. The article and the aorist/imperfect distinction in Bulgarian: an analysis based on cross-language 'aspect' parallelisms. *Linguistics* 22, 643–72. Mouton Publishers.
Kabakciev, K. 2000. *Aspect in English*. Kluwer.
Kadmon, N. 2001. *Formal Pragmatics*. Blackwell.
Kamp, H. 1981. A theory of truth and semantic representation. Groenendijk, J.A.G., T.M.V. Janssen, and M.B.J. Stokhof, eds., *Formal Methods in the Study of Language*, 277–322.
Kamp, H. and Uwe Reyle. 1993. *From Discourse to Logic*. Kluwer.
Kato, Y. and T. Fukuchi. 1989. *Tensu, Asupekuto, Muudo*. Aratake Shuppan.
Kindaichi, H. 1976. *Nihongo Dooshi No Asupekuto*. (Aspects of Verbs in Japanese) Tokyo: Mugi Shobo.
Kindaichi, H. 1988. *Nihongo Shinpan (Ge)*. Iwanami Shoten.
Kindaichi, H. 1998. *Nihongo Kyoshitsu*. Chikuma Shobo.
Kitahara, Y. 1981. *Nihongo Jyodoshi No Kenkyu*. Taishukan Shoten.
Koike, S. 1994. *Nihongo Wa Donna Gengo Ka.* (What Kind of Language Is Japanese?)

Tokyo: Chikuma Shobo.
Koizumi, M. 1994. Secondary predicates. *Journal of East Asian Linguistics* 3, 25–79.
Kokuritsu Kokugo Kenkyujyo. 1985. *Gendai Nihongo Doshi No Asupekuto.* Shuei Shuppan.
Konoshima, M. 1973. *Kokugo Jyodoshi No Kenkyu.* Ouhusha.
Kratzer, A. 1989. Stage-level and individual-level predicates. In *Papers on Quontification, NSF Grant Report.* Department of Linguistics, University of Massachusetts at Amherst.
Krifka, M. 1989. Nominal reference, temporal constitution, and quantification in event semantics. In Bartsch, R., J. van Benthem, and P. van Emde Boas, eds., *Semantics and Contextual Expression.* Dordrecht: Foris Publications.
Krifka, M. 1992. Thematic relations as links between nominal reference and temporal constitution. Sag, Ivan A. and A. Szabolcsi, eds., *Lexical Matters.* CSLI/Stanford Univ.
Kuno, S. 1973. *The structure of the Japanese language.* MIT Press.
Kuno, S. 1973b. *Nihon Bunpoo Kenkyu.* Tokyo: Taishukan.
Kuroda, S-Y. 1972. The categorical and the thetic judgment. *Foundations of Language* 9, 153–185.
Kuroda, S-Y. 1974. Pivot-independent relativization in Japanese I. *Papers in Japanese Linguistics* 3: 59–93.
Kuroda, S-Y. 1992. *Japanese Syntax and Semantics.* (This includes his paper in 1974 on the HIR.) Dordrecht: Kluwer.
Ladusaw, W. 1994. Thetic and categorical, stage and individual, weak and strong. SALT IV. Also reprinted in Horn, L. & Y. Kato (2000), eds., *Negation and Polarity,* 232–42. Oxford University Press.
Lambrecht, K. 1987. Sentence focus, information structure, and the thetic-categorical distinction. *BLS* 13, 366–382.
Lambrecht, K. 1994. *Information Structure and Sentence Form.* Cambridge University Press.
Lambrecht, K. 1996. On the formal and functional relationship between topics and vocatives: evidence from French. In Goldberg, A. E. ed., *Conceptual Structure, Discourse and Language,* 267–288. CSLI Publications.
Landman, F. 1992. The progressive. *Natural Language Semantics,* Vol. 1, No. 1, 1–32. Kluwer.
Langacker, R. 1969. On pronominalization and the chain of commands. In Reibel, D. and S. Schane, eds., *Modern Studies in English.* Prentice-Hall.
Larson, R. 1988. On the double object construction. *Linguistic Inquiry* 19: 235–89.
Lascarides, A. and N. Asher. 1993. Temporal interpretation, discourse relations and commonsense entailment. *Linguistics and Philosophy,*16, 437–93.
Lascarides, A. and A. Copestake. 1998. Pragmatics and word meaning. *Journal of Linguistics,* 34, 387–414.
Lascarides, A., A. Copestake, and T. Briscoe. 1996. Ambiguity and coherence. *Journal of Semantics,* 13, 1, 41–65.
Lasnik, H. and M. Saito. 1984. On the nature of proper government. *Linguistic Inquiry* 15, 235–289.
Lewis, D. 1979. Scorekeeping in a language game. *Journal of Philosophical Logic* 8, 339–59.
Levinson, S. C. 1983. *Pragmatics.* Cambridge University Press.
Levinson, S. C. 1996. Relativity in spatial conception and description. In: Gumperz, J. and S.

Levinson, eds., *Rethinking Linguistic Relativity*, 177–202. Cambridge University Press.

Makino, S. 1987. How relevant is a functional notion of communicative orientation to *ga* and *wa*? In Hinds, J., S. K. Maynard, and S. Iwasaki.

Martin, S. E. 1975 & 1988. *A Reference Grammar of Japanese*. New Haven: Yale University Press & Tokyo: Charles E. Tuttle Company.

Masuoka, T., Y. Nitta, T. Gunji, and S. Kinsui. 1997. *Bunpo*. Iwanami Shoten.

Masuoka, T. and Y. Takubo. 1989. *Kiso Nihongo Bunpo*. Kuroshio Shuppan.

Matsuda, Y. 1993. On the so-called Japanese headless relative clauses. ms., USC.

Matsui, T. 1995. *Bridging and Relevance*. Ph. D. dissertation, UCL.

Matsumoto, Y-K. 1997. *Noun-Modifying Constructions in Japanese: A Frame-Semantic Approach*. John Benjamins.

Matsushita, D. 1930. *Hyojun Nihon Kogoho*. Chubunkan Shoten.

McCawley, J. 1971. Tense and time reference in English. In Fillmore, C. & D.T. Langendoen, eds., *Studies in Linguistic Semantics*, 97–113. New York: Holt Reinhart.

McCawley, J. 1981. Notes on the English perfect. *Australian Journal of Linguistics* 1, 81–90.

McNally, L. 1997. *A Semantics for The English Existential Construction*. Garland Publishing.

McNally, L. 1998. Stativity and theticity. In Rothstein, S., ed., *Events and Grammar*, 293–307. Kluwer Academic Publishers.

Michaelis, L. 1994. The ambiguity of the English present perfect. *Journal of Linguistics*.

Mihara, K. 1994. *Nihongo-no toogo koozoo*. Tokyo: Shohaku-sha.

Mihara, K. & K. Hiraiwa. 2006. *Shin Nihongo-no toogo koozoo*. Tokyo: Shohaku-sha.

Milsark, G. 1974. *Existential Sentences in English*. Ph.D. dissertation, MIT.

Milsark, G. 1977. Toward an explanation of certain peculiarities of the existential construction in English. *Linguistic Analysis* 3: 1–29.

Minsky, M. 1977. Frame-system theory. Johnson-Laird, P.N. and P.C. Wason, eds., *Thinking: Readings in Cognitive Science*. Cambridge Univ. Press.

Miyagawa, K. 1992. The head-internal relative clauses in Japanese. ms., USC.

Miyagawa, S. 1987. *Wa* and the wh phrase. In Hinds, J., S. K. Maynard, and S. Iwasaki, eds., 185–217.

Miyagawa, S. 1993. Case, agreement, and *ga/no* conversion. In *Japanese/Korean Linguistics* 3, 221–235.

Morita, Y. 1977. *Kiso Nihongo* (Fundamental Japanese Grammar): vol.1. Tokyo: Kadokawa Shoten.

Morita, Y. 1994. *Dooshi-No Imiron-Teki Bunpoo Kenkyuu* (A Semantic Study of Verb Grammar). Tokyo: Meiji Shoin.

Moriyama, T. 1988. *Nihongo Doshi Jyutsugo-Bun No Kenkyu*. Meiji Shoin.

Murasugi, K. 1991. *Noun Phrases in Japanese and English: A Study in Syntax, Learnability, and Acquisition*, Ph.D. dissertation. University of Connecticut.

Murasugi, K. 1994. Head-internal relative clauses as adjunct pure complex NPs. In *Synchronic and Diachronic Approaches to Language: A Festschrift for Toshio Nakao on the Occasion of His Sixtieth Birthday*.

Nakau, M. 1980. Tensu, asupekuto no hikaku. In Kunihiro, T., ed., *Nichieigo Hikaku Kooza* 2: *Bunpoo*, 101–155.

Nitta, Y. 1997. *Nihon Bunpo Kenkyu Jyosetsu*. Kuroshio Shuppan.

Noda, H. 1991. *Hajimete No Hito No Nihongo Bunpoo*. (Japanese Grammar for Beginners) Tokyo: Kuroshio Shuppan.
Ogihara, T. 1997. The ambiguity of the *-te iru* forms in Japanese. *Journal of East Asian Linguistics*.
Ohara, H. K. 1992. On Japanese internally headed relative clauses. *BLS* 18, 100–108.
Ohara, H. K. 1994. An event-reporting relative construction in Japanese. *BLS* 20.
Okuda, Y. 1985. *Kotoba No Kenkyu Jyosetsu*. Mugi Shobo.
Okutsu, K. 1996. *Shuui Nihon Bunporon*. Hituzi Syobo.
Parsons, T. 1989. The progressive in English: events, states and processes. *Linguistics and Philosophy* 12, 213–41.
Parsons, T. 1990. *Events in the Semantics of English*. Cambridge: MIT Press.
Partee, B. 1973. Some structural analogies between tenses and pronouns in English. *Journal of Philosophy* 70, 601–9.
Partee, B. 1984. Nominal and temporal anaphora. *Linguistics and Philosophy* 7, 243–86.
Pelletier, J.F. and N. Asher. 1997. Generics and defaults. In Benthem, J. van and A. ter Meulen, eds., *Handbook of Logic and Language*. Elsevier Science B.V.
Pesetsky, D. 1987. Wh-in-situ: movement and unselective binding. In Reuland, E. J. and G.B. ter Meulen, eds., *The Representation of (In)definiteness*, 98–129. MIT Press.
Poesio, M. 1993. A situation-theoretic formalization of definite description interpretation in plan elaboration dialogues. In Aczel, P., D. Israel, Y. Katagiri, & S. Peters, eds., *Situation Theory and Its Applications*, Vol. 3, 339–59.
Portner, P. and K. Yabushita. 1998. The semantics and pragmatics of topic phrases. *Linguistics and Philosophy* 21: 117–157.
Potts, C. 2005. *The Logic of Conventional Implicatures*. Oxford University Press.
Prince, E. 1981. Toward a taxonomy of given/new Information. In Cole, P., ed., *Radical Pragmatics*, 223–54. Academic Press.
Prince, E. 1986. On the syntactic marking of presupposed open propositions. *CLS* 22, 208–222.
Prince, E. 1992. The ZPG letter: subjects, definiteness, and information-status. In Thompson, S. A. & W. C. Mann, eds., *Discourse Description: Diverse Analyses of a Fundraising Text*, 295–325. John Benjamins.
Pustejovsky, J. 1991. The generative lexicon. *Computational Linguistics*, 17, 409–41.
Pustejovsky, J. 1995. *The Generative Lexicon*. MIT Press.
Reinhart, T. 1983. *Anaphora and Semantic Interpretation*. London: Croom Helm.
Reinhart, T. 2006. *Interface Strategies: Optimal and Costly Computations*. Cambridge, MA: MIT Press.
Ross, J. R. 1969. On the cyclic nature of English pronominalization. In Reibel, D. and S. Schane, eds., *Modern Studies in English*. Prentice-Hall.
Rothstein, S. 1998. *Events and Grammar*. Kluwer.
Saito, M. 1985. *Some Asymmetries in Japanese and Their Theoretical Implications*. Ph.D. dissertation, MIT.
Sakuma, K. 1966. *Gendai Nihongo No Hyogen To Goho, Zohoban*. Koseisha Koseikaku.
van der Sandt, R. 1992. Presupposition projection as anaphora resolution. *Journal of Semantics* 9, 4.

Shibatani, M. 1990. *The Languages of Japan*. Cambridge University Press.
Shirota, S. 1998. *Nihongo Keitairon*. Hituzi Syobo.
Smith, C. S. 1991. *The Parameter of Aspect*. Kluwer.
Soga, M. 1983. *Tense and Aspect in Modern Colloquial Japanese*. Vancouver: University of British Columbia.
Spejewski, B. 1996. Temporal subordination and the English perfect. *Proceedings from Semantics and Linguistic Theory (SALT)* 6. Ithaca: Cornell University.
Sperber, D., and D. Wilson. 1986. *Relevance: Communication and Cognition*. Blackwell.
Stowell, T. 1981. *Origins of Phrase Structure*. Ph.D. dissertation, MIT.
Suzuki, S. 1979. Gendai nihongo no doshi no tensu. In Gengogaku Kenkyukai, ed., *Gengo No Kenkyu*, 5–59. Mugi Shobo.
de Swart, H. 1996. (In)definites and genericity. In Kanazawa, M., C. Pinon, and H. de Swart, eds., *Quantifiers, Deduction, and Context*, 171–194. CSLI Publications.
de Swart, H. and A. Molendijk. 1999. Negation and the temporal structure of narrative discourse. *Journal of Semantics* 16, 1–42. Oxford University Press.
Takahashi, T. 1990. Tensu, asupekuto, voisu. Kondo, T., ed., *Nihongo To Nihongo Kyoiku* 12. Meiji Shoin.
Takezawa, K. 1987. *A Configurational Approach to Case-Marking in Japanese*. Ph.D. dissertation, University of Washington.
Tateishi, K. 1994. *The Syntax of Subjects*. Tokyo: Kuroshio Publishers.
Tenny, C. L. 1994. *Aspectual Roles and the Syntax-Semantics Interface*. Kluwer.
Tenny, C. L. and J. Pustejovsky. 2000. *Events as Grammatical Objects*. CSLI.
Teramura, H. 1980. Meishi shuushokubu no hikaku. In Kunihiro, T., ed., *Nchieigo Hikaku Kooza* 2: *Bunpoo*, 221–266.
Teramura, H. 1984. *Nohongo No Sintakusu To Imi* 1. Tokyo: Kuroshio Shuppan.
Teramura, H. 1989. Tensu to asupekuto. In Inoue, K., ed., *Nihon Bunpoo Shoo Jiten*. Tokyo: Taishuukan Shoten.
Teramura, H. 1993. *Teramura Hideo Ronbun Shu* 1: *Nihongo Bunpoo Hen*. Tokyo: Kuroshio Shuppan.
Teramura, H. et al. 1987. *Keesu Sutadii Nihongo Bunpoo*. Tokyo: Ouhuu.
Tomioka, S. 1993. Verb movement and tense specification in Japanese. *WCCFL* 11, 482–94.
Tsubomoto, A. 1981. It's all "no": unifying function of "no" in Japanese. *CLS* 17.
Tsujimura, N. 1996. *An Introduction to Japanese Linguistics*. Blackwell.
Uchibori, A. 1992. Head-internal relatives and null operator binding. ms., University of Connecticut.
Vallduvi, E. 1992. *The Informational Component*. New York: Garland.
Vallduvi, E. and E. Engdahl. 1995. Information packaging and grammar architecture. *NELS* 25, 519–33.
van Valin, R. 1990. Semantic parameters of split intransitivity. *Language* 66, 221–260.
Veltman, F. 1996. Defaults in update semantics. *Journal of Philosophical Logic*. Kluwer.
Vendler, Z. 1957. Verbs and times. *Philosophical Review* 56, 143–160.
Vendler, Z. 1967. *Linguistics in Philosophy*. Ithaca, New York: Cornell University Press.
Vlach, F. 1981. The semantics of the progressive. *Syntax and Semantics* 14, 271–92.

Walker, M. A., A. K. Joshi, and E. F. Prince. 1998. *Centering Theory in Discourse*. Clarendon Press/Oxford University Press.
Watanabe, A. 1991. Wh-in-situ, subjacency, and chain formation. ms., Syntax Generals paper, MIT.
Watanabe, A. 1992. Subjacency and S-structure movement of wh-in-situ. *Journal of East Asian Linguistics* 1:3.
Williams, E. 1981. Argument structure and morphology. *The Linguistic Review* 1, 81–114.
Williamson, J. S. 1987. An indefiniteness restriction for relative clauses in Lakhota. In Reuland, E. J. and G.B. ter Meulen, eds., *The Representation of (In)definiteness*. MIT Press.
Wilson, D. 1975. *Presupposition and Non-Truth Conditional Semantics*. New York: Academic Press.
Yoshikawa, T. 1989. *Nihongo Bunpoo Nyuumon* (Introduction to Japanese Grammar): *NAFL Sensho* 6. Tokyo: ALC.

INDEX OF TOPICS

a

accommodation   111, 123
Accomplishment   64, 65, 75, 83, 84, 85, 118, 120
Achievement   65, 75, 83, 84, 87, 89, 118, 120
Activity   64, 65, 74, 81
Ancash Quechua   2, 30
antecedent government   16
aspectual shift   120, 122
Axiom   104, 105, 106, 107, 114, 116–119

b

Bridging   108, 109, 110, 112, 123

c

canonical relative clause   2, 4, 11, 17, 18
categorical judgment   130, 151
Cause-Result   110, 119
coherence/coherent   103–107, 110–118, 124
COMP (complementizer)   19, 20, 21, 32
Conditional Topic   138
contiguity   8, 73, 92, 115–122, 125, 151

Continuative   62–64, 72
contraindexed   40, 41
Contrast   117, 126
contrastive -*wa*   116, 126
conventional implicature   155
conversational implicature (C.I.)   149–150, 152, 154
Correction   108
Culminated   44, 45, 46, 47, 79, 121
culmination   79, 80, 81-84, 86

d

default (nominative) case   45, 56
default matching   86, 90, 110, 112, 113, 114, 117–123, 125, 151–152
default measurement   83, 87, 91, 92, 108, 115
default reasoning   86, 91, 108, 112, 115
defeasibility   124
DGC (Double -*ga-case* constraint)   33
DICE   100, 107, 112–114, 122, 123, 124
Diegueno   30
discourse (event) relations   104–107, 112, 116, 118–120, 124
discourse default   99, 102–104, 118, 123
discourse-initial   72
discourse-new   132, 153
discourse-old   132, 153
Distinct Common Topic   104, 106

division of labor   130
DOC (Double -*o* constraint)   23–28, 30

e

E-card   42, 43, 44, 47, 50, 52, 55, 103
ECP   14–17
EL (Exhaustive Listing)   128, 137, 140–150, 152, 154
Elaboration   102, 112
event argument/variable   42, 43
event time   73
existential   72
existential individuation   138–140, 145, 146, 150, 152
existential quantification   51, 126, 136, 154
existentiality   52, 64, 68, 73, 76, 78, 81, 87, 137, 143
Explanation   107, 124
external argument   29

f

focus(ing)   128, 133, 141–153
formal noun   9, 31
French articles   154

g

global focus   151

h

head-internal   6, 14

i

I-card   42, 43
Imbabura Quechua   30

Imperfective 37, 39, 40, 48, 90
imperfective paradox 90
inchoative 89
individual-level (predicate)/ILP 47, 143, 144
information structure 128, 132, 139–140, 145
inheritance structure 95, 112
In-progress (state) 44, 48–50, 53, 59–61, 82–86, 91, 92, 115–122
intentional structure 124
internal argument 29
internal head 6
iterative 121, 122

k

koto 21, 32

l

Lakhota 2, 30
left/right boundaries 45
lexical default 94, 97–98, 102–105, 110, 112–118, 123
LF(-)movement 2, 11, 13, 30
LF-extraction 14, 16
light verb(s) 135
listener-oriented 131
L-mark(ing) 14–17, 31
logical metonymy 93, 123

m

Mad Magazine register 50, 52
Mapping Hypothesis 143
Milsarkian generalization 143

mono 21, 32

n

Narration 106, 107, 114–120
narrow focus 151
narrow(-)scope 15–17, 31, 82
ND (Neutral Description) 127, 140
non-monotonic inference 123
NP(-)movement 12, 14, 18
Numeral Quantifier Float 140

p

Perfective 37, 39, 40, 48, 49, 56, 60, 62, 69, 70, 88
plan 112, 124
prenominal complement 1, 11, 14, 18, 19
present routine act 70
presupposition 50–53, 55, 109–115, 121–123, 128, 145, 150
pro(-based) approach 11, 18, 22, 28, 29, 30, 33–34
proper government 15
property-denoting/-denotation 135, 140–143, 145–147, 150, 152
prosodic (forces) 140–149, 152, 153

q

Q Principle 149–150, 152
qualia structure 93, 96, 98, 105, 107, 112, 113
quirky case 23

r

R Principle 149
reference time 73
referent 6, 18, 31, 32, 43, 53, 54, 101–103, 108, 115, 117, 139
relativized noun 2, 4, 5
relevancy condition 46, 120
Resultant (state) 44, 47–50, 53, 59–62, 77, 83–86, 91, 92, 115, 116, 121, 122
resultative 72–74, 76–78
rhetorical relations 102, 104
right boundary 73, 81, 83
root-infinitive (RI) 41–47, 50, 53–55, 56, 60
Russian 41, 45–47, 53, 54

s

saliency/salient 139
scalar implicatures 154
SDRS 100, 101, 103–108, 112, 113
semantic head 6, 13, 30
simultaneity 8
speaker-oriented 131
Specificity Principle 103, 124
speech time 73, 78, 82, 88
stage-level (predicate)/SLP 47, 56, 143, 144
strong (NP) 142, 143

t

telic (role) 93, 94, 97, 98, 101, 102, 112, 113, 118–122
temporal coreference 56
Tense chain 42

termination 79, 80, 83, 85
theta role 15, 16, 18, 31, 32, 53
thetic judgment 130, 135, 145, 150–152
tokoro 21, 24, 25, 28, 32, 126, 153
topic-comment 130
Toyama dialect 32
transport 110, 113
truth-conditional 107
-tsu 70

u

uniqueness constraint 124
universal quantification 51, 52, 56, 138, 154

v

variable index 42
vocative 138, 139

w

weak (NP) 142
wide(-)scope 15–17

INDEX OF AUTHORS

a

Abbott 154
Ando 128, 141, 144
Asher (& Lascarides) 90, 99, 100, 104–107, 108, 111, 113, 124, 126
Avrutin 41–45, 50, 52, 55

b

Babyonyshev 33, 56
Barwise and Seligman 90
Basilico 2, 11, 12, 30
Birner & Ward 126, 128
Breivik 154
Briscoe 93, 95, 97

c

Chafe 128
Chierchia 108
Chung and Timberlake 38
Chomsky 14–16, 31, 41
Clark 108–109
Cole 2, 6, 11, 12, 30, 33
Cole & Herman 30
Comrie 38
Copestake 96
Culy 11, 30

d

Davidson 42

Diesing 143–144

f

Fernald 144
Fukui 14–16, 31

g

Giorgi and Pianesi 45
Glasbey 90
Grice 149
Grimshaw 31
Grosz & Sidner 124, 126
Gueron and Hoekstra 40, 42
Gundel, Hedberg & Zacharski 139

h

Haegeman 15
Harada 22
Hasegawa 87
Hashimoto 62, 68–70, 78
Heim 42
Herburger 142, 144–145, 154
Heycock 128, 144, 146, 149, 153
Higginbotham 42
Hobbs 108, 126
Horie 8, 21, 32
Horn 75, 88, 89, 123, 149–150, 154
Hoshi 8, 11, 17, 19, 21, 22, 28, 33
Hyams 40, 41, 56

i

Iida 31
Ikegami 89

Ishii 1, 8, 11
Ishikawa 43, 90, 150, 154
Ito 1, 11, 19
Iwasaki 128–130, 136, 141, 145, 153

j

Josephs 53, 56

k

Kadmon 103
Kamp (& Reyle) 124
Kindaichi 69, 70
Kratzer 42
Kuno 89, 128, 133, 140, 142, 144, 149, 153
Kuroda 6, 8, 19, 46, 118–120, 130, 135

l

Ladusaw 135, 142, 144, 151
Lambrecht 128, 139
Landman 90, 93, 124
Larson 23
Lascarides & Copestake 94, 97–99, 103, 106, 124
Lascarides (& Asher) 99
Lascarides, Copestake & Briscoe 105
Lasnik & Saito 15
Levinson 149
Lewis 105

m

Makino 87, 128, 131, 153, 154
Masuoka & Takubo 62
Matsuda 8, 14, 17, 21, 30, 31, 32
Matsui 108
Matsushita 70, 78
McCawley 68, 76
McNally 135, 136, 145, 151
Michaelis 68, 72, 75–77
Mihara 17, 33
Mihara & Hiraiwa 17
Milsark 87, 137, 142–145
Minsky 93, 124
Miyagawa 128, 136, 149
Morita 89
Moriyama 62
Murasugi 6, 8, 11, 17, 19-21, 22–28, 32, 33

n

Nitta 62, 64–68, 76, 77

o

Ohara 6
Okuda 62

p

Parsons 42, 44, 48
Pelletier & Asher 93, 124
Poesio 93, 124
Portner & Yabushita 155
Potts 155
Prince 132, 139, 153
Pustejovsky 90, 93, 94

r

Reinhart 56, 154

s

Sakuma 70, 78
Sandt, van der 108, 111
Shibatani 128, 141
Shirota 64, 70
Soga 36, 39
Sperber & Wilson 108
Stowell 31
Suzuki 62, 63, 88, 89
Swart, de 154
Swart, de & Molendijk 124

t

Takahashi 62
Tateishi 138
Teramura 69–71, 78, 89
Tsubomoto 8
Tsujimura 4, 5, 18

u

Uchibori 8, 56

v

Vallduvi 126, 128
Vallduvi & Engdahl 128
Veltman 93, 124

w

Watanabe 1, 11
Williamson 2, 6, 11, 30

【著者紹介】

石川 邦芳 (いしかわくによし)

[経歴] 東京学芸大学・同大学院英語科(学士・修士).イエール(Yale)大学院言語学科(哲学修士・言語学博士)。カリフォルニア大学院(バークレー校)客員研究員(1990-1)。MIT 大学院言語学科・脳認知科学科研究員(1996-7)。東京電機大学、宇都宮大学、東京家政学院大学人文学部(助教授)にて教え、現在、明治大学情報コミュニケーション学部准教授。

[主要な研究・出版] "Overriding Effects of Focus on Weak NPs in Thetic Sentences" (*CLS* 40, 2008) シカゴ大学。"Discourse Event-Representation With an Untensed Bi-Clausal Construction" (*LACUS FORUM* 33, 2007) カナダ・米国言語学会。"談話解釈理論による、過少表示でのディフォールト意味解釈" (*JELS* 20, 2003) 日本英語学会。"Path and Implicature in Go and Come Complex Predicates" (「意味と形のインターフェイス」) くろしお出版。研究発表：米国言語学会 (2000, 2006)、日本英文学会 (1999)、日本コミュニケーション学会 (2005) 等。談話構造、情報構造、統語・韻律インターフェイス領域、認知と意味、談話とコミュニケーション等を研究。

Hituzi Linguistics in English No. 13

Discourse Representation of Temporal Relations in the So-Called Head-Internal Relatives

発行	2009 年 2 月 14 日　初版 1 刷
定価	9400 円＋税
著者	© 石川邦芳
発行者	松本　功
装丁	向井裕一（glyph）
印刷所	互恵印刷株式会社
製本所	田中製本印刷株式会社
発行所	株式会社 ひつじ書房

〒 112-0011 東京都文京区千石 2-1-2 大和ビル 2F
Tel.03-5319-4916　Fax 03-5319-4917
郵便振替 00120-8-142852
toiawase@hituzi.co.jp　http://www.hituzi.co.jp/

ISBN978-4-89476-406-4　C3080

造本には充分注意しておりますが、落丁・乱丁などがございましたら、小社かお買上げ書店にておとりかえいたします。ご意見、ご感想など、小社までお寄せ下されば幸いです。

刊行案内

Hituzi Linguistics in English No.10
The Development of the Nominal Plural Forms in Early Middle English
堀田隆一 著
978-4-89476-403-3　定価 13000 円＋税

Hituzi Linguistics in English No.11
Chunking and Instruction
The Place of Sounds, Lexis, and Grammar in English Language Teaching
中森誉之 著
978-4-89476-404-0　定価 8800 円＋税

Hituzi Linguistics in English No.12
Detecting and Sharing Perspectives Using Causals in Japanese
宇野良子 著
978-4-89476-405-7　定価 12000 円＋税

Hituzi Linguistics in English No.13
Discourse Representation of Temporal Relations in the So-Called Head-Internal Relatives
石川邦芳 著
978-4-89476-406-4　定価 9400 円＋税

Hituzi Linguistics in English No.14
Features and Roles of Filled Pauses in Speech Communication
A corpus-based study of spontaneous speech
渡辺美知子 著
978-4-89476-407-1　定価 11000 円＋税

刊行案内

講座社会言語科学　全6巻
各巻 A5 判上製カバー装　定価 3200 円＋税

講座社会言語科学 第1巻　異文化とコミュニケーション
井出祥子・平賀正子 編

講座社会言語科学 第2巻　メディア
橋元良明 編

講座社会言語科学 第3巻　関係とコミュニケーション
大坊郁夫・永瀬治郎 編

講座社会言語科学 第4巻　教育・学習
西原鈴子・西郡仁朗 編

講座社会言語科学 第5巻　社会・行動システム
片桐恭弘・片岡邦好 編

講座社会言語科学 第6巻　方法
伝康晴・田中ゆかり 編

シリーズ文と発話　全3巻　串田秀也・定延利之・伝康晴 編
各巻 A5 判上製カバー装　定価 3200 円＋税

第1巻　活動としての文と発話
第2巻　「単位」としての文と発話
第3巻　時間の中の文と発話

刊行案内

国際交流基金日本語教授法シリーズ　全 14 巻
各巻 B5 判並製（* は 2009 年 2 月現在未刊）

　第 1 巻　日本語教師の役割／コースデザイン　定価 580 円＋税
　第 2 巻　音声を教える　定価 1500 円＋税
*第 3 巻　文字・語彙を教える
*第 4 巻　文法を教える
　第 5 巻　聞くことを教える　定価 1000 円＋税
　第 6 巻　話すことを教える　定価 800 円＋税
　第 7 巻　読むことを教える　定価 700 円＋税
*第 8 巻　書くことを教える
　第 9 巻　初級を教える　定価 700 円＋税
*第 10 巻　中・上級を教える
*第 11 巻　日本事情・日本文化を教える
*第 12 巻　学習を評価する
*第 13 巻　教え方を改善する
　第 14 巻　教材開発　定価 800 円＋税